Beckett: Waiting for Godot

Waiting for Godot is a byword in every major world language. No other twentieth-century play has achieved such global currency. In *Waiting for Godot* Samuel Beckett challenged conventional wisdoms concerning the whole process of play production. His innovations have affected not only the writing of plays, but all aspects of their staging. In this book David Bradby explores the impact of the play and its influence on acting, directing, design and the role of theatre in society. David Bradby begins with an analysis of the play and its historical context. After discussing the first productions in France, Britain and America, he examines subsequent productions in Africa, Eastern Europe, Israel, America, China and Japan. The play has become a proving ground for actors and directors, and this book assesses interpretations by actors such as Bert Lahr, David Warrilow, Georges Wilson, Barry McGovern and Ben Kingsley, and directors Roger Blin, Susan Sontag, Sir Peter Hall, Luc Bondy, Yukio Ninagawa and Beckett himself. It also contains an extensive production chronology, bibliography and illustrations from major productions.

PLAYS IN PRODUCTION

Series editor: Michael Robinson

PUBLISHED VOLUMES

Ibsen: *A Doll's House* by Egil Törnqvist
Miller: *Death of a Salesman* by Brenda Murphy
Molière: *Don Juan* by David Whitton
Wilde: *Salome* by William Tydeman and Steven Price
Brecht: *Mother Courage and Her Children* by Peter Thomson
Williams: *A Streetcar Named Desire* by Philip C. Kolin
O'Neill: *Long Day's Journey into Night* by Brenda Murphy
Albee: *Who's Afraid of Virginia Woolf?* by Stephen J. Bottoms
Beckett: *Waiting for Godot* by David Bradby

BECKETT
Waiting for Godot

*

DAVID BRADBY

Royal Holloway, University of London

CAMBRIDGE
UNIVERSITY PRESS

PUBLISHED BY THE PRESS SYNDICATE OF THE UNIVERSITY OF CAMBRIDGE
The Pitt Building, Trumpington Street, Cambridge, United Kingdom

CAMBRIDGE UNIVERSITY PRESS
The Edinburgh Building, Cambridge CB2 2RU, UK
40 West 20th Street, New York, NY 10011–4211, USA
477 Williamstown Road, Port Melbourne, VIC 3207, Australia
Ruiz de Alarcón 13, 28014 Madrid, Spain
Dock House, The Waterfront, Cape Town 8001, South Africa

http://www.cambridge.org

First published 2001

Printed in the United Kingdom at the University Press, Cambridge

Typeface 10.75/14 pt. Adobe Garamond   *System* LaTeX 2$_\varepsilon$ [TB]

A catalogue record for this book is available from the British Library.

Library of Congress Cataloguing in Publication data

Bradby, David.
Beckett, Waiting for Godot / David Bradby.
p.   cm. – (Plays in production)
Includes bibliographical references and index.
ISBN 0 521 59429 4 – ISBN 0 521 59510 X (pbk.)
1. Beckett, Samuel, 1906–. En attendant Godot.   2. Beckett, Samuel, 1906– – Dramatic
production.   3. Beckett, Samuel, 1906– – Stage history.   I. Title: Beckett.   II. Title.
III. Series.
PQ2603.E378 E62 2001   842'.914–dc21   2001035591

ISBN 0 521 59429 4 hardback
ISBN 0 521 59510 X paperback

CONTENTS

List of illustrations	*page* viii
General preface	xi
Acknowledgements	xii
Introduction	1
1 Beckett before *Waiting for Godot*	11
2 *Waiting for Godot* – the play	24
3 The first production: Théâtre de Babylone, Paris, January 1953, directed by Roger Blin	45
4 The first productions in English	67
5 Early productions in the United States	86
6 Beckett's own production: Schiller-Theater, Berlin, March 1975	106
7 'Fail again. Fail better.'	135
8 *Godot* in political context	162
9 Productions at the end of the twentieth century	180
Conclusion	209
Select production chronology	213
Notes	221
Select bibliography	243
Index	249

ILLUSTRATIONS

1. The first production by Roger Blin, Théâtre
   de Babylone, Paris, 1953. (Photo: Agence
   Bernand, Paris.)   *page* 63
2. The first English production by Peter Hall,
   Arts Theatre, London, 1955. (Photo: Houston
   Rogers collection at the Theatre Museum, London.)   80
3. The production by Herb Blau at the San Francisco
   Actors Workshop, 1957. (Photo: courtesy of
   Alan Mandell.)   99
4. The production by Samuel Beckett, Schiller-Theater,
   Berlin, 1975. (Photo: Ilse Buhs Sammlung at the
   Deutsches Theatermuseum, Munich.)   111
5. The production by Samuel Beckett, Schiller-Theater,
   Berlin, 1975. (Photo: Ilse Buhs Sammlung at the
   Deutsches Theatermuseum, Munich.)   118
6. The production by Samuel Beckett, Schiller-Theater,
   Berlin, 1975. (Photo: Ilse Buhs Sammlung at the
   Deutsches Theatermuseum, Munich.)   130
7. The production by Otomar Krejča, Papal Palace,
   Avignon Theatre Festival, 1978. (Photo: Collection
   Fernand Michaud, Département des Arts du Spectacle,
   Bnf., Paris.)   143
8. The production by Sir Peter Hall, Old Vic, London,
   1997. (Photo: John Haynes, London.)   183
9. The production by Walter Asmus, Gate Theatre
   (Dublin) at the Barbican, London, 1999.
   (Photo: John Haynes, London.)   191

10. The production by Walter Asmus, Gate Theatre
   (Dublin) at the Barbican, London, 1999.
   (Photo: John Haynes, London.)   193
11. The production by Luc Bondy, Théâtre Vidy,
   Lausanne, 1999. (Photo: Laurence Mullenders,
   courtesy of Théâtre Vidy.)   204
12. The production by Luc Bondy, Théâtre Vidy,
   Lausanne, 1999. (Photo: Mario del Curto, courtesy
   of Théâtre Vidy.)   206

FIGURES

1. Sketch by Beckett of the stage (courtesy of the
   Beckett International Foundation).   *page* 108
2. Beckett's sketch for 'Inspection [of] Place' (courtesy
   of the Beckett International Foundation).   122

GENERAL PREFACE

Volumes in the series Plays in Production take major dramatic texts and examine their transposition, firstly on to the stage and, secondly, where appropriate, into other media. Each book includes concise but informed studies of individual dramatic texts, focusing on the original theatrical and historical context of a play in relation to its initial performance and reception followed by subsequent major interpretations on stage, both under the impact of changing social, political and cultural values, and in response to developments in the theatre generally.

Many of the plays also have been transposed into other media – film, opera, television, ballet – which may well be the form in which they are first encountered by a contemporary audience. Thus, a substantial study of the play-text and the issues it raises for theatrical realization is supplemented by an assessment of such adaptations as well as the production history, where the emphasis is on the development of a performance tradition for each work, including staging and acting styles, rather than simply the archaeological reconstruction of past performances.

Plays included in the series are all likely to receive regular performance and individual volumes will be of interest to the informed reader as well as to students of theatre history and literature. Each book also contains an annotated production chronology as well as numerous photographs from key performances.

Michael Robinson
University of East Anglia

ACKNOWLEDGEMENTS

My thanks go first of all to the many Beckett scholars who have so generously helped me with materials for this book, especially to James Knowlson, Ruby Cohn, Katharine Worth and Michael Robinson. Secondly, I wish to thank those who helped in other ways, notably Timothy Bateson and Peter Woodthorpe who spoke to me about their memories of the first English production, Rick Cluchey and Alan Mandell of the San Francisco and San Quentin workshops, Mary Bryden and Julian Garforth of the Beckett International Foundation at the University of Reading, Béatrice Picon-Vallin of the CNRS in Paris, Marie-Claude Billard of the Maison Jean Vilar in Avignon, Mark Batty, Jon Brokering, Maria Delgado, Elin Diamond, Dina Djurović, Matthijs Engelberts, Anna Ganev, Jean-Claude Lallias, Dan Urian and James Woodall. Finally, I am grateful to Barbara Bradby, Mika Sato and David Short for their translations from Spanish, Japanese and Czech.

I wish to record my gratitude for material assistance in the research and writing of this book to the AHRB and the Camargo Foundation. The Arts and Humanities Research Board granted me an extra sabbatical term for research, and the Camargo Foundation provided a residency for writing up in Cassis, France.

INTRODUCTION

> Cette pièce a changé l'état du théâtre. (This play has changed the
> condition of theatre.)
>
> Roger Blin[1]
>
> Beckett has changed the way we do Shakespeare, the way we act,
> the way we write and the way we direct in the theatre.
>
> Peter Hall[2]

Beckett's work for the theatre has changed the way in which we think
about the art of the stage. His extraordinary challenge to all the accepted conventions of the theatre in his day is already present in the
text of *Waiting for Godot*, which he wrote between 9 October 1948
and 29 January 1949. It took the productions of the next twenty-five
years, however, for the extent of this challenge to become clear. Beginning with the early realisations of Roger Blin (who was responsible
for the first production in 1953) and Peter Hall (in 1955), and culminating in Beckett's own production of the play in 1975, the radical
originality of Beckett's theatrical vision, and its implications for every
aspect of stagecraft were gradually revealed. The plays which followed
Waiting for Godot, and the production work on which he had em-
barked, show Beckett refining and developing his new approach to
the art of theatre. This study will draw on such work where appropriate, but its chief purpose is to examine the history of productions
of *Waiting for Godot* in order to come to a better understanding of
just how Beckett has, in Peter Hall's words, changed everything about
our approach to theatre.

Waiting for Godot is one of the defining works of twentieth-century
European culture. Theatre in the last century was the great chronicler

of failure and defeat. Two images stand out with special starkness: Brecht's Mother Courage pulling her cart doggedly across the battle-fields, despite the loss of her three sons, and Beckett's two tramps waiting endlessly for Godot who never comes. Both are images of people going nowhere and both were created midway through the century.[3] In its style as well as in its content, *Waiting for Godot* is a very European play: like Pirandello's *Six Characters in Search of an Author* (1921), Beckett's play turns the conventions of European theatre in upon themselves, revealing their inner contradictions. Through questioning fundamental Western assumptions about theatrical re-presentation, it implicitly poses an equally fundamental challenge to received ideas about the meaning of life. Like Pirandello's play, Beckett's was written shortly after the conclusion of a world war that had shaken traditional beliefs and provoked massive migrations of people, leaving millions uprooted and starving. Horror at the cruel-ties of life, as well as anguish at its uncertainties, are feelings never far from the surface of *Waiting for Godot*.

In the course of the early 1950s, productions of the play took place in most European countries and in the USA. *Godot* became a kind of litmus test for the state of the theatre in each new place where it was performed. It was understood (and misunderstood) differently in the different theatrical cultures. In countries as different as Spain and Yugoslavia it was banned as being subversive. In Florida it was adver-tised as 'the laugh sensation of two continents' but flopped, whereas in California it made an astonishing impact on the prisoners of the San Quentin penitentiary. In Sarajevo under siege it had an impor-tant morale-boosting effect. The play struck such different chords in its various audiences, and influenced theatrical cultures in so many ways, that the study of this play in production turns out to reveal as much about the traditions, habits and expectations of the different theatrical cultures as it does about the play itself.

An intriguing problem facing anyone assessing the significance of Beckett's work for theatre production is to be found in the apparent rigidity of Beckett's views on how his plays should be performed. Stories of actors and directors being refused the right to perform his plays circulate freely, especially since Deborah Warner's production of *Footfalls* was brought to a halt in 1996.[4] In this Beckett resembles Brecht, who also tended to stipulate conditions for the production of his plays and would send his representatives to make sure his wishes were respected. In the same month that Peter Hall was rehearsing his London production of *Waiting for Godot*, Joan Littlewood was staging the first English production of *Mother Courage* by Brecht, under the watchful eye of Carl Weber, sent over from the Berliner Ensemble.[5]

In the case of Brecht, the motivation for concern about the manner in which his plays were produced was principally political. As someone who frequently used folk-tales or parables, he was painfully conscious of the way the manner of their representation could affect the meanings they conveyed to an audience. Elements not recorded in the written text, such as the grouping of characters, the rhythm of delivery and the use of costumes and of settings, all needed to be selected from a conscious political standpoint; the dialogue alone could not put across the dramatist's understanding of what it is to live in society. In the case of Beckett, the manner of production is just as crucial. His plays are not concerned with exploring social and political relationships in the same way as Brecht's – their depiction of humanity is more general – but they imply a specific manner of production which is every bit as vital to their effect on an audience. Pierre Chabert, who acted and directed with Beckett, has expressed it by saying that Beckett 'carried through the work of *mise en scène* at the stage when he was composing the play'.[6] In other words, *Waiting for Godot* carries its own production within it, waiting to be activated by director, actors, designers and all the other people with a creative input into the production of the play. Paradoxically, this has not led most theatre practitioners to complain of lack of freedom: on the contrary, many have spoken of the extraordinary sense of creative freedom they have experienced through respecting Beckett's precisely annotated directions.

THEATRE PRODUCTION AND THE ROLE OF THE DIRECTOR

The idea that the stage directions are as central to the play's integrity as the dialogue between characters is far from self-evident, and requires some examination of the evolution of theatre production in Europe if it is to be clarified. The key development in the theatre of the last century and a half has been the rise of the artistic director, a figure who hardly existed in previous ages. In earlier times, actors were largely responsible for the staging of plays. They would provide their own costumes and make their own decisions about how to move and speak and which gestures to employ. Rehearsals were not often overseen by any one guiding hand, and consisted, for the most part, in making sure that all the cast knew their exits and their entrances. The first people to maintain that actors, designers, costumiers, stage painters and the rest needed someone called a director to co-ordinate their artistic efforts emerged towards the end of the nineteenth century. It was a time when technological advances, especially in lighting, were making it possible to create ever more realistic depictions of human environments on stage.

The emphasis of early theatre directors, especially the man often seen as the father of modern directing, Duke Georg II of Saxe-Meiningen, was on recreating spectacular tableaux of historical periods and of civilisations distant from their own. Duke Georg's company was founded in 1866 and had a considerable influence on theatre practice all over Europe. But in the course of the 1880s new directors began to believe that a greater challenge lay in perfecting the more subtle art of representing the daily life of their own period in all its complexity. In France, Emile Zola campaigned vigorously for this vision of what theatre might achieve and his call was taken up by directors in all the major artistic centres of Europe, notably André Antoine in Paris, Otto Brahm in Berlin and Konstantin Stanislavski in Moscow. The partnership of Stanislavski and Chekhov brought this form of theatre to a high point of perfection in the closing years of the last century.[7]

Concurrently with these advances in realistic theatre production, however, other theatre artists were inferring quite different possibilities from the developments in lighting, sound and other technologies of the stage. Of these, the most influential and charismatic was Edward Gordon Craig. In 1905, he published a short dialogue entitled 'The Art of the Theatre'.[8] This dialogue pitted a 'Playgoer' against a 'Stage-Director'. The Playgoer begins by asserting that Acting and the Play are the essential elements making up the Art of Theatre. But the Stage-Director convinces him that 'the Art of the Theatre is neither acting nor the play, it is not scene nor dance, but it consists of all the elements of which these things are composed: action, which is the very spirit of acting; words, which are the body of the play; line and colour, which are the very heart of the scene; rhythm, which is the very essence of dance.'[9] After arguing through the implications of these statements, the Stage-Director concludes with the following words: 'I am now going to tell you out of what material an artist of the theatre of the future will create his masterpieces. Out of ACTION, SCENE, and VOICE.' Under the heading 'Action' Craig includes gesture, movement, rhythm, pace; under 'Scene', everything that is visible to the spectator, including lighting, colour, costume, stage settings and any objects employed in the performance. Under 'Voice', Craig writes: 'I mean the spoken word or the word which is sung, in contradiction to the word which is read, for the word written to be spoken and the word written to be read are two entirely different things.'[10]

Craig's vision, close to that of the Symbolist poets, painters and theorists, was of an art form in which all these elements combined to create a poetic whole which was greater than the sum of its parts. The Symbolists had found this artistic ideal embodied in the *Gesamtkunstwerk* of Wagnerian opera. But although Craig directed some opera, notably his influential *Dido and Aeneas* (1900), he was more interested in discovering a new form of theatre which would combine elements of dance and spoken drama, as well as singing, music and dance. He was fascinated by the Japanese Noh theatre, by masks and by marionettes. He considered that the purpose of theatre was not to mirror life, but to open the doors of perception to its inner essence, to be found only on the threshold of death. Some of his most radical ideas concerned the actor, whom he wished to do away with, at least in the Stanislavskian conception. For Stanislavski's notion of realistic performance, it was essential to find (or to train) sensitive actors, expert in calling up and recreating true emotional states. But for Craig most of the unsatisfactory aspects of theatre were to be traced to the egotism and emotional instability of actors. He concluded that 'the actor must go, and in his place comes the inanimate figure – the Über-marionette we may call him, until he has won for himself a better name'.[11]

Craig's theories were widely disseminated and discussed among the avant-garde theatres of Europe and had a liberating effect on many practitioners, such as the Russian director Vsevolod Meyerhold. Having been an actor in Stanislavski's company, Meyerhold understood the demands placed on the naturalistic actor. He believed that Stanislavski's method was mistaken in that by putting so much emphasis on creating the illusion of reality it sacrificed the most fundamental quality of the art of theatre: play. Meyerhold studied the traditions of popular performance: clowning, acrobatics, juggling, mime and *commedia dell'arte*. In the acting method he developed, known as 'biomechanics', he encouraged outward, physical expressions of inner emotions. Instead of internalising and relying on emotion memory, like Stanislavski's actors, Meyerhold trained his actors in acrobatic displays which could symbolise mental states through physical means. His stage sets were never realistic images of everyday environments, but complex structures with different levels, ramps and staircases, facilitating a wide range of complex movements for his actors. In Meyerhold's productions, especially those of the first decade after the Russian Revolution, the director's creative contribution became almost entirely separable from the text of the play; it was an art form in its own right, a language of the body, of movement in space, with its own peculiar syntactical and stylistic methods.

It was the French poet, actor and director Antonin Artaud, however, who took this idea to its logical conclusion. Artaud considered that the Western theatre tradition had become irretrievably corrupted by plays of discussion and debate, whereas the art of theatre, properly understood, was as all-engulfing as an epidemic of bubonic plague. Like the plague, he believed, theatre should have the effect of a great collective nightmare, from which few would emerge unscathed, but which would have a purgative effect on society as a whole. Like the plague, its impact would be felt, in the first instance, in the body. Only after a physical trial bringing one close to death, could the mental and spiritual dimension of theatre be reached. In this way, Artaud believed, people might escape from the inauthenticity and hypocrisy of modern life into an intense experience of life, and discover the deep, painful truths to which our minds are normally closed.

Although Artaud had little practical success as a director, his theories, like those of Craig, Meyerhold and many others, have contributed to the construction of a new concept of what it is to be a theatre director. The modern director is seen as an all-controlling magus, having powers and spirits to command like Prospero on his magic island. In this way Craig's words about the 'artist of the theatre of the future' have proved to be prophetic: today's artistic directors have won for themselves a position of control over all the other creative processes which go to make up the art of theatre. At least as much attention is now given to the director as to the author or to the actors, both in critical discussion and in theatre publicity. It is common to discuss 'Peter Stein's *Oresteia*', or 'Ariane Mnouchkine's *Tartuffe*', or even 'Peter Hall's *Waiting for Godot*', though the habit is less ingrained in British cultural life than it is in other parts of Europe. Many of the most successful directors have been attracted to opera at least as much as to straight theatre, since it offers greater opportunities for enlisting dance and music, as indicated by Craig.[12]

So important has the director become, that he has been able to lay claim to being recognised as an 'author' in his own right. Just as the film directors of the French New Wave claimed the title of *auteurs* (authors), so theatre directors in France have claimed responsibility for *l'écriture scénique* (scenic or stage writing) having an importance equal to that of *l'écriture dramatique* (the writing of the play). Craig would have understood this language, since it gives credit to the interplay of action, line, colour and rhythm in building up the meaning and the emotional force of a performance, as much as to the words written by the dramatist. It also minimises the contribution made by individuals with outstanding acting talent.

The principle that the art of the director is separable from yet just as important as that of the playwright has given rise to paradoxically contradictory productions on stage. On the one hand, it has had a liberating effect, visible in such masterpieces as Peter Brook's production of *A Midsummer Night's Dream*, set in a bare, white playing space, or Giorgio Strehler's *The Illusion*, in which the figure of Alcandre, the magician, was clearly intended to represent a theatre director. On the other hand, it has led to excesses of wilful distortion, and, worse still, has imposed an unspoken pressure on all directors to come up with an original vision or unexpected setting every time they decide to mount a classic play.

The period during which theatre directors were laying claim to the status of *auteurs* was also the period in which literary theorists were mounting an attack on the objective authority of the literary author. Indeed, one of the strongest voices proclaiming the 'death of the author' was Roland Barthes, who was also one of the chief defenders of the autonomy of the art of the director. In the course of the 1950s, as one of the editors and leading contributors to the French journal *Théâtre Populaire*, Barthes argued repeatedly that Brecht provided the model for modern theatre practice. And although he acknowledged

Brecht's importance as a writer and thinker, his main enthusiasm was reserved for Brecht's understanding that every element of theatre production could be enlisted in constructing a complex, meaningful work of art. He especially appreciated Brecht's ability to make meaning emerge from the discontinuities between 'scenic writing' and 'dramatic writing'.[13]

As a result, since the middle of the twentieth century the work of the director has come to be seen as a necessary complement to that of the playwright. The playwright has been thought of as supplying not a self-sufficient text but a 'script', on the analogy of a film script. In other words it is seen as an artefact not complete in itself but which requires the work of the director and his team to bring it fully to life. This view fits well with post-structuralist literary theory, in which the author's intention is less important than the act of reading, by which each new person who comes to any given text gives it new life, meaning and context. It is also a view which has generated much that is enriching in our theatrical culture. The long-running London production by Stephen Daldry of J. B. Priestly's play *An Inspector Calls* is a case in point. The setting, action, lighting, performances, in fact the whole staging of this play are very far from what Priestley can have intended or imagined. And yet they have given the play a new life and relevance, bringing its themes sharply into focus for audiences since the end of the Thatcher era. The successful 're-visioning' of a text like this can achieve star status for its director, and the institutional structures in Western theatre now reflect the general acceptance that the key to a vital theatre is a dynamic director. There is an expectation that he or (in a few cases) she will provide the main creative force.

Beckett's work does not fit comfortably into this organisation of the theatre enterprise, because it challenges the dominant position of the director. Integral to Beckett's way of writing plays is the assumption that the playwright, not the director, is the *auteur* of the final, staged work, every bit as much as he is author of the play text. It further assumes that the tasks of the director, the actors, the designer and others must all be subordinated to his controlling vision, since he, not the director, has become the 'artist of the future' envisioned by Craig. A detailed explanation of what this means must be allowed to emerge from study of the different productions discussed in this book.

CHAPTER 1

BECKETT BEFORE *WAITING FOR GODOT*

Samuel Barclay Beckett was born on 13 April 1906 (Good Friday). The anguish that pervades his plays has no discernible root in his childhood experiences. On the contrary, he appears to have enjoyed a happy childhood, despite being somewhat introverted and reclusive. He had a gift for games and enjoyed excelling in all kinds of sporting contests: he was light heavyweight boxing champion and opening batsman for his school as well as being a passionate chess and bridge player.[1] At Trinity College, Dublin, he achieved first-class honours in French and Italian before going on to spend a couple of years as *lecteur* at the prestigious Ecole Normale Supérieure in Paris. Here he met James Joyce and his friends, and published his first essay ('Dante . . . Bruno. Vico . . . Joyce') as well as his first short story. When in 1930 he returned to Trinity College, to a lectureship in French, all seemed set for a glittering career.

But after only four terms at Trinity, at Christmas 1931, he resigned his post, leaving Ireland for Germany, and then Paris, where he spent several months writing his first novel, *Dream of Fair to Middling Women* (not published until 1993). From then on, with brief visits home, he was to live in exile throughout his life, gradually fixing on Paris as his permanent place of abode. He spent time with his uncle's family in Kassel in Germany, where he became emotionally attached to his cousin Peggy Sinclair and extended his interest in fine art, since his uncle was at this time a picture dealer. On visits home, he maintained a good relationship with his father, but found his mother harder to relate to, both desiring her affection and approval but shrinking from her Protestant middle-class values. In early Summer 1933, he lost the two people he cared for most in quick succession: in May, Peggy Sinclair died of tuberculosis, and the following month his father suffered a fatal heart attack. Beckett went into a period of prolonged depression. He was in London during 1934 and 1935, where he underwent psychiatry for a short time. He also published a collection of stories entitled *More Pricks than Kicks* with Chatto and Windus, and wrote his second novel, *Murphy*. In 1936–7 he spent six months travelling around Germany, visiting acquaintances and art galleries. It was during this period that he saw Caspar David Friedrich's painting *Two Men Observing the Moon* in Dresden (a painting to which he referred in the production notebook for *Godot*), and also met the Munich dialect comedian Karl Valentin.

He returned home to Ireland for another six months before taking up residence again in Paris. An embarrassing return to Dublin to stand as witness in a family libel case at the end of 1937 resulted in his being publicly branded a 'bawd and blasphemer from Paris' and strengthened his dislike of Irish parochialism. In Paris, he renewed and extended his earlier acquaintance with Joyce's circle and with a number of avant-garde artists, began to write poems in French and, in 1938, had the satisfaction of seeing his novel *Murphy* published in London by Routledge. He had a brief affair with the American heiress and art collector Peggy Guggenheim, was stabbed in a street brawl and, while he was recovering in hospital, began a close friendship with Suzanne Deschevaux-Dumesnil, who was to become his lifelong partner. When war broke out he was visiting his mother in Ireland, but immediately returned to stay in France with Suzanne. In 1941 he joined a resistance group, recruited by his close friend Alfred Péron. A year later, when the network was betrayed to the Gestapo and Péron was arrested, Beckett and Suzanne took refuge in Provence, in a village of the Vaucluse called Roussillon d'Apt. *Waiting for Godot* contains several references to this part of France, including the name of the farmer for whom Beckett worked, Bonnelly, and the peculiar red colour of the earth.[2] During this time, he wrote *Watt* as a kind of escape from the dreadful times he was living through.

The war years had a decisive influence on Beckett. A new note of urgency begins to replace the self-consciously clever verbal pyrotechnics of some of his early writing, and his vision no longer seems so exclusively private in its inspiration. His biographer James Knowlson wrote that 'it is difficult to imagine him writing the stories, novels and plays that he produced in the creative maelstrom of the immediate postwar period without the experience of those five years. It was one thing to appreciate fear, danger, anxiety and deprivation intellectually. It was quite another to live them himself.'[3] Stanley Gontarski went further, noting that 'war is latent in much of Beckett's work', and that 'despite very little direct reference to the war itself, *Waiting for Godot* grew out of Beckett's war experiences'.[4] These experiences included the channelling of secret information (for which he was awarded the Croix de Guerre in 1945), all the anguish of waiting for contacts in dangerous circumstances, of seeing friends betrayed, hearing of their torture and death, of hiding in fields and ditches, and of being permanently hungry. Even after the Liberation of France, Beckett accepted hard physical labour and a share in the sufferings of others, when he volunteered to work for five months in a hospital being run by the Irish Red Cross at Saint-Lô in Normandy.

When he finally settled back into his Paris flat in 1946, he experienced an extraordinarily fertile period. He described it as 'a frenzy of writing' and, in the course of the next four years, he found time for little else. Between 1946 and 1950, Beckett wrote his first novel in French, *Mercier et Camier*, four short *nouvelles*, and the three novels of the trilogy *Molloy; Malone meurt; L'Innommable*, as well as two complete plays, *Eleutheria* and *En attendant Godot*. The change of language (from English to French) together with the enthusiasm of Jérôme Lindon, then a young publisher who had recently founded Editions de Minuit, led to his becoming as much a French author as an Irish one. His novels and plays were taken up in France before they became famous in the English-speaking world, and he continued to live in Paris, until his death in 1989.

Much has been written about Beckett's friendship with the Joyce family and his links with significant figures in the literary avant-garde at this time. There is comparatively little evidence about his theatrical tastes. He was always something of a recluse, and the extrovert exuberance commonly associated with theatre circles was not for him. He was drawn to both painting and music, spending many hours in art galleries, and, especially after he met Suzanne (a pianist), attending concerts. But his visits to the theatre were rarer. As a young man in Dublin he had been a regular attender at the Abbey Theatre, where he was impressed by the plays of O'Casey, W. B. Yeats and, especially, J. M. Synge. When asked by Knowlson which playwrights had influenced him, he mentioned only Synge.[5] Katharine Worth comments on 'the affinities between the blind couple who make the world for themselves from words in [Synge's] *The Well of the Saints* and Beckett's lonely tale-spinners',[6] and also recalls Beckett telling her that *At the Hawk's Well* was his favourite among Yeats' plays. His theatre-going in Dublin was not limited to literary theatre, however: he had also attended the music hall, circus and cinema, and developed a special admiration for Buster Keaton and Charlie Chaplin. He was always drawn to melancholy clowns, and was deeply moved by his meeting with Karl Valentin in Munich in 1937; after seeing him perform he wrote that he was a 'real quality comedian, exuding depression, perhaps past his best'.[7] Although his circle of acquaintances included few actors, many of his friends were artists who had been active in the performance events of the Dada and early Surrealist movements, such as Marcel Duchamp, Francis Picabia and the founding father of Dada, Tristan Tzara. Their importance is discussed below, in the section on avant-garde performance.

During the war years, Beckett had little opportunity for attending artistic functions of any kind, especially after 1942, when he and Suzanne were hiding from the Gestapo in the Vaucluse. In the second half of 1945 his work at Saint-Lô kept him fully occupied, and after his return to Paris in 1946 conditions were very difficult: he and Suzanne lived from hand to mouth on her earnings as a piano teacher, and he seldom attended public functions of any kind. For *Eleutheria* and *En attendant Godot*, he appears to have drawn not on the theatre life of contemporary Paris but on his friendship with men such as Tristan Tzara and his own earliest experiment in dramatic performance. This had been when he was still lecturing at Trinity in 1931, when he had collaborated on a burlesque parody of Corneille's masterpiece *Le Cid*, retitled *Le Kid*, which is discussed in the next section.

Why Beckett turned to drama at this point in his writing life is an intriguing question which may be answered in a number of different ways. To Colin Duckworth (editor of the first scholarly edition of *En attendant Godot*) he said, 'I began to write *Godot* as a relaxation, to get away from the awful prose I was writing at that time.'[8] This may be true, but says nothing about why he had already begun and completed *Eleutheria* early in 1947. *En attendant Godot* was written over a comparatively short period: the first page of the manuscript is dated '9 October 1948' and the last '29 January 1949'. The 'awful prose' to which he referred was the trilogy of novels on which he was working at this time, novels grounded in despair at the failure of language to give meaning to human existence. Michael Robinson sums it up: 'By the end of the trilogy, the dichotomy of which Beckett speaks in the *Three Dialogues*, the obligation to write and the nothing to write, becomes irreconcilable. The hero is forced into repeatedly denying a valid meaning to his words: Beckett is left with a voice in the void that can never know itself, must find itself, has only words with which to achieve this and yet lies in every word it speaks.'[9]

Robinson considers that 'Beckett's decision to turn to the theatre arose from this situation'. If language was fundamentally untrustworthy, then perhaps he could expect more of an art form in which language is not the only means of communication, but which can orchestrate all the different elements invoked by Edward Gordon Craig and can use each to comment upon the other. 'The theatre allows Beckett a double freedom; the opportunity to explore the blank spaces between the words and the ability to provide visual evidence of the untrustworthiness of language.'[10] Above all, theatre introduces the element of time in a concrete, experiential form not possible in prose fiction. Ross Chambers points to a sentence from Molloy:

> My life, my life, now I speak of it as something over, now as of a joke which still goes on, and it is neither, for at the same time it is over and it goes on, and is there any tense for that?[11]

Chambers suggests that it was 'this failure of language to express a certain experience of time that turned Beckett's attention to the theatre, where he was able to create that experience with a fragment of actual time instead of trying to capture it in a linguistic structure that, in fact, denied its existence'.[12]

These accounts of Beckett turning to theatre as the solution to a creative and artistic impasse are persuasive, but in turn raise a further question: what theatre would he turn to? For Beckett's prose (and poetry) had showed him to be at the forefront of the avant-garde of his day, and he was not likely to slip comfortably into traditional models of dramatic construction. This was especially true if, as Robinson and Chambers suggest, his interest was drawn less to the dramatic text than to all the other dimensions of performance and production. His first full-length drama, *Eleutheria*, shows him very clearly experimenting with the avant-garde theatrical forms of the 1920s and 1930s as a sort of 'clearing of the decks' before arriving at his own theatrical style with *En attendant Godot*. In particular, he drew inspiration from the experiments of the Dada and Surrealist movements, just as he had done in his poetry.

DADA, SURREALISM AND THE AVANT-GARDE PERFORMANCE TRADITION IN FRANCE

The Dada movement, which flourished in Zurich from 1916 until 1920 and then continued in Paris, transforming itself into Surrealism, was based on a group of what would now be termed performance artists. The prime mover, Tristan Tzara, was the first twentieth-century artist to make protest and provocation a fundamental principle of all that he did, and the first to enlist sculpture, painting, poetry and music as well as theatre performance in this venture. Annabelle Melzer, the historian of Dada and Surrealist performance, has written that 'there is hardly a theatrical "innovation" perpetrated on our contemporary audiences by the environmental and psycho-physical theatres, the happening and the event, which had not been explored before 1924 by Tzara, his cohorts and disciples'.[13]

The performances given by members of the Dada group in Zurich and, later, in Paris, were carefully designed to outrage and provoke their audiences in every possible way, but especially by attacking their belief in the value of art itself. 'Art is useless and impossible to justify', declared Francis Picabia.[14] The very name Dada was chosen for its lack of meaning or definition (though many attempts have been made to give it one – almost as many meanings as have been suggested for Godot) and Tzara's manifestos demonstrate Dada's careful attempt to avoid definition.[15] Beckett has described *Godot* as a play striving all the time to avoid definition but this concern to avoid definition is most flagrantly evident in the central character of *Eleutheria*, whose refusal to define himself provokes all the other characters to fury: 'Prenez un peu de contour, pour l'amour de Dieu' ('Take on some sort of shape, for the love of God'), says one of them.[16]

Dada's originality lay in its systematic reversal of every quality assumed to contribute to a work of art. As well as hurling verbal insults at their audience, the performers at the Cabaret Voltaire in Zurich insulted their expectations of what a performance should consist of, exploiting the captive nature of any live audience, and using this to provoke them in every way possible. One of these was to devalue language; Hugo Ball's declamation of nonsense poems became a regular feature of Dada evenings, when he would stand up dressed in a cardboard hat and costume and declaim, for example:

> gadji beri bimba
> glandridi lauri lonni cadori
> gadjama bim beri glassala ... [17]

Melzer writes that 'for Ball, words were conceived of as being meaningful by being reminiscent of other words, or rather sounds "touching lightly on a hundred ideas without naming them"'. In August 1916 Ball wrote: 'Language is not the only means of expression. It is not capable of communicating the most profound experiences.'[18] Dada's search for ways of overcoming this perceived failure of language through live performance has obvious links with the preoccupations of Beckett in 1947 and 1948.

Since Dada's aim was to disrupt every established canon and to avoid definition, it was bound to burn out after a short time. Indeed, the provocative effect of performances which abuse their audiences is quickly lost when the audiences come expecting to be abused. Tristan Tzara moved to Paris in 1920 and various *manifestations* and *soirées* took place whose chief purpose was again provocation. Members of the group involved went on to found the Surrealist movement. In the first four years of the 1920s, a number of plays and sketches of combined Surrealist and Dada inspiration were performed, including Cocteau's *Les Mariés de la Tour Eiffel* (1921), Ribemont-Dessaignes' *Le Serin muet, Le Zizi de Dada* and *Le Partage des os* (1921), Tzara's *Le Coeur à gaz* (1922), Vitrac's *Entrée libre* (1922) and *Les Mystères de l'amour* (1923) and Artaud's *Le Jet de sang* (1924). These performances, though very different from one another, all shared an underlying ambition, which was to shock or destabilise their audiences. The only one who proved sufficiently commercial to have his work regularly performed was Jean Cocteau, whose work Beckett certainly knew.

Among Cocteau's plays, *Orphée* (1926) stands out for its mixture of classical theme with Surrealist dramatic technique and music-hall jokes. A key character introduced by Cocteau is Heurtebise, a glazier. He appears in Scene 2 in response to Orphée's deliberate smashing of a window-pane and retains a central role throughout the play. In *Eleutheria*, Beckett must surely intend an echo of Cocteau's work when Victor deliberately breaks a window (at the start of Act II) only to find that a glazier appears, as if by magic. As in Cocteau's play, the glazier then remains, playing a central role throughout the remaining two acts. Both glaziers might be traced back to a common origin in Strindberg's *Dream Play*, were it not for the fact that Beckett denied having read Strindberg's work before writing *Eleutheria* and *Godot*.[19]

LE KID AND ELEUTHERIA

These experiments of the avant-garde theatre in Paris filtered through to members of the Trinity College French department with the usual time-lapse of a few years that it takes for academic institutions to wake up to new artistic developments. They clearly inspired a student production given in 1931. This was devised by Beckett, in collaboration with Georges Pelorson (the department's French language assistant), and parodied Corneille's *Le Cid*, under the punning title *Le Kid* (Charlie Chaplin's film *The Kid* had come out ten years earlier). Since the text of this parody is lost, information about it can only be gleaned from contemporary accounts and the memories of those involved. According to Georges Pelorson, who was responsible for the production, it was he and not Beckett who did the work of cutting up Corneille's text, while Beckett's only original contribution was the title.[20]

Whatever the truth, it is certain that Beckett took part, playing the role of Don Diègue and delivering his famous speech at the end of the first act, 'O rage! ô désespoir! ô vieillesse ennemie!', to a strict time limit set by an alarm clock. The alarm began to ring before he had finished, and so his delivery of the last part of the speech became faster and faster 'until he built up a wild, crazy momentum, producing a torrent of sound that has been aptly compared with the effect of Lucky's extravagant monologue in *Waiting for Godot*'.[21] Other contemporary accounts quoted by Knowlson make it clear that the performance relied on a series of comic gags which recalled the provocative performances of the Dada movement, in which everything to do with military glory was mocked. As Don Diègue, Beckett carried an umbrella in place of a sword. Don Gomès was played by Pelorson in the uniform of a German general borrowed from the previous year's production, which had been Giraudoux's *Siegfried*. Balloons were released on stage and, as in Apollinaire's *Les Mamelles de Tirésias*, the general leapt off the stage and ran all over the auditorium, trying to burst them with his sabre. Corneille's heroes all wore modern dress and Corneille's heroic glorification of both love and war were treated in grotesque, deflating style. Above all the burlesque reduction of a grand hero to a Chaplinesque child is entirely in the Dada spirit.

Taking their cue from the historic seventeenth-century quarrel about whether Corneille's play observed the classical unities of time, place and action, many of the jokes drew on conventions of time. Beckett was dressed up to look like Old Father Time, with a long white beard. A silent figure seated on a ladder was supposed to turn the hands of a large clock face through twenty-four hours in the course of the action. He kept falling asleep and having to be prodded awake by the actors. The play concluded with a barman uttering the traditional cry used to indicate the imminent closing of a pub: 'Time, Gentlemen, please!'. Much of this was clearly inspired, as Knowlson points out, by the irreverence and iconoclasm of early Dada performance. Irreverence and iconoclasm were permanent features of Beckett's writing, especially his writing of the 1930s. Mostly, these tendencies found expression in scatological word play and in aggressive challenges to traditional expectations of poetic or narrative structure. The exploitation of performance as a means of undermining or destroying traditional assumptions seems not to have occurred to Beckett again until after the war.

Human existence within time is demonstrably the theme Beckett felt could most appropriately find expression on stage, from Don Diègue's alarm clock in *Le Kid*, to the endless wait of Vladimir and Estragon and beyond. What *Eleutheria* demonstrates is that, just as he had done in *Le Kid*, Beckett at first turned to the techniques of Dada and Surrealist performance before he was able to discover his own. Knowlson detects in *Eleutheria* echoes of Pirandello, Sheridan, Strindberg, Sophocles, Molière, Ibsen, Yeats, Hauptmann and Shakespeare, but fails to allude to the more obvious recent antecedents.[22] These can be found in the work of those who had mounted the most radical challenge to performance conventions – just as in the novel he was drawn to Joyce, who was challenging its very structure.

Although the Surrealist movement produced relatively little performance work to match the force and explosive energy of Dada, several of the Surrealists wrote sketches or plays, and Antonin Artaud, the most radical reformer of all, was a member of the Surrealist group from 1924 to 1926. The fact that Beckett seldom attended theatre performances was no bar to his knowing the work of Artaud and other Surrealists, since they were so seldom performed on the Paris stage. But they were much discussed, especially in the circles frequented by Beckett, and he certainly knew their work: he translated poems by Breton, Eluard, Crevel and Tzara for various literary journals, and, as John Fletcher has pointed out, 'his verse throughout his career shows the influence of Surrealist technique'.[23] *Eleutheria* presents many similarities with the Surrealist sketches of Breton and Soupault, of Ribemont-Dessaignes, of Tzara and of Vitrac. In the first place, it follows the Surrealist fashion in setting the action in a dream space. The dream is suggested by the fact that the anti-hero, Victor, is present throughout, even when the action does not concern him, and is shown asleep at the start of the first and third acts. Beckett anticipates a device which Adamov was to use some years later in *Le Professeur Taranne*: part of the stage space is left empty, with the action confined to the other part. The empty space becomes that of the dreamer.

Many of the Surrealist plays employed passages of dialogue derived from the technique known as automatic writing – Vitrac's *Les Mystères de l'amour* is a prime example. In writing *Eleutheria*, Beckett does not appear to have made use of automatic writing, but much of the play is reminiscent of it, using dialogue that borders on the absurd, bearing strong similarities to Ionesco's early plays. This is partly because, as in *La Cantatrice chauve* or *Jacques*, its nonsense dialogue is used to send up respectable middle-class society – also a feature of many Surrealist plays of the pre-war period. Another device often used in Surrealist plays, which Beckett borrows in *Eleutheria,* is that of an audience member who jumps on stage to protest about the incomprehensibility or irrelevance of the action. In *Eleutheria,* the interloper from the audience remains on stage for the greater part of the third act.

Most striking of all, however, is the debt that *Eleutheria* owes to the play generally considered the most successful dramatic manifestation of Surrealism, Vitrac's *Victor, ou les Enfants au pouvoir.* Like Vitrac's play, Beckett's is constructed in the shape of a self-conscious and rather heavy-handed parody of the bourgeois *drame.* Like Vitrac's hero, Beckett's is named Victor, and there is much to suggest that Beckett intended his Victor as a counterpart to the Victor of Vitrac. Both are figures of the rebellious son who upsets the expectations of his respectable bourgeois family and reveals their double standards. But whereas Vitrac's child is more advanced and more active and more intelligent than the adults, Beckett's character is just the reverse: he is completely passive, refuses to move from his bed, and rejects all attempts to cajole him into joining 'normal' life or into explaining what he stands for. Vitrac's Victor represents the libido freed from the normal constraints imposed on it; Beckett's Victor desires only to be left alone.

Vitrac was Artaud's partner in establishing a theatre named after Alfred Jarry in 1927. Here, they presented two of Vitrac's plays: *Les Mystères de l'amour* and *Victor, ou les Enfants au pouvoir,* as well as others including Strindberg's *Dream Play.* Although Artaud had very little active involvement with theatre after his production of *Les Cenci* in 1935, he continued to be an influential presence through his writings (*Le Théâtre et son double* first appeared in 1938) and through his friends, on whom he made great demands. These included Roger Blin and Arthur Adamov, who edited a literary review, *L'Heure Nouvelle* (two issues only, in 1945 and 1946), which expressed an attitude to language not unlike that of Beckett at this period.

Adamov, like Beckett, had spent the 1930s on the fringes of literary and artistic circles in Paris, occasionally earning money from translations. Like Beckett, too, he did not begin to write plays until the late 1940s. When he did turn to theatre, his plays bore the stamp of both the Surrealist experiments and the theories of Artaud. In a preface first published in 1950, he argued that 'theatre as I understand it is linked utterly and absolutely to performance'.[24] Like Artaud, he believed that the only theatre worthy of the name was one 'in which everything, from conception to achievement, only has value or existence to the extent that it takes concrete shape on the stage'.[25]

Adamov went on to designate this desired quality as 'literality': 'What I should like to see in the theatre, and what I have attempted to put into practice in my plays, is for the manifestation of content to coincide literally, concretely, physically, with the content itself.'[26] This recalls Beckett's approving comment on Joyce: 'here form *is* content, content *is* form'.[27] Beckett's plays all demonstrate a similar striving for mastery of theatrical form in which the play only achieves full expression when it takes place in real time and space on the stage. No doubt Blin's close involvement with both Artaud and Adamov enabled him to understand from the very beginning this quality in Beckett's work when, in 1949, he was given his first two plays to read. For Blin, the principles of Artaud continued to be vital to his understanding of Beckett. To Beckett's first biographer, Deirdre Bair, Blin said that Beckett was 'one of the two most important people in my life. He and Artaud divide my sentiments between them.'[28] When Blin's production of *En attendant Godot* opened at the Théâtre de Babylone in 1953, it took its place, quite deliberately and self-consciously, in this tradition of French avant-garde theatre. This will be examined in more detail in chapter 3.

CHAPTER 2

WAITING FOR GODOT – THE PLAY

Waiting for Godot cannot be approached in the traditional critical fashion by first summarising the plot, then discussing the characters, and finally considering different directors' visions of these elements. Even to give a plot summary is awkward, somehow missing the point of the play, and the reason is simple: the play's purpose is precisely to dynamite traditional notions of plot, utterly rejecting the type of dramatic construction whose development through exposition, crisis and dénouement can be summarised in such a way as to allow a meaning to be extracted. This is not to say that the play does not secrete meaning. Peter Hall likens it to poetry, which is a helpful way to approach the play. Its meanings are allusive, multilayered, often ambiguous, as in any poetic writing, and, like poetry, it makes a direct personal appeal to members of its audience.

This quality is well captured by Ruby Cohn, who summarised the play in a single paragraph which manages the *tour de force* of explaining what happens in the play without appearing to explain it away:

> The seed of *Waiting for Godot* is St. Luke's account of the crucifixion, as summarised by St. Augustine (although no one has found the passage to which Beckett refers): 'Do not despair: one of the thieves was saved. Do not presume: one of the thieves was damned.' The two thieves are Didi and Gogo; the two thieves are Pozzo and Lucky; the two thieves are Mr. Godot's goatherd and his off-stage shepherd brother; the two thieves might be you and me. Beckett shaped the play to reflect that fearful symmetry – in text and performance.[1]

If we look for plot as conventionally understood – that is, as a series of events following upon and explaining one another – we shall be frustrated. As Cohn goes on to say, the play consists of two acts, the second repeating the outline of the first: two friends wait uncertainly for Godot, are visited by a master and his slave, who then move on, leaving them alone and longing for night to fall. A young boy arrives with a message from Godot that he will not come that day but surely the next. Night falls, the moon rises and the two friends decide to go but do not move. It is natural for an audience to worry uneasily about the meaning of these unexplained events, since the two friends, Didi and Gogo, are themselves in a state of perpetual anxiety about what they are doing there, whether they are in the right place, on the right day, and what may come of their long wait. But the expectation of a traditional dramatic plot, which is that it will resolve such questions, is forever deferred.

Before Beckett, drama was synonymous with action: a plot in which nothing happens was inconceivable. Beckett is the first dramatist to focus exclusively on the act of waiting and to make this into his dominant metaphor for existence. At the same time he obliges his audience to share the experience, in real time, of what it is to wait. To wait is to experience time passing slowly or coming to a standstill. Beckett makes use of this experience of time to dramatise not a story but a state of mind, as Martin Esslin pointed out in 1961: '[Beckett] is trying to capture the basic experience of being "in the world", having been thrust into it without a by-your-leave, and having, somehow, to come to terms with "being there", *Dasein* itself, in Heidegger's sense.'[2]

This aspect of the play was well expressed by Alain Robbe-Grillet, a leading novelist of the Nouveau Roman school, whose own work explored similar themes. In an article entitled 'Samuel Beckett, or "Presence" in the Theatre',[3] he points out that Vladimir and Estragon 'do nothing, say practically nothing, have no other property but that of being there'.[4] In other words, their function is to show, in its most elemental state, what it is to exist, to 'be there'. Moreover, he continues, 'What does *Waiting for Godot* offer? To say nothing happens in it is an understatement . . . But here *less than nothing* happens. It is as if we were watching a sort of regression beyond nothing . . . "This is becoming really insignificant," says one of the principals at that point. "Not enough," replies the other. His answer is followed by a long silence.'[5] Not only has Beckett succeeded in stripping away all the traditional paraphernalia of plot, story and characters, in order to concentrate solely on 'being there', he also manages to demonstrate how presence inevitably entails decay.

This is achieved by the play's emphasis on the dimension of time and on how our sense of identity is governed by it. The close links between identity and memory are investigated more deeply in some of Beckett's subsequent plays (for example, *Krapp's Last Tape*). But already in *Godot* the problem fuels much of the dialogue between Vladimir and Estragon. If they cannot be sure that they were in this place, by this tree, on the previous day, then how can they be sure that they are in the place appointed by Godot? Indeed, how can they be sure of anything, including their own identity? Not being sure of any of the events or people they allude to, they frequently lapse into self-conscious verbal or physical routines just to fill the silence and to ward off their fear of the void. The function of many of these games or routines is, as Estragon says, 'to give us the impression we exist' (Faber 69).[6]

Such attempts seldom get them very far, and, rather than being discussed, the theme of being in time is *experienced* by characters and audience alike. For Vladimir and Estragon, as for anyone who waits for an event which never occurs, time almost seems to have stopped. Between Acts I and II they change very little, although there are small clues pointing towards slow deterioration, such as the fact that carrots have given way to turnips and black radishes. But Pozzo and Lucky appear to be ageing at a different rate. Their appearance in Act II represents a major degeneration by comparison with Act I: Pozzo has gone blind, Lucky has lost the power of speech, and both are so decrepit they can hardly stand. This contrast between two apparently different developments in time encourages the audience to think about what it is to live through time. As well as reflecting on it, the audience is made to experience the passage of time by the constant recurrence of the leitmotif:

ESTRAGON: Let's go.
VLADIMIR: We can't.
ESTRAGON: Why not?
VLADIMIR: We're waiting for Godot.
ESTRAGON: (*despairingly*). Ah! (Faber 14)

At first it seems that, as Lucky says, 'time will tell' and the outcome of the waiting will be revelation. But the idea of time as a reassuring provider of answers is gradually eroded. Even a simple question about why Lucky doesn't put down his bags becomes confused, since, by the time Pozzo answers it, Lucky has in fact put down his bags and so, argues Vladimir, 'Since he has put down his bags it is impossible we should have asked why he does not do so' (Faber 41). As Robbe-Grillet commented, 'in this universe where time stands still, the words *before* and *after* have no meaning. All that counts is the present: the bags *are* down, and so it is as if they always had been.'[7] There is a contrast between the audience's perception of minute changes, such as the bags being put down, and the characters' sense of stasis. It is by exploiting this contrast that Beckett achieves the dynamic force required to give his play the minimum necessary forward movement, avoiding total paralysis. And it is because the play obliges its audience to share the characters' experience of time that the pace and rhythm of performance is so crucial to its success in production.

For the way Beckett links the treatment of self-awareness to his treatment of the time dimension demonstrates his mastery of the specific qualities of theatre performance. His constant reminders to the audience of the time ticking away induces in them exactly the same uneasy self-consciousness of opportunities missed which tortures the characters in the play. Pozzo's speech at the end of Act II expresses forcefully the anguish which has, by this point in the evening, invaded the auditorium as well as the stage:

> Have you not done tormenting me with your accursed time! It's abominable! When! When! One day, is that not enough for you, one day like any other day, one day he went dumb, one day I went blind, one day we'll go deaf, one day we were born, one day we shall die, the same day, the same second, is that not enough for you? (*Calmer.*) They give birth astride of a grave, the light gleams an instant, then it's night once more.
> (Faber 89)

These considerations lead us to the conclusion that a discussion of plot couched in the form of the question 'What is this play about?' will provide no answers. Beckett himself described it as 'a play which strove at all cost to avoid definition'.[8] As Alec Reid has written, '*Waiting for Godot* is not about Godot or even about waiting. It *is* waiting and ignorance and impotence and boredom, all made visible and audible on the stage before us.'[9]

Because this study is concerned with the play in production, it will avoid following up the many thematic leads suggested by the play and will concentrate on the experiential dimension encapsulated in the above statement by Alec Reid. Chapter 1 has shown that Beckett was not the only writer to be preoccupied with how to liberate the theatre from inherited conventions and to introduce to the stage some of the innovations characteristic of Modernism in the fine arts, in poetry or in the novel. His first play, *Eleutheria*, shows him working through many of the solutions that had been adopted by other writers, especially those active in the Dada and Surrealist movements. Their plays had challenged coherent plots by allowing a proliferation of dream-like events, lacking rational or logical structure, and characters who were unstable, liable to dissolve at any moment, or to transform themselves in contradictory ways.

The power and originality of *Godot* is that all such reactive devices have been whittled away until we are left with nothing but what Geneviève Serreau termed 'le jeu pur' ('pure play').[10] Serreau, whose husband Jean-Marie had welcomed Blin's production to his Théâtre de Babylone, was the first of many theatre professionals to write about Beckett's original approach to dramatic character in *Waiting for Godot*. The key, she considered, was in the obvious affinities Beckett's characters share with clowns or music-hall performers. What distinguishes an act between two clowns or comedians is precisely the absence of plot or character. Their performance does not have the ambition to be *about* any given subject (unless they are in satire). The mainspring of a clown act is the play instinct at its most fundamental, and its working lever can be a mere difference in size or temperament: for example, one clown may be tall while the other is short, or one sad and the other happy, and from this simple difference can spring a whole series of playful routines. The effect of such acts may be predominantly comic, but it may equally well suggest pathos or even tragedy. Beckett chose the subtitle 'tragicomedy' for his play, which aptly conveys its range, including moments of farce as well as passages evoking a mood of deeply felt anguish.

None of the four major characters of *Waiting for Godot* possesses the usual defining characteristics of stage characters. Their histories and relationships to one another are full of doubts and uncertainties. They do not share dynastic family histories, like the characters of Racine, whose tragedies Beckett admired. Nor do they talk very much of their private memories, like so many characters of modern drama. They can hardly remember where they come from, despite isolated fragments, such as a memory of going up the Eiffel tower, and although Pozzo asserts confidently, as he departs, that he has a manor house ('le château' in the original French), the audience has begun to suspect that this is just talk.

Rather than seeing them as realistic depictions, it is best to approach each of the pairs of characters as two halves of a single theatrical dynamic. We do not get to know them through building up an understanding of their histories, but through the pure theatrical categories alluded to by Edward Gordon Craig: their movements, gestures and physical and vocal rhythms. These appear first and foremost in the way they relate to one another. Pozzo and Lucky are linked by the classic interdependence of master and slave. They are tied to one another by the rope knotted around Lucky's neck, which Pozzo manipulates like a dog-leash. Lucky repeatedly demonstrates his dependency through obedience to a series of elaborately demeaning orders from Pozzo and appears to be in a state close to physical collapse. Pozzo, on the other hand, is well-fed, well-dressed and claims ownership of the land on which Vladimir and Estragon are waiting. Lucky not only carries Pozzo's coat, his bag, his stool and picnic hamper, but also responds to the order to provide entertainment in the form of a dance and a discourse. Nevertheless, Pozzo hints more than once that he depends on Lucky as much as Lucky does on him. He claims that Lucky has taught him how to think and also that Lucky's hold over him is so strong that he is making his life a misery.

Vladimir and Estragon are linked by an equally symbiotic relationship,[11] although their interdependence is of a different kind. It is that of any couple where there is no obvious imbalance of power (unlike Pozzo and Lucky) and where very small differences therefore take on great significance, leading to a division of roles. Vladimir is the more wakeful and alert of the two: he becomes the provider (of carrots, radishes and turnips). Estragon is the more lethargic: he becomes the one who accepts help and support from Vladimir, giving him a sense of purpose by listening to his stories, occasionally amusing him with his sardonic sayings. Both are visibly old, dirty and decrepit, although there are suggestions that they have seen better days. As characters, there is little to distinguish them, but their physical and temperamental differences provide material for a sequence of tragi-comic routines and dialogues which account for half of the play's two hours or so of running time.

These differences, which emerge in the course of the play, are themselves organised as comic pairs or contrasts. When Pozzo asks which of them smells so bad, he is told that Vladimir has stinking breath while Estragon has stinking feet. Vladimir wishes to hear Lucky think, Estragon to see him dance. As Estragon munches a carrot, he says, 'Funny, the more you eat the worse it gets', to which Vladimir replies,

'I get used to the muck as I go along' (Faber 21). Estragon suffers from painful swollen feet, while Vladimir has a painful prostate condition. Vladimir is nervous and agitated while Estragon is sleepy and bored. Vladimir is the one who insists that he remembers the place, the tree, the events of the previous day, while Estragon always doubts him. Vladimir worries over stories from the Bible, Estragon tries to tell salacious jokes. Vladimir has sometimes been seen as the 'straight man' to Estragon's comic, but this only captures a small part of their relationship and ignores the fact that occasionally they exchange roles, each taking on the characteristics the audience had begun to associate with the other. To the person reading the text, this can be disconcerting, and it is common for readers to find it hard to distinguish between the two. On stage, however, it presents no such difficulty, since the physical distinction between the two is clearly visible, and so it serves to increase the subtle interplay of similarity and difference on which their relationship is built.

Waiting for Godot achieves more perfectly than any other play of the late 1940s the quality of literality expounded by Adamov and inspired by Artaud. Coming to Beckett's writing from the standpoint of linguistic philosophy, Stanley Cavell found a quality which he too called literality.[12] For Cavell, this was to be found in the way the language used by Beckett's characters means exactly what it says, no more and no less. This literality is also present at the level of performance. Instead of there being, as in Stanislavskian naturalism, an artful hinting at everything presumed to lie *behind* a character's words or actions, there is instead a literal authority about the performance: *all* that there is to see and hear is openly displayed before the audience. Beckett's plays encourage us not to look beyond the words and actions for hidden meanings, but to experience the presentation itself as the only meaning offered. Beckett himself provided clear guidance as to how to understand his work when he spoke of the importance to him of the *shape* of certain ideas. Ruby Cohn makes this explicit when she starts her summary of the play with the celebrated sentence from St Augustine: 'Do not despair: one of the thieves was saved. Do not presume: one of the thieves was damned.' This condensed, almost poetic shaping of human beings' deepest hopes and fears paradoxically stresses both symmetry and difference in the very structure of the statement. Beckett's inventiveness as a playwright can be seen in the variety and complexity of his shaping devices. These can be examined under the three main categories identified by Edward Gordon Craig: Action, Scene and Voice.

To begin with 'Voice', all of Beckett's characters are haunted by voices, and the tramps are no exception. Estragon evokes 'all the dead voices', and the noise they make is likened to wings, to sand, to leaves, to ashes:

> VLADIMIR: What do they say?
> ESTRAGON: They talk about their lives.
> VLADIMIR: To have lived is not enough for them.
> ESTRAGON: They have to talk about it.
> VLADIMIR: To be dead is not enough for them.
> ESTRAGON: It is not sufficient. (Faber 63)

This lyrical evocation of the voices which babble in the head, and can never be silenced, is the exception. As a rule, Vladimir and Estragon's talk is very much more down-to-earth, centred on the concrete objects of immediate concern to them – their boots and hats, their physical complaints, the place they are in. Yet even in the middle of such discussions, the tone will often modulate from the physical to the metaphysical. In the play's opening sequence, having at last managed to remove his boot, Estragon complains that it has caused his foot to swell. Vladimir's response is: 'There's man all over for you, blaming on his boots the faults of his feet' (Faber 11). The same modulation recurs, more abruptly, at the end of the act in the following exchange:

> VLADIMIR: But you can't go barefoot!
> ESTRAGON: Christ did. (Faber 52)

Craig was emphatic about the difference between the word written to be read and the word written to be spoken. The way that Beckett shapes the words for the characters of *Godot* never lets us forget that they are words to be performed. Pozzo, especially, cannot speak without being sure that he has an audience. His elaborate preparations for his pompously self-conscious disquisition on evening contrast with Lucky's sudden launching into his parody of a lecture which, significantly, is described as his 'Think', since we are incapable of thinking without verbalising. Although Pozzo and Lucky are so different from Vladimir and Estragon, their speech shares the same tendency to modulate from the concrete to the abstract, the physical to the metaphysical. This can create difficulties for actors, especially those who are accustomed to base their performance on discovering a sub-text. The speeches of *Godot* are almost entirely devoid of sub-text, since the characters are not characters in the naturalistic sense. Instead of pointing inwards to a hidden reality, their speeches seem to point outwards to a poetic overview. A good term for describing this was devised by the American critic Bert O. States, when he wrote that they display a 'peculiar co-operation of text and metatext': 'we hear the pace and detail of real speech, speech concerned with a real out there; but we also have the feeling that speech is referring to another landscape that can be seen only with the metaphysical eye.'[13]

The shaping of vocal delivery in which we hear this 'co-operation of text and metatext' is especially evident in devices such as the song Vladimir sings at the beginning of Act II. The fact that Beckett particularly enjoyed this song is shown by its reappearance in *The Unnamable*, the novel he began immediately after completing *Godot*. The song is used, not primarily because of the meaning to be found in its words, but because it embodies, in a peculiarly vivid form (not without a certain mystery), a particular shape or structure: the shape of the endless cycle. This is the shape on which the whole play is structured, since, just like the song, it repeats the same sequence of actions.

Most complex of all, as shaping devices, are those speeches on which Beckett has imprinted the form of a disintegrating intellect. Attempts to decode the meaning of Lucky's 'Think' (or the mouth's rambling monologue in *Not I*) will give only limited results, since they are not written in discursive, rational mode. But the overall shape of their disjointed fragments conveys something both vivid and clear. In the case of Lucky's monologue, it is the shape of a mind that shrinks, pines and dies as a result of the failure of the world, as perceived, to meet the demands of the enquiring mind. Where academic discourse claims to discern order, logic and even progress, the 'Think' resembles a lecture as it might be given in a bad dream. The monologue enacts a struggle between an attempt to impose a structure of scientific research and philosophical discourse on experience, which is constantly disrupted by the breaking through of phrases (such as 'abode of stones') suggesting brute natural forces quite indifferent to human logic or consciousness.

Moving on to Craig's category of 'Scene', Beckett's theatre work shows his remarkably fertile ability to invent scenic images which take on a condensed, almost proverbial status: Nagg and Nell in their dustbins, or Winnie, half buried in a mound of earth. *Waiting for Godot* is the only one of Beckett's plays not to confine its characters in some physically restrictive fashion. Critics have suggested that this is because his central theme of waiting drew on plays such as Synge's *The Well of the Saints* or Maeterlinck's *The Blind*, which are set in open country. It is possible that Beckett was also thinking of limbo, as presented by Dante; Beckett's debt to Dante, as well as to many other thinkers, including Descartes, Pascal, Geulincx and Jung, are very fully explored by Colin Duckworth in his introduction to the edition of *En attendant Godot* published by Harrap in 1966. But the most important aspect of the setting is its neutrality: it provides an empty space, neither historically conditioned nor socially appropriated. In Peter Hall's words, it enables him to escape from naturalism[14] and becomes a metaphor for the whole uncertainty within which Vladimir and Estragon flounder. When Pozzo comes along he claims that the land is his, but the audience is left in some doubt as to whether this is so. Beckett once commented that the key word in his play was 'perhaps',[15] and the setting contributes to the general ambiguities and uncertainties.

For a play which operates on a metaphorical level, the stage setting 'a country road' has obvious advantages. A road is normally expected to lead to a destination, but this one goes nowhere: it is the spatial equivalent of the temporal waiting for Godot who never comes. The tree which is the only other given item also has a metaphorical force, suggesting the cross on which the two thieves were executed on either side of our Saviour, as discussed by Vladimir in the play's opening pages. This association is strengthened at the end of each act when Vladimir and Estragon contemplate hanging themselves from it. Paradoxically, it also suggests the tree of life found in Norse legends, since it has sprouted a few leaves by the start of Act II. For his production at the Schiller-Theater in 1975, and for subsequent productions, Beckett added 'A stone'.[16] This stone may be seen to have many associations, among which the most evident are the grave and the recurring motif of 'the earth abode of stones' in Lucky's monologue. Beckett himself commented that the stone completed the three orders of animal, vegetable and mineral present on the stage.[17]

Just as the performance of the characters repeatedly calls attention to itself as 'pure play', so the stage setting is given an additional self-referential aspect. In Pirandellian style, Beckett repeatedly reminds us that we are not really faced with a country road at all, but quite simply with a stage in a theatre. The tramps refer to the place called 'the board' ('le plateau' in the original French, which is a term used by French theatre professionals for a stage). They allude to the existence of the audience in several places, and, on one of the occasions when Vladimir has to rush offstage to relieve himself, Estragon shouts 'End of the corridor, on the left', to which, as he exits, Vladimir replies, 'Keep my seat' (Faber 35). The self-consciousness of the setting is underlined by other scenic elements, such as the hats and the boots. We have seen how these everyday objects may be given metaphysical associations, but they also speak on yet another level of the playful world of the great music-hall comics: the hat and the boots that were Charlie Chaplin's trademark, or the hat-swopping routines borrowed from the Marx Brothers and from Laurel and Hardy.

Turning finally to Craig's 'Action', the dominant shape imposed on *Godot* is that of repetition, or circularity. Repetition emphasises sameness, and the monotonous quality of the play is an important part of its effect. In Beckett's theatre monotony is always complicated, however, by the introduction of paradox. As the voice at the end of Beckett's trilogy of novels states: 'You must go on, I can't go on, you must go on, I'll go on.'[18] The very first line of the play emphasises Estragon's sense that there is 'Nothing to be done', even as it sets in motion the sequence of actions that *must* be done, and repeated, over the next two hours. In so far as both halves of the play repeat the same pattern of actions, the structure can be termed cyclical. In so far as they both enact a something with no outcome, it can be seen as, paradoxically, the opposite of cyclical: static. Thus its structure is both cyclical and static. The action at the conclusion of both acts clarifies this paradoxical shape: the appearance of the boy brings hope, while at the same time confirming that Godot will not come; the discussion of suicide implies an ending, but the absence of the requisite rope means death must be deferred. Finally, the conclusion fixes the shape as Estragon (Vladimir in Act II) says, 'Well, shall we go?', and Vladimir (Estragon in Act II) replies, 'Yes, let's go', but they do not move. So the paradoxical shape, both cyclical and motionless, underlies everything: dialogue, movement and structure.

The evident difficulties entailed in analysing dramatic action and structure in such paradoxical terms are reduced if we turn instead to the vocabulary of music criticism. Musical form is impossible without repetition, while at the same time constantly varying the rhythm, dynamics or tonality, so that each repetition is subtly different. The usefulness of musical terminology was demonstrated by John Fletcher, who insisted that the play 'may not be constructed along traditional lines, with exposition, development, peripeteia and dénouement, but it *has* a firm structure, albeit of a different kind, a structure based on repetition, the return of leitmotifs, and on the exact balancing of variable elements, and it is this structure which must be brought out in production'.[19] He comments on the way the writing in the play modulates from one tone to its opposite and brings out the emotional force of Beckett's use of repeated leitmotifs.

The emotional high points of the play are all achieved by repeating elements already used, bringing them back in a way that their force increases with each repetition. The theme of time is one such example, building to the articulation of despair in Vladimir's speech at the end of Act II. Filled with anguish at seeing Estragon asleep, while the boy once again comes to announce that Godot will not appear that day, he summarises existence in a repeat of and variation on Pozzo's words: 'Astride of a grave and a difficult birth. Down in the hole, lingeringly, the grave-digger puts on the forceps' (Faber 90–1). This paradoxical image, bringing together in one brutal phrase the birth that marks the beginning of a life and the death that ends it, condenses the emotional shape of the whole performance. The shaping device to which Beckett attached special importance was the moment, just before the play's conclusion, when Estragon is planning to hang himself and pulls out the rope that was round his waist, so that his trousers fall round his ankles. In a letter written to Roger Blin (see chapter 3), Beckett made it plain that the spirit of the play was 'that nothing is more grotesque than the tragic'. This image of Estragon, at his most ridiculous (in the classic pose with his pants down) at precisely the point when he is also most tragic (contemplating suicide), is the conclusive example of the paradoxical shaping devices so evident at every level of the play.

In conclusion, Beckett presents his audience with a shape that is not just endlessly cyclical (like Vladimir's song) or paradoxical (like the statement 'let's go' combined with the stage direction 'they do not move') or condensed (like the grave-digger/midwife image) but also self-conscious, a shape that comments upon itself – and that is the shape of a performance. To ask Why? What does it mean? is to commit the same error as the people to whom Winnie so scornfully refers in *Happy Days*: 'What does it mean? he says – What's it meant to mean? – and so on – lot more stuff like that – usual drivel.'[20] The reason why Beckett's plays call attention to their own shape is that this is another, more concrete way of warning the audience not to look for meanings behind or beyond the work, but to consider it for what it is: 'a matter of fundamental sounds (no joke intended) made as fully as possible'.[21] This comment must draw our attention not only to the 'fundamental sounds' but also to the manner in which they are made.

Waiting for Godot has become a modern classic because it gives us *both* a human situation expressed with an emotional force that draws us into its own orbit *and* a reflection on the theatrical means used to achieve this. It dares to do away with the reassuring structures of traditional plot and character, and to plunge audiences into the same uncertainty that had previously been reserved for characters in plays. Vladimir and Estragon come from nowhere, have nowhere to go and are sustained only by a hope that is shown to be at best a comforting illusion, at worst a cruel deception. What then is their interest? It lies in how they manage the *tour de force* of filling the space, both temporal and physical, which they are assigned. Their situation becomes a total image for existence; not just the imagined situation of the country road beside the tree, which they conjure up for us by the power of their acting, but their actual situation on stage. This has complex and fascinating consequences for actors and directors who produce the play, as this history of different productions aims to show.

AFTERWORD: *WAITING FOR GODOT* IN THE ENGLISH-SPEAKING THEATRE

Chapter 1 situated the play in its European context and demonstrated its debt to the avant-garde tradition going back through Surrealism and Dada to the Symbolist theatre at the turn of the century. Both *Eleutheria* and *Waiting for Godot* demonstrate clearly their debt to this tradition. But when Beckett translated *Godot* into English, another set of influences revealed themselves: those of the Irish theatre and of English-language variety or music-hall productions on both sides of the Atlantic. Soon after the success of *En attendant Godot* in Paris,

Jérôme Lindon (the publisher) began to receive requests for English-language rights or for permission to translate the play. The prospect of being performed in English must have attracted Beckett, because he quickly began to work on a translation and had completed a first draft by June 1953. The complex story of the battle over rights for the first productions in England, Ireland and the United States is well told by James Knowlson in his biography.[22]

Beckett's English version was first published by Grove Press in 1954. It has a subtly different tone from that of the French original. All of Beckett's work in French benefits from the smaller vocabulary and tendency towards abstraction characteristic of that language. The special quality of the dialogue between Vladimir and Estragon, in which commonplace statements become infused with cosmic significance, depends on this abstract, or neutral quality in the language. When translating into English, Beckett could not avoid the 'earthier', more concrete qualities of English. An example is the exchange about the carrot in Act I. The French uses proverbial formulations which are close to being clichés:

> ESTRAGON: . . . C'est curieux, plus on va, moins c'est bon.
> VLADIMIR: Pour moi c'est le contraire.
> ESTRAGON: C'est-à-dire?
> VLADIMIR: Je me fais au goût au fur et à mesure.[23]

In English, the phrases are less part of a received stock of sayings and come across as cruder:

> ESTRAGON: . . . Funny, the more you eat the worse it gets.
> VLADIMIR: With me it's just the opposite.
> ESTRAGON: In other words?
> VLADIMIR: I get used to the muck as I go along. (Faber 21)

Another example of a similar coarsening of tone is the conclusion of the first long discussion about the two thieves. Estragon's closing statement in the English version is 'People are bloody ignorant apes' (Faber 13). There is a violence implied in this phrase which is not so evident in the more conventional French: 'Les gens sont des cons.'[24] Beckett also introduced a few 'Irishisms' into his English version, showing that he was translating into a very particular English idiom – that of Dubliners. These vary from colloquial expressions such as Vladimir's 'Get up till I embrace you' (Faber 9) and Estragon's references to Godot as 'your man', to Irish names or special words such as 'Kapp and Peterson', the trade name of Pozzo's pipe, and the word 'dudeen', used to describe it by Estragon, and slang expressions such as 'cod' and 'banjaxed'. There are other pointers suggesting that Beckett was hearing Irish voices in his head when he made his translation, such as the phrase 'stark naked in stockinged feet in Connemara' for 'déshabillé en Normandie' in the original text of Lucky's monologue.

The fact that the Irish-English text is perhaps a little more colourful, more idiosyncratic, than the French helps to bring out another feature that was again not so obvious in the original, though guessed at by Blin.[25] This was the debt it owes to popular entertainment and especially to music-hall cross-talk acts. These were a characteristic feature of both American, British and Irish variety shows but were not so common in France. They consisted of short comic routines which relied for their dynamic on exchanges between two contrasted comics. Often a 'funny man' was partnered by a 'straight man', whose task was to appear puzzled or unmoved by all the jokes or strange ideas or enthusiasms of his partner. Hardy, for example, played the straight man to Laurel, just as a generation later Wise played straight man to Morecambe.

Whereas a 'double-act' could be used to describe any partnership in which comedy was derived from such differences, the 'cross-talk act' indicated a particular form of humour in which the partners began by understanding each other well enough, but quickly lost the thread as the words themselves proved treacherous. This kind of comedy was an element in numerous acts, which often verged on the surreal. An example was the couple Nat Mills and Bobbie MacCauley, a comedy double-act which was popular in the variety shows of the 1930s. Their cross-talk routines often turned on a failure of everyday language to guarantee identity, developed in a style that cannot help reminding one of Beckett:

> NAT: Listen – you can talk, but at the right time.
> BOBBIE: Well, who's talking now?
> NAT: Me.
> BOBBIE: Oh no – *I'm* 'me'.
> NAT: No – I'm 'me'.
> BOBBIE: Then who am I ?
> NAT: You're 'you'.
> BOBBIE: I can't be you – I must be me!
> NAT: You're only 'me' to you! I'm 'me' to me and I'm 'you' to you.
> BOBBIE: What relation does that make me to Aunt Polly?
> NAT Aunt Polly my foot!
> BOBBIE: Oh – I've got two.
> NAT: Two *what*?
> BOBBIE: Two feet. Give me one more and I'll have a yard.
> NAT: You've got hold of the wrong end of the stick.
> BOBBIE: What stick?
> NAT: When I say, 'You've got hold of the wrong end of the stick', I don't mean there *is* a stick, I mean there *isn't* a stick!
> BOBBIE: You're talking through your hat.
> NAT: *What* hat?
> BOBBIE: When I say, 'You're talking through your hat', I don't mean there is a hat, I mean there *isn't* a hat!
> NAT: Oh, let's – get – *on* – with – it.[26]

This dialogue shows the most elementary speech particles breaking free and losing their normal contours in a way that recalls not only Vladimir and Estragon but also much French Surrealist humour. Nat and Bobbie's dialogues would be punctuated by moments when Nat's frustration with Bobby reached breaking point and he would bring the discussion to a halt with a frustrated 'Let's get *on* with it', which became a common catch phrase. Its similarity to the repeated 'Let's go' punctuating the dialogue of *Godot* is obvious. Nat and Bobby were a husband-and-wife team and much of the comedy in their cross-talk came from the accurate reproduction of the low-level bickering which sustains a great many married couples. Several critics have made the obvious point that the dialogue between Vladimir and Estragon, indeed their whole relationship, resembles that of an old married couple.

This is because they share intimacies of even the most embarrassing kind in a way that makes it plain they have been doing so for decades. In addition, like some long-married couples, their expression of fundamental needs suggests a reversion to childhood (reversion to childhood was a common feature of plays by Adamov and Ionesco, as it had been in the Surrealist theatre). Like Vladimir and Estragon, the paired comedians of the music-hall double-acts often combined qualities of experience and naiveté which made them react, paradoxically, like children one moment and like old people the next. This permitted an alternation between cruelty and care which made for humorous effects. All the most successful double-acts, such as Laurel and Hardy, Abbott and Costello, Flannagan and Allen or Morecambe and Wise, exhibit this alternation.

It is not only Vladimir and Estragon who are modelled on the comic double-act: a reference in the first French text of the play shows that Beckett associated Pozzo and Lucky with a Russian double-act. In the first act, when Pozzo has just been complaining about Lucky, the following exchange takes place:

> ESTRAGON: It's awful.
> VLADIMIR: Worse than the pantomime.
> ESTRAGON: The circus.
> VLADIMIR: The music-hall.
> ESTRAGON: The circus. (Faber 35)

In the original manuscript, there was no mention of pantomime or circus. Instead, the exchange went: 'On se croirait au spectacle./ Au music-hall./ Avec Bim et Bom./ Les comiques russes.' ('you'd think we were at a show./ At a music hall./ With Bim and Bom./ The Russian comics.') In the first published text, Beckett changed the last word from 'russes' to 'staliniens', only to excise all reference to Bim and

Bom from the English translation as well as from subsequent French editions.[27] Clearly he thought that the reference to Russian or Stalinist comedians gave too precise a political overtone to Pozzo and Lucky. Bim and Bom were, in reality, a Russian double-act whose material satirised some of the absurdities of life in the Soviet Union under Stalin, and the fact that Beckett first associated them in his mind with Pozzo and Lucky shows that the cruelty of their relationship was also tinged, for him, with the comedy of a clown act.

The significance of the rich culture of popular comic performance and cross-talk acts, which can be seen to lie behind *Waiting for Godot*, is that it helps us to understand why the play is able to achieve such a poignant mix of the tragic and the comic while remaining in a thoroughly down-to-earth, everyday situation. Because it employs recognisable structures of comic dialogue, it sets up the expectation that we shall all be amused and entertained. Because the special comedy of the cross-talk act invariably involves frustration and misunderstanding, the audience is prepared for interruptions and incomplete stories (such as the one about the Englishman going to the brothel in Act I). Because Beckett ruthlessly pares away all sentimentality and refuses to allow his performers to ingratiate themselves with the audience (as most comics do), the stark despair of the situation emerges all the more cruelly from the structure, since it sets up expectations of comic relief. For Vladimir and Estragon, ultimately, relief never comes. They suffer the worst fate imaginable for all comedians – not to be able to bring their act to a climax and so leave the stage. After their 'let's go' at the end of each act, 'they do not move'.

The debt the play so clearly owes to music hall and the English-language tradition of the cross-talk act does not mean, however, that the play can be performed as pure comedy. Its distinctive tone and atmosphere derives from the way it sets up particular expectations, including the expectation of comic repartee, and then disappoints them by taking the dramatic development to an unexpected conclusion. Productions in which famous clowns have tried to use the play to showcase their own comic trademarks have usually failed for this reason. Only when the actors have been prepared to face the rather frightening challenge of going on stage with no character to act and nothing but Beckett's 'shapes' to sustain them has the play succeeded in exerting its spell. The echoes of comic dialogues discussed above are offset by the play's debt to the Irish literary theatre of the early twentieth century and to its characters, who, though they may look like tramps, often express deep metaphysical truths. Many commentators have pointed out that the play's opening stage direction ('A country road. A tree. Evening.') suggests a landscape and atmosphere similar to that required for the plays of Yeats or Synge. As James Knowlson has written, both are playwrights who make a key feature of fruitless waiting, and the lineage of the tramps is unmistakeably Irish. He adds that 'as so often with Beckett, his inspiration is literary': he has borrowed more from the beggars and tinkers of John Millington Synge than from any real-life tramps.[28] The rhythms of Beckett's dialogue demonstrate most clearly his debt to Irish theatre, as was clear to the play's first Irish director, Alan Simpson (see chapter 4). This has led many directors of English-language productions outside Ireland (including Peter Hall in 1997) to make their casts adopt Irish accents. The production by the Gate Theatre discussed below in chapter 9 benefited greatly from the vocal intonations and rhythmic pacing given to the dialogue by the Irish actors performing Vladimir, Estragon and Lucky.

CHAPTER 3

THE FIRST PRODUCTION: THEATRE DE BABYLONE, PARIS, JANUARY 1953, DIRECTED BY ROGER BLIN

THE GENESIS OF ROGER BLIN'S PRODUCTION

Blin had never planned to become a director, having worked as an actor in both theatre and films during the 1930s and 1940s. But in 1948 he became, technically, the director of the small Gaîté-Montparnasse theatre. The lease on the theatre was, in fact, paid for by an actress friend, Christine Tsingos, and her husband, but because they were Greek, French law required them to work through association with someone of French nationality. In this way, for two years (until the theatre burnt down) Blin was the nominal director. He was never to repeat the experience and was paying off the debts incurred by the theatre for most of the rest of his life.

His plan at the Gaîté-Montparnasse was to continue performing contemporary plays, as he had done before the war, but he also wanted to explore some of the lesser-known writers whose work had prepared the way for the modern theatre, including Strindberg and Büchner. He produced *The Ghost Sonata* by Strindberg and performed in *Woyzeck* by Büchner (though *Woyzeck* was an artistic disaster and was taken off after its opening night). The choice of these two authors was certainly influenced by Blin's close friendship with Adamov, who was gradually developing his own oppositional theatre, which he defined by reference to Büchner, Strindberg, Grabbe, and other playwrights whose work was hardly known at the time or who were considered to be only marginal figures in the history of drama.

Beckett's decision to allow Blin the rights to produce *Godot* probably had less to do with seeing himself as part of this attempt to redefine a new genealogy for the modern theatre than with his admiration for the artistic courage of a director who chose to put on uncommercial plays by writers such as Strindberg and Beckett's friend Dennis Johnstone. Johnstone's *The Moon in the Yellow River* had been Blin's first choice as a director, put on in May 1949 at the Gaîté-Montparnasse and followed in October of the same year by *The Ghost Sonata*, which was seen by Beckett and Suzanne. At this time, Suzanne was busy offering the manuscripts of both *Eleutheria* and *En attendant Godot* to any director she thought might be interested. They had already been turned down a number of times – for example, by the Grenier-Hussenot company, who specialised in cabaret, and by Georges Vitaly, another young actor-turned-director who had championed the plays of both Pichette and Audiberti.[1] Jean Vilar had seriously considered a production of *Eleutheria* as early as 1948.[2] Late in 1949 Suzanne gave Blin the manuscripts of both *Eleutheria* and *En attendant Godot*.

Tristan Tzara, who had read the manuscript of *Godot*, had already spoken to Blin of his admiration for the play. In addition, Blin had some slight acquaintance with Beckett's work, having read one of his poems on the radio, and knew of his friendship with the Surrealists. He was excited by *Eleutheria*, calling it 'cette très belle première pièce' ('this very fine first play'), but he realised he could never afford the seventeen actors it required. 'In *Godot*,' he went on, 'there are only four characters plus a child and a tree, it was simpler.'[3] The qualities that excited him in *Godot* were 'l'humour et la provocation'.[4] The French word 'provocation' has a stronger meaning than its English homonym, conveying a challenge or even an incitement. Blin emphasised how much he valued this subversive quality in Beckett's work by repeating that what aroused his interest in the play was 'Beckett's gift for provocation'.[5] He went on to enlarge on this: 'I am always excited by the prospect of being a pain in the arse. I put on *Les Nègres* against the Whites, *Les Paravents* against the army, *Boesman and Lena* against apartheid. Eighty per cent of my motives for doing the play derive from its value and ten per cent from its powers of provocation. With *Godot*, I was sure that we would shake up a lot of people, especially the playwrights of the time, the theatre directors and a section of the audience.'[6]

Early in 1950 Blin met with Beckett for the first time to discuss ideas for production. He was able to convince Beckett of his real enthusiasm for both plays, though he explained that considerations of cast size ruled out *Eleutheria*. So, with Beckett's blessing, Blin set about finding a theatre manager who would allow him to direct a production of *En attendant Godot*. At this time he was still technically director of the Gaîté-Montparnasse, but Christine Tsingos was not impressed by the play, just as she failed to share Blin's enthusiasm for Adamov. Blin, on the other hand, felt very strongly that Adamov and Beckett belonged to the same artistic family: both were erudite, charismatic men, yet completely uninterested in fashion, fame or fortune. Blin described Adamov at this time as a beggar-prince;[7] he lived in considerable poverty but was a well-known figure in the literary world of the Left Bank, valued for his passionate commitment to marginalised writers, whether long dead, such as Büchner and Strindberg, or still living, such as Artaud, whom he helped sustain for much of the 1940s. Beckett, who lived hand-to-mouth throughout the 1940s, had a similar lifestyle and frequented the same milieu (as well as some of the same cafés). Both Adamov and Beckett followed the latest movements in poetry and painting; both took on translating jobs for cash. More important still, both men wrote from a perspective of solidarity with the down-and-outs of society which challenged the trappings of bourgeois success in a deliberately provocative style. But most important of all, in Blin's eyes, both were dedicated, as Artaud had been, to developing a new stage language – a dramatic style which Blin called 'poetic' and whose poetry was very different from the verse drama current at that time.

Beckett had to wait four years after completing *En attendant Godot* before it was first produced on the Paris stage. He might have had

to wait a great deal longer had it not been for a cluster of very small
'art' theatres, mostly situated in the Latin Quarter and all dedicated
to avant-garde performance work. These tiny *salles* were a distinctive feature of the Paris theatre in the 1940s and 1950s; they have
been chronicled in loving detail by Ruby Cohn in her admirable
book *From 'Desire' to 'Godot': Pocket Theater of Postwar Paris.*[8] Often
built in converted shops, most of these theatres held fewer than one
hundred spectators, had very low running costs, and so were able to
take risks on new and experimental work. In order to increase their
profitability they would put on two shows in the same evening, one
at 6 or 6.30 p.m. and the second at the more normal Parisian hour of
9 p.m. (a practice still maintained at the Lucernaire theatre today).
Many of them were converted into cinemas in the 1950s and 1960s
(for example, the Noctambules, where Ionesco's first play *La Cantatrice chauve* had its première). Others were pulled down or turned
back into shops; only one survives as a theatre – La Huchette in the
rue de la Huchette, where *La Cantatrice chauve* and *La Leçon* have
been playing uninterrupted since they were revived in a double bill
in 1957.

The actors, directors and playwrights who were active in these
theatres were very conscious of working towards a new form of theatre. They saw themselves as part of the avant-garde tradition discussed in chapter 1, going back through Artaud and the Surrealists
to Alfred Jarry and the Symbolists. Their reference points included
Lautréamont, Mallarmé and the metaphysics of absence, and the
Cubist painters, especially Picasso and Braque. They did not expect
their work to be taken up by the big, established theatres, glory-
ing instead in the semi-clandestinity of the small Left Bank theatres
which made up what would now be called a 'fringe' or 'alternative'
theatre circuit. This feeling was summed up by Adamov, looking back
a decade later: 'What a great time the fifties were. We were forced to
beg for everything; we talked about producing a play without even
knowing what theatre would accept it ... But all of us – Serreau,
Roche, Blin of course, others, myself – shared a similar idea of what

theatre should be. We were the playwrights, actors, directors of the active avant-garde, opposed to the old theatre of dialogue, which we condemned.'[9] This evokes the artistic context in which men like Blin were striving to develop a new theatre, in which movement, gesture, mime, all the physical language of bodies in space, assumed as much importance as the dialogue.

By 1950, when Blin took on *En attendant Godot*, he had been searching for a theatre in which to mount a production of Adamov's first play, *La Parodie*, for three years. A system of state subsidy for new theatre work was only just beginning to be put in place. The normal way to get a new play on stage was to find a patron, someone with money to spare and who wished, for whatever reason, to be associated with the latest developments in the arts. Blin and Adamov together spent considerable energy writing begging letters to friends who might be persuaded to help and courting possible patrons.[10] In the meantime, Blin took the leading role in another Adamov play, *La Grande et la Petite Manoeuvre*, directed by Jean-Marie Serreau at the Théâtre des Noctambules. Blin was hoping that it would prove possible to mount *En attendant Godot* in the same theatre 'as soon as Adamov's *La Grande et la Petite Manoeuvre* has exhausted its admirers',[11] but this did not happen. In fact it was not for another two and a half years that the same combination of Blin and Serreau resulted in the production of *En attendant Godot*.

In the course of those years other productions were preparing a climate that would be favourable to *Godot*. Maurice Blanchot, for example, reflecting on *L'Invasion* by Adamov, directed by Jean Vilar, wrote that the necessary condition for a renewal of theatre was that 'language can become simple and transparent enough to render completely visible this strange absence that is dramatic space'.[12] Comments of this kind show intellectuals groping towards a new concept of how the stage might operate as signifying space, a concept that would enable them to respond to the works of Beckett. A key production in this evolving process was that of Ionesco's *Les Chaises* at the Lancry theatre in April 1952, which turned into a *cause célèbre* in theatre circles. Following a hostile reception from most of the theatre reviewers, the fortnightly journal *Arts* (17 May 1952) published a page of statements in defence of Ionesco's play by a number of literary or theatrical luminaries, including Beckett and Adamov. The contribution by Beckett was in the form of an open letter: 'I have just seen *Les Chaises*. I wish to let you know that I was deeply moved.' Adamov saluted 'the image of decrepitude that reduces existence to a wail without relief from cradle to grave'.[13] Neither to Beckett nor to Adamov did Ionesco's play seem absurd; on the contrary, it presented an image of the world that was all too real, rather than appearing as a grotesque exaggeration. Parody was central to their conception of avant-garde theatre, but they had left behind the absurdity and nonsense of Surrealism in favour of a harsher representation of the predicament of modern humanity.

Throughout this period Blin was working on *En attendant Godot*. Always sensitive to the poetic rhythms of a text, he was haunted by the power of Beckett's dialogue and began to rehearse sections of it with different actor friends long before he had secured a theatre in which to put on the production. For the role of Vladimir he chose Lucien Raimbourg, a former music-hall artist who had performed a programme of cabaret sketches entitled *Quatre Pas dans le cirage* at the Gaîté-Montparnasse at the time when Blin was rehearsing *The Moon in the Yellow River*. For Estragon, he took on another actor he had known for some time, Pierre Latour. Various different actors tried the role of Lucky, many of whom abandoned it in disgust, until Blin was able to persuade another old friend, Jean Martin, to do the role.

Although he was at first unsuccessful in persuading any theatre manager to accept the play, Blin's persistence brought rewards in other ways. In 1951 a copy of the play was submitted to Georges Neveux, president of a committee which existed to assist the production of first plays by new playwrights, the Commission d'Aide à la Création. The committee made a positive recommendation and the official announcement that a subsidy would be available for the production of the play was made on 7 June 1951.[14] In January 1952, the wheels of bureaucracy having turned their slow circles, Blin received a letter from Georges Neveux announcing both his personal enthusiasm and the precise sum allocated: 700,000 francs. At this stage Blin had hopes that Jean-Marie Serreau would choose the play for the opening production at the Théâtre de Babylone, but when Serreau settled on a different play Blin accepted a promise from Mme France Guy, manager of the Théâtre de Poche, that the play could go on there as soon as her current production came to an end. An agreement was signed to this effect on 23 July. But the production running at the time (*Uncle Vanya*, directed by Sacha Pitoeff) proved to be unexpectedly successful; Mme Guy did not want to take off a show that was pulling in the crowds and certainly did not imagine that *En attendant Godot* would do as well. She and Blin fell out over the interpretation of the contract.

Although Blin had such difficulty in persuading theatre managers to back the play, he had some modest success with the Organisation de la Radio-Télévision Française. In February 1952 an abridged version of the play was performed in the studio of the Club d'Essai de la Radio and broadcast on the radio.[15] This in turn helped to persuade Jérôme Lindon, director of Editions de Minuit, to announce publication of the play for October 1952. Blin's search for a theatre finally brought him back to his friend Jean-Marie Serreau, whose Théâtre de Babylone had just completed its first season. He still had the promise of government subsidy, and a number of private individuals, including Delphine Seyrig, put up additional sums.[16] On 2 November 1952 contracts were signed for a production of *En attendant Godot* due to open the following January. By this time, Serreau could already foresee the coming financial collapse. Blin quotes him as saying: 'I shall have to close down anyway, so why not go out on a high note?'[17]

The Babylone was emblematic of all that was most energetic and visionary about the pocket theatres of the Parisian postwar period. It had been converted from a former shop at 38 Boulevard Raspail by Serreau and a group of friends. Since they had no grants or private resources, they had to beg or borrow materials from whatever source offered itself. The 223 seats, for example, were liberated from an unused cinema nearby. Serreau was always a man of broad vision. He opened the theatre with an art exhibition, hoping that 'the Babylone would be a home for avant-garde artists in music, painting and film as well as theater'. Ruby Cohn's evocative description continues:

> The Babylone was located at the end of a cobblestone courtyard. To the right slumbered two stone lions that looked as though they had been sculpted by Douanier Rousseau. Before the door of the theater arched four acacia trees, as though patterned after the set of O'Neill's *Desire under the Elms*. The interior of the theater was red and pale gray. Long, narrow, and relatively bare, the Babylone clearly belonged to the same family as the Vieux-Colombier, but the red seats were a departure. The stage was six meters wide and five deep; despite Serreau's ambitious plans, there was no money for curtain or lights.[18]

Serreau never allowed the penury in which he worked to dim his ambitions. As well as putting on numerous productions of new plays in less than three years (before he went bankrupt) Serreau also founded a festival of Left Bank theatres. He was also the first director to introduce Brecht on the avant-garde circuit. The list of authors presented at the Babylone reveals a far-sighted choice of playwrights who were to prove central in forming the theatrical sensibility of the 1950s and 1960s: Jarry, Strindberg, Kafka, Pirandello, Brecht, Ionesco, Adamov and Beckett.

Given Serreau's reputation, the critics came to the first night of *Godot* knowing what sort of event to expect. Not all of the reviews were positive, but almost every one acknowledged that the play was something out of the ordinary. Added to Serreau's reputation, Beckett was becoming known as the author of *Molloy* and *Malone meurt*, both published by Editions de Minuit in 1951. These novels had provoked a number of major review articles in high-profile journals by critical heavyweights.[19] All the major papers carried reviews of *En attendant Godot*. A few were puzzled or hostile, but most were favourable, and more than one mentioned the subversive quality which had appealed to Blin. Guy Dumur, for example, who was later to become one of the most respected of French theatre critics, wrote: 'Samuel Beckett is a subversive spirit; you can't imagine how comforting that is' (*Combat*, 12 January 1953). *Arts*, whose policy was to champion the avant-garde theatre, and which had published a defence of *Les Chaises*, carried several articles: on 16 January Audiberti wrote that *En attendant Godot* was 'a perfect work which deserves a triumph', and on 27 February Anouilh wrote his famous defence, in which he claimed that the production was as important as that of Pirandello's *Six Characters in Search of an Author* (brought to Paris by Georges Pitoëff exactly thirty years earlier), summing it up as 'the music-hall sketch of Pascal's *Pensées* as played by the Fratellini clowns'. In the same issue of *Arts* Salacrou wrote that this was 'the play of our time for which we have been waiting'.[20] And as early as February 1953 Alain Robbe-Grillet published a long, thoughtful article in the respected journal *Critique*. This is still one of the profoundest critical meditations on the play (see chapter 1).

The significant thing about this list is that it includes three of the most important and forward-looking playwrights of the period. No doubt their enthusiasm for the play was partly motivated by the knowledge that (as recent examples such as *Les Chaises* had shown) the play was extremely unlikely to outlast its initial run of a month and that Serreau was on the verge of financial collapse. But even taking this into account, the number and the acuity of the tributes from fellow-writers was remarkable. Many of the critics also succeeded in grasping what was important about the play. Jacques Lemarchand, one of the most consistent defenders of the new playwrights, wrote a particularly prescient review:

> *En attendant Godot* is a profoundly original work; as such, it will not
> fail to disturb. It will charm some and inspire others to scorn and even

fury . . . [It] indicates the true direction of a whole dramatic movement that is still in a period of research.[21]

Marcel Frère, writing a preview article for *Combat*, made the following very perceptive comment:

> *En attendant Godot* often moves at the pace of farce. Its realistic dialogue consists of everyday words in short lines. Without an ounce of literature – I mean self-conscious literature – Samuel Beckett gives us a profoundly poetic work.[22]

Renée Saurel, critic of the Communist Party's arts review *Les Lettres Françaises* (whose founder editor was Louis Aragon), also insisted that 'Samuel Beckett is a poet. He has written intelligible, lively dialogue, made up of small, familiar phrases. His very subtle art is full of tenderness, reserve, burning love of life under the surface of a bitter clown show.'[23]

The result of all this critical interest was that, after a slow start with audiences, the play caught on and became the success of the season. People went in a spirit of curiosity to see whether the play lived up to its reputation and whether it was really possible to sustain an evening in the theatre with no dramatic action, only waiting. This led to an atmosphere in which members of the audience would mutter to one another, occasionally walk out noisily, or even get into arguments with one another in mid-performance. The play acquired a reputation as the latest Parisian *succès de scandale*, taking its place in the mythology of theatre-going alongside famous predecessors such as Hugo's *Hernani*, Jarry's *Ubu Roi*, Apollinaire's *Les Mamelles de Tirésias* and a number of Artaud's productions. It continued to attract full houses until the *fermeture annuelle* in the summer, and then re-opened in the autumn and ran for a further year; the same production did short tours to Germany, Switzerland and Italy. But even a year and a half of full houses could not provide the sums necessary to pay off Serreau's debts and the Babylone finally closed down in November 1954.

THE PRODUCTION

Considering the major significance this production was to assume in the development of twentieth-century theatre, its poverty of means seems almost unbelievable. Of course all such judgements are relative: audiences in the 1940s and early 1950s did not expect lavish staging, especially in a pocket theatre of the Left Bank. Moreover, Copeau's influence was still strong, and austere staging was seen as something of a virtue.[24] Even so, the equipment available to Blin was so rudimentary that it might shame even an amateur production. The tree, designed by Blin, was made by wrapping tissue paper that had been painted brown round a framework of wire coat-hangers twisted together. The spindly result was anchored in a piece of foam rubber. This and the technical running of the show was the responsibility of Sergio Gerstein. In the interval between the acts he added bits of green paper to the tree to suggest leaves.

The lighting consisted of three spotlights suspended above the stage area and directed at the backcloth from above. There was also a ground row at the back of the stage, illuminating from below the backcloth made up of old sheets sewn together. This back-lighting helped to create some sense of space despite the restrictions of the tiny stage. Additional lights were improvised for the occasion by fixing light bulbs into empty oil cans.[25] Two of these were held by stagehands at the back of the auditorium and directed at the performers' faces so as to make them visible, against the silhouette effect of the back wash. They were also used for atmosphere: to represent the moon rising a stagehand behind the backcloth directed another similar light onto the cloth while raising it in a relatively rapid arc, suggesting a sudden, unrealistic arrival of night. Another light placed offstage left was used to illuminate the tree from the side, giving the impression of the setting sun. Blin's talent for design was thus given very little scope: the most he could do was to create a strong distinction in the colour of the lights, from yellow (the sunset) to blue (the moon). For the rest, the play's stage direction, which specifies

evening, justified the relative obscurity in which most of the action
was performed.

The props were even more improvised, being scavenged from dustbins by the costume mistress's husband who was a rubbish collector.[26]
Ruby Cohn writes that 'Blin stole from his own father (a doctor)
a wedding jacket for Vladimir-Raimbourg'.[27] This morning coat
looked rather too large on Raimbourg and was worn over a loose shirt-
front, a celluloid butterfly collar and a thin black tie; underneath he
wore nondescript black trousers. Estragon had a tighter black jacket,
with no shirt underneath but a grubby white neck scarf, and very
baggy black trousers held up by a piece of rope. His boots were old
and broken down and visibly too big for him. As Odette Aslan has
commented, 'These two characters were not really dressed in rags,
but their clothing appeared completely incongruous in this desert.
A picture of civilisation in an end-of-the-world setting. Vagabonds,
decrepit but dignified.'[28] Lucky was in a scarlet old-fashioned footman's jacket, trimmed with braid and worn over a striped vest and
old black trousers which had been messily cut away just below the
knees, leaving his shins bare. The footman's jacket had been found
lying around at the theatre and so was appropriated. He carried a
suitcase in one hand and a plain round wicker basket in the other.
Under his arm was a simple folding stool and the cord tied round
his neck was long and thin. While the aspect of these three was
dowdy and broken-down in the extreme, Blin's costume as Pozzo was
clean and new: a checked macfarlane with cape, a smart collar and
tie, a fancy waistcoat, neat jodhpurs and knee-length leather boots
gave him the air of a well-to-do English country squire. All four wore
bowler hats, which was the one explicit instruction Blin received from
Beckett.

As a director, Blin's policy was always (and unfashionably) to seek to
impose himself as little as possible on the conception provided for him
by the author: 'I have never attempted to mark my productions with a
sort of Blin continuity.'[29] This modest statement reflects faithfully the
determination which sustained Blin throughout his life: it was a refusal

of everything which would now be called mainstream, including the development of a characteristic production style or a set of theories by means of which he could be 'pigeon-holed'. If this seems a rather negative ambition, it is true that there was something austere and uncomfortable about Blin. This was one of the qualities he shared with Beckett – he expressed it by saying that Beckett and he discovered a 'solidarity in leanness'.[30] But this quality also had its positive side, which was to fight for whomever or whatever was marginalised by the establishment.

Blin's reputation in the later years of his life was such that he was frequently interviewed by journalists, academics, writers and research students. He was always happy to reminisce about the long gestation period of his production and, despite some small variations in detail, he always based his account on the same salient points:

1. The large number of theatre professionals (actors as well as direc-tors) who had read the play but could see no future for it and declined to become involved, hence the courage and commitment shown by those who did agree to join him in putting it on.
2. The different ideas that came to him for how to visualise the characters and their actions on stage.
3. The physical process through which each actor grew into his part, especially during the last weeks, when rehearsals were taking place full time. Those who witnessed the first production all speak of the outstanding quality of the performances and it seems likely that the long rehearsal period enabled the actors, especially Raimbourg and Latour, to reach a point of far greater perfection than was common in pocket theatre productions of the time.

Blin's first idea was to present the characters as clowns and construct a circus ring on stage. He imagined the actors coming on in dressing gowns, bringing on a potted tree, doing some limbering-up exercises, rubbing their shoes in a resin box (as clowns did when they had to perform acrobatic tricks on boards) and only after this would the play begin. He claimed that it was the relationship between Vladimir and Estragon and the rapid-fire cross-talk dialogue that had made him think of clowns and of the American film comedians he particularly admired: Harry Langdon and Buster Keaton. He attributed these qualities to the Irish and English music-hall traditions which he assumed must have influenced Beckett. This reaction demonstrates the sureness and accuracy of Blin's reading.

He soon realised, however, that despite the circus 'feel' of the play it would be far too restrictive to costume the characters as clowns and have them perform in a ring. Despite the fact that this would provide a good visual metaphor of the cyclical nature of the play, he realised that the second act, especially the last few pages, when Vladimir almost seems to wake up to the real horror of his situation, would lose much of its emotional force if performed as a piece of clowning. He was to find a more deliberate application of clowning in Genet's play *Les Nègres* (subtitled *Clownerie* by Genet) when he directed its first production six years later. He decided that to see Vladimir and Estragon as clowns was a false trail, or, worse, a trap: 'Ninety per cent of the *Godots* put on in the world fall into this trap.'[31]

Next, he veered towards a tragic reading of the play. He began to see Vladimir as a figure resembling some of Adamov's early characters: a man crushed by forces outside his control about which he could do nothing, however hard he might try. This he called the tearful trap ('piège larmoyant'), especially for Vladimir, and one which he decided also had to be avoided. In the last analysis, he came to believe that the richness of the play lay precisely in its multilayered quality and that its ambiguity was a way of obliging an audience to respond in complex ways which could not be reduced to a single emotion. He summed up the whole rehearsal process with the words: 'essentially, the work we did during the rehearsal period was to find the correct balance between laughter and emotion, not tipping over into farce, nor into weepiness'.[32]

Psychological analysis of character did not form part of Blin's preferred method for preparing a role. Instead, he enjoyed experimenting with movement, gesture, vocal tone and register, exploring the play's peculiar music through trial and error in performance. This method was derived from his experiences of working with Artaud and the October Group before the war, and with Adamov more recently. He never came to rehearsals with a plan of action set out in advance; he never (unlike Beckett when he came to direct his own work) sketched out suggested moves for his actors in the margin of the text. Instead, he would improvise with the rhythm and music of the text and with the actors' movements and use of the stage. He described his production work on *En attendant Godot* as 'the long perfecting of a sort of ballet',[33] and his method was one of working 'from the outside in'. This meant that rehearsals did not involve sitting down and discussing the meaning of the play or the thoughts of the characters. Rather, they were constantly active, running through sections of dialogue, trying out different voices, rhythms, movements, and trusting to intuition rather than to any conceptualised plan in order to pick on some solutions while others were rejected.

Nevertheless, there were of course guiding ideas behind his approach. One of these had to do with the physical condition of the characters. He noticed that each of them suffered from some sort of affliction, and encouraged his actors to start by exploring the consequences of these for the way they moved. Vladimir, for example, has prostate trouble. Constantly feeling the need to urinate, he is permanently on the move, finding it difficult to remain still for very long, sometimes doubled up with pain, and rushing off stage every so often to relieve himself. Estragon, on the other hand, has painful feet, and so avoids moving about as much as he can; he is sleepy and hungry all the time and can be seen as 'a lump of recalcitrance, a man with a leaden arse'.[34] In the role of Vladimir, Raimbourg used all the charisma he had developed as a cabaret comic. For example, he would move rapidly around the stage, then stop suddenly, bending his legs outwards in a movement which was irresistibly comic and had occasionally to be restrained. He was also capable of raising a laugh just by the way he looked at someone. According to Blin, Pierre Latour felt that he was sometimes sacrificed to Raimbourg, becoming nothing more than his sidekick because of his stolid, sleepy immovability. But it was the relationship between the two which elicited both the comedy and the pathos remarked on by those who saw them.

Blin was particularly insistent on the physical nature of this relationship:

> Physically, it seems to me, these two vagabonds must fit exactly into each other, for their relationship is that of an old couple, and works at the level of physical interlocking at the same time as that of rejection. They need one another, cannot be apart for long, but can no longer put up with one another.[35]

The image which they brought to mind for him was of two monkeys he had once seen in a miserable cage, clinging desperately to one another 'with a sort of infinite distress'.[36] Vladimir and Estragon have been seen by commentators as a 'pseudo-couple' and as the separated halves of a single personality. Beckett himself was to emphasise their physical connectedness when he came to direct the play – no doubt he had learned from Blin's very concrete approach (see chapter 6). Blin exploited the contrasts between the physical build of the two actors, and between their movements and gestures, to emphasise their physical complementarity. As Estragon, Pierre Latour moved relatively little, remaining curled up by the mound downstage right whenever he could, suggesting, as well as his inertia, a residual slyness, which made him constantly on the lookout for ways to frustrate the activities thought up by Vladimir. Raimbourg, on the other hand, was extremely active, constantly moving from one side of the stage to the other, from back to front, never giving up hope of seeing Godot appear at any moment. After each of these movements he would return anxiously to Estragon and in these moments of reconciliation and togetherness Blin allowed his original circus-inspiration to influence the playing. Their professions of friendship were highly physicalised, with exaggerated embraces and rather childlike body movements. Blin remembered Beckett saying that despite 'this filth that surrounds us, in spite of his pessimism about the human condition, there are nevertheless moments when one can take someone's hand, when something happens'.[37]

For Pozzo, Blin had difficulty in finding an actor who satisfied him. He eventually settled on one, but he departed in mid-December, either because he hated the play (as Peter Bull, the first English Pozzo, was to do) or because he received a better offer. Blin was persuaded to take on the role himself instead of that of Lucky, which he had been rehearsing. Since Beckett saw the character as 'a mound of flesh',[38] he padded out his costume with a false stomach, wore a false bald head, and assumed a voice that was heavy and brutal. He decided that Pozzo suffered from a heart condition with a tendency to run short of breath. He also gave him flat feet, walking awkwardly, with his feet splayed out : 'He is led by his belly.'[39] With only three weeks to go before the opening, Blin decided to ask his old friend Jean Martin to take on the role of Lucky in his place. Martin was immediately struck by the play and agreed to do the part. In line with the physiological approach to characterisation, Martin performed Lucky with a constant, uncontrollable trembling and slavering, as if he were afflicted by Parkinson's disease. He arrived at this solution by describing to a friend who was a doctor the posture and muscular quivering of the character as it had been indicated to him by Beckett at rehearsals. The doctor identified the movements as being the physical symptoms of Parkinson's disease. When he saw Martin trembling, Beckett apparently said nothing by way of approval or disapproval (his mother had recently died with Parkinson's, and the movements must have brought back painful memories). Blin was uncertain until the dress rehearsal, when the costume mistress, witnessing his performance for the first time, was seized with uncontrollable nervous laughter and then began to vomit, crying that it was unbearable. That was the point at which Blin confirmed 'that's the way to do it'.[40]

Martin's delivery of Lucky's monologue was particularly impressive. In French the speech begins with the words 'étant donné l'existence...'. Martin began it by repeating the first syllable 'é' more than a dozen times with a quavering but rather staccato sound, evoking a damp motor engine stuttering unreliably into life. As he continued, the words emerged at the same rhythm as the trembling spasms which convulsed his body, so that the whole speech was imprinted with the image of physical breakdown. His delivery broke up the words into their component syllables, stressing each syllable without necessarily attending to the shape of the words, like someone who had learned a poem by heart but forgotten its meaning. As the monologue progressed, and the pace of his delivery increased, his trembling became more and more pronounced, so that by the end he was swaying and jerking wildly, making it quite difficult for Vladimir and Estragon to get hold of his hat. Physically, Martin was much taller than Latour or Raimbourg, which helped to make this moment all the more grotesque.

Contemporary reports indicate that the feelings of extreme horror and revulsion provoked by Jean Martin's apparently uncontrollable trembling and slavering continued to be experienced by audiences throughout the run. No doubt a sense of horror was provoked as much by the attitude of Pozzo as by the appearance and behaviour of Lucky. Memories of the Nazi occupation were still fresh in people's minds. Indeed the full horror of the death camps had emerged only gradually in the postwar years. The image of a poor, broken-down slave, suffering from a terminal medical condition but obliged to continue to perform whatever tasks he could still manage by an arrogant master, was not so very far removed from realities which were only too vivid in the memories of many in the audience. Blin's production helped to emphasise such responses by differentiating very sharply between the two couples. Where Vladimir and Estragon were similar in many ways, Pozzo and Lucky were presented as extremely different: Pozzo clean, elegant, well-fed, upper-class; Lucky dirty, half-starved, sickly and servant-class. The clear class differentiation was one of the aspects where Beckett felt that Blin had pushed his interpretation too far, and in his own production (twenty-two years later) he costumed them in a more similar style and suggested a greater interdependence between them. But in

1. The first production by Roger Blin, Théâtre de Babylone, Paris, 1953.
Standing left to right: Pierre Latour (Estragon), Roger Blin (Pozzo), Lucien
Raimbourg (Vladimir). On the ground: Jean Martin (Lucky).

Blin's performance there was no doubt about the cruelty and class-
superiority of Pozzo.

The flagrant sadism of Pozzo's treatment of Lucky contrasted with
the strong interdependence of Vladimir and Estragon. Through this
frankly theatrical patterning of the two couples, their actions and relationships, Blin helped to convey in his production the poetic force
of Beckett's text. This was necessary because its absence of poetic
language, its ordinary, everyday quality, especially its occasional cru-
dities, were in danger of misleading audiences into thinking that they

were faced with a sort of documentary on *clochards*. The poetic horror
of the everyday, in which the most ordinary situation can suddenly
present itself to the mind clothed in all the nameless horror of a dream,
was a relatively new technique in the theatre of the time. Its most notable literary exponent was Kafka, and some of his works were adapted
for the stage at this period (Jean-Louis Barrault, for example, who had
worked with Blin, performed adaptations of *The Trial* in 1947 and
The Castle in 1952). But others who had used this technique, such as
Adamov and Ionesco, had not, as yet, had any success with audiences,
who expected grotesque situations to be matched with grotesque language, as in the plays of Michel de Ghelderode, which were popular
at the time. The combination of nightmare situation and everyday
language was still very novel.

Once the contract with the Théâtre de Babylone was signed, Beckett attended many of Blin's rehearsals. Conscious of his own lack of
experience in theatre production, Beckett was willing to go along
with most of Blin's suggestions and was also prepared to make cuts
and changes in his text.[41] For the most part, Blin and his actors were
content to take the text as they found it, and confined their input
to working out the movements, gestures and pacing. Like Beckett,
Blin was interested in painting (he was a gifted draughtsman) and
approached stage production in terms of images. Mark Batty comments that he worked 'through a sort of stage sculpture', building
up sequences of visual images designed to create palpable emotion.[42]
A prime example was the moment when Vladimir and Estragon are
trying to decide whether they should help Pozzo and Lucky get up
after they have fallen in a heap in Act II. As they walked up and down
in the confined space, they found themselves marching straight over
the bodies, stamping on Pozzo's back on the words 'l'humanité c'est
nous' (Faber 79). Another was the exit of Pozzo and Lucky in Act I:
they made a complete circuit of the stage before leaving, suggesting
the circus image of ringmaster and trained animal, making one last
circuit before their exit from the arena.

Beckett never intervened in the course of the rehearsals, preferring to discuss things quietly with Blin after the day's work. If asked a direct question, he tended to say nothing, or to give a temporising reply, and so the actors soon realised that it would not help to ask him for the meaning of any given line or motivation. In fact the approach that seems to have worked best was that of Raimbourg, whose performance was described by many observers as having a kind of innocence. Jean Martin commented that 'Raimbourg, to the end of his days, never understood his part in *Godot*, yet he was brilliant.'[43] An exceptional team spirit appears to have grown up among the cast, who all trusted Blin's instinctive approach to the play. This quality of trust and harmony was witnessed by many, including Renée Saurel, who wrote: 'It is rare to find profound and intimate agreement between text, production and interpretation. This miraculous coincidence has nevertheless occurred with *En attendant Godot*.'[44]

No doubt Blin's unusual combination of commitment to serving an author he admired and visual insight into how to shape his vision in production contributed a great deal to the success of *Godot* and taught Beckett much about the art of stage production. But there was one instance in which Beckett had to put his foot down and insist that his own shaping vision be respected. This was the very end of the play, when Estragon, hoping to hang himself, removes the rope that serves as a belt, with the result that his trousers drop round his ankles. Latour felt that this was an indignity too far, and contrived the moment so that his trousers simply drooped a little. Beckett, who had fled to his house outside Paris to avoid the publicity of the first night, received a report about this from Suzanne and fired off the following letter:

> One thing troubles me, the pants of Estragon. I naturally asked Suzanne if they fell well, and she told me that he keeps them half on. He mustn't. He absolutely mustn't. It doesn't suit the circumstances. He really doesn't have the mind for that then. He doesn't even realize they're fallen. As for the laughter, which could greet their complete fall, there is nothing

to object to in the great gift of this touching final tableau; it would be of the same order as the preceding scenes. The spirit of the play, to the extent to which it has one, is that nothing is more grotesque than the tragic. One must express it up to the end, and especially at the end. I have a lot of other reasons why this action should not be tampered with but I will spare you them. Just be good enough to reestablish it as it is in the text and as we always foresaw it during rehearsals. And that the pants fall completely around the ankles. That might seem stupid to you but for me it's capital.[45]

CHAPTER 4

THE FIRST PRODUCTIONS IN ENGLISH

THE ARTS THEATRE, LONDON, AUGUST 1955, DIRECTED BY PETER HALL

In English-speaking countries, *Waiting for Godot* quickly acquired a reputation as a 'difficult' play. From the very beginning it was picked on by critics as an example of everything that was wrong with twentieth-century art. Terms such as 'pretentious' and 'tedious' were used. In the *Evening Standard*, Milton Shulman called it 'another of those plays that tries to lift superficiality to significance through obscurity'.[1] Until the positive reviews of Harold Hobson and Kenneth Tynan appeared (in the *Sunday Times* and the *Observer* respectively), almost every critic conveyed the sense that here was something impossible to understand and probably undesirable if you did. Even Peter Hall, the director of the play, announced: 'I haven't the foggiest idea what some of it means.'[2]

These reactions need to be set in context. The English theatre of the early 1950s was going through an awkward period of transition. Its role as a provider of mass popular entertainment had almost entirely disappeared and the star comic performers who had once drawn large audiences were to be found on the radio or in films, rather than in the live theatre. A few theatres were still able to put on variety shows until the early 1960s, but the spread of television wiped them out in all but isolated instances (such as the Royal Variety Show). The need to subsidise theatre was beginning to be recognised, but was only applied in a very limited way. The Arts Council, founded in 1946, still distributed comparatively small sums of money, mostly to what would now be called 'heritage theatre'. It was not until the late 1960s that significant subsidies became available to theatre companies of all kinds.

In the 1950s, Arts Council policy was to support only work judged to be of the highest standards and most professional qualities. This was interpreted to mean art that appealed to educated middle-class taste, seeking out whatever was ennobling and uplifting. It favoured the universal over the particular and the traditional over the experimental, and specifically excluded performances which drew on popular traditions. In music, jazz was not supported. In theatre, the vaudeville, music-hall and variety performers, who had been part of the ENSA organisation (set up to entertain the troops during the war), were not eligible for Arts Council support. Even Joan Littlewood's Theatre Workshop (founded in 1945) could not persuade the Arts Council to fund it to any significant degree, despite international success and constant invitations to perform at European festivals. It took the cultural revolution of the 1960s to change the climate of opinion, and establish the principle that all forms of live performance should be eligible for subsidy.

The whole attitude of the Arts Council in the 1950s made it unthinkable that it should support an avant-garde play of dubious Franco-Irish origins. There is evidence that the Arts Council's drama officer did in fact see the text of *Waiting for Godot* in 1954, when it was still in search of a theatre: Colin Chambers reports that Peggy Ramsay, then just setting up as a play agent, was passionate about the play, and felt she should campaign for it to be produced. 'She sent the play to the Arts Council's drama officer and recalled receiving a rude reply in which the play was described as drivel.'[3] It was seen as degrading and squalid – quite the opposite of the uplifting function art was supposed to have in the new Britain, where all levels of society were infused with a sense of rectitude and moral superiority following the victory against Nazism. This national mood was bolstered by events such as the Festival of Britain (1951) and the coronation of Queen Elizabeth II (1953), in which the whole country celebrated its sense of achievement despite continuing austerity. Far from seeing themselves as the impotent plaything of uncontrollable historical forces, many Britons felt confident that they had demonstrated the possibilities of intervention in the world scene, and that it was now their responsibility to maintain a positive, even an optimistic approach to life.

Nevertheless, as the 1950s unfolded, a mood of disillusionment began to corrode some of this self-confidence. In 1956, the Suez crisis opened many people's eyes to the fact that Britain was relatively powerless in the world scene and induced a movement of national soul-searching. This found expression in the plays of John Osborne: *Look Back in Anger* (1956) and *The Entertainer* (1957). Osborne's plays, like Beckett's, were criticised for their 'sordid' qualities and *Waiting for Godot* became linked in the minds of some critics with the 'kitchen sink' drama which followed in the second half of the 1950s. J. W. Lambert, a respected theatre reviewer, suggested in 1956 that Osborne's *Look Back in Anger* 'might have been subtitled *Waiting for Godot in Wolverhampton*'.[4] Ivor Brown, the former theatre critic of the *Observer* but by then supplanted by the more percipient Kenneth Tynan, saw in both plays 'a genuine appetite for the seamy and the shabby sides of life'. 'Must we,' he asked, 'make a deliberate cult of squalor?'[5]

These comments point to the fact that in London's West End, where *Waiting for Godot* was produced in 1955, theatre had still not entirely shaken off the tone of polite drawing-room comedy and 'Anyone for tennis?' which had predominated in the pre-war period. Midway through the 1950s, the plays of Osborne, Wesker and Arden had not yet burst onto the stage of the Royal Court and Brecht, whose Berliner Ensemble first visited Britain in 1956, was relatively unknown. Yet it would be wrong to imagine that cross-channel influences were unimportant. French theatre in particular was extremely popular with audiences. Between 1949 and 1955 there were major professional performances of ten plays by Anouilh, five by Giraudoux, two by Cocteau and two by André Roussin, as well as a large number of other translations of works by French, German and Italian authors. Anouilh and Giraudoux were both translated by Christopher Fry, whose own plays were also being produced, and whose poetic drama was seen by some commentators as the way forward, especially in the light of the success of T. S. Eliot's *The Cocktail Party* (1949) and the 1953 revival of *Murder in the Cathedral* at the Old Vic with Robert Donat. It is to Peter Hall's credit that he recognised the poetry of *Waiting for Godot* although it was so different from that of Fry and Eliot.

London had no equivalent of the small pocket theatres of the Left Bank in Paris, in which Adamov, Ionesco and others had flourished and whose modest means had been sufficient for Blin's production of *Godot*. The fact that no such concentration of centres for dramatic experiment existed (and London had seen relatively few innovatory avant-garde performances in the earlier part of the century) could be attributed to the legal status of theatre censorship in Britain, where every play script had to be submitted to the Office of the Lord Chamberlain before a performance licence was granted. This had long been an inhibiting factor on experimental performance, since any deviation by an actor from the words precisely set down in the script seen by the Lord Chamberlain was punishable by law. The only way to avoid this was to set up a theatre club, which took the performance out of the public domain, making it a private event and thus subject to less stringent controls.

The history of such theatrical innovation as did occur in London is closely linked to these clubs, since the attitude of the Lord Chamberlain was always intensely conservative, refusing to license anything which challenged socially accepted norms; it was only by setting up club performances that plays by most of the innovative twentieth-century playwrights could be produced at all. The list of those refused licences is long and includes writers as different as Wilde, Ibsen, Shaw, Strindberg, Wedekind, Pirandello, O'Neill, Miller and Osborne. Two of the most active clubs were the Gate Theatre, set up in 1925, and the Arts Theatre, set up in 1927. Until the abolition of the Lord Chamberlain's censorship duties in 1968, many of the productions given by the English Stage Company at the Royal Court from

1956 onwards also had to be 'club' performances, because the Lord Chamberlain refused to license plays by Osborne, Arden and Bond, among others. Beckett himself suffered considerably at the hands of the Lord Chamberlain and at first thought a production would be impossible because of the cuts he had been asked to make. Once again the problem was circumvented by making the Arts Theatre production a 'private club' event.[6]

The circumstances of the entry of *Waiting for Godot* into the repertoire of the English-speaking theatre were thus very different from the slow maturing process it had enjoyed at the hands of Roger Blin. Whereas Blin was a living link to the history of the European avant-garde, and understood the subversive potential of Beckett's writing, the play's first English and American directors were both young and neither shared Blin's radical political views. Whereas the French production benefited from a government subsidy designed to encourage new writing, no such subsidy was available either in London or across the Atlantic. In England (and even more so in America) the play was seen principally as commercial property: it was picked up by impresarios who recognised its powerful theatrical qualities but who thought in commercial terms, and who believed that it needed star performers if it was to attract an audience. In London, early in 1954, Donald Albery bought a six-month option on the play for £250, and expended a great deal of energy trying to recruit Ralph Richardson and Alec Guinness for the parts of Vladimir and Estragon. Albery's negotiations proved fruitless and the six-month period provided for by his contract elapsed. So he paid a second £250 advance for a further six months, with an option again including the United States. Only when he again failed to attract a cast of recognisable star actors did he offer the play to the twenty-four-year-old Peter Hall, who had just taken over as artistic director of the Arts Theatre.

The choice of Hall was an admission that the play did not fit the established theatrical taste of the time and required the advocacy of a young turk with new ideas. In the previous two seasons, Hall had been successfully promoting his belief that the English theatre had become impoverished and needed to look to continental Europe for fresh inspiration. After completing his degree at Cambridge, where he had directed four different plays in his last year, he put on a summer season at the Arts Theatre in Cambridge, then went to work as assistant to John Fernald at the London Arts Theatre, and also directed several productions at the Oxford Playhouse. The plays he chose for these theatres were mostly drawn from the European repertoire: plays by Anouilh, Gide, Giraudoux, Gogol, Goldoni, Lorca and Julien Green. He stated in an interview that the only significant dramatist writing in English was John Whiting, whereas he could name at least half a dozen major new French playwrights. When he took over direction of the Arts from John Fernald in 1955, he chose as his first production *The Lesson* by Ionesco, thus clearly identifying his own innovatory projects with those of the French avant-garde theatre. He received the support and encouragement of Ionesco's young play agent, Margaret Ramsay (though she was never to act as Beckett's agent).[7]

The Arts Theatre in Monmouth Street was far better equipped than Serreau's Babylone. In the late 1940s, the Arts had been managed by Alec Clunes, and had acquired a reputation for giving the premières of new plays which went on to further success in other theatres. In size, however, it was not so different from the Babylone, holding only 347 seats facing a very cramped stage. The audience it attracted thought of themselves as discriminating and literate. In such an atmosphere, the provocation of Beckett's text was bound to be felt keenly, though it came across as a different kind of shock from the one that had had such an impact in Paris. French audiences had come to the play with images of starvation, sickness and exploitation all too vividly present in their memories of the Nazi occupation. To audiences in such a frame of mind, the plight of Vladimir and Estragon did not seem so very strange or unusual, and the violence implicit in the Pozzo–Lucky relationship needed no underlining to exert its sinister power. In London, audiences found the images less familiar, and it sometimes seemed that the chief anxiety provoked by the production was to do with whether its meaning had been understood. When Beckett visited London, Harold Hobson (who had championed the play in the *Sunday Times*) remarked to him: 'What we are all arguing about in London is the meaning of *Waiting for Godot*', to which Beckett famously replied: 'I take no sides about that.'[8]

Today, half a century after it was written, the play no longer seems so obscure; its frequent revivals demonstrate that it speaks strongly to contemporary audiences. While its many layers of meanings may be difficult to exhaust, its general thematic concerns are clear: waiting, uncertainty and the problem of human existence in time; the symbiotic relationship of couples who have lived together for many years; the contrast between human aspirations and the realities of most human lives; the tension between comedy and tragedy in the most everyday situations. If the play's original audiences found these commonplace themes hard to grasp, maybe it was because, simple though they may be, they were not commonly the stuff of 'high art'. On the contrary, they were seen to belong to the popular cultural tradition at a time when, as we have seen, popular culture was often dismissed as unimportant by critics and other doorkeepers of the arts in England. The theme of waiting was certainly not unfamiliar, but its best-known enactment was probably the George Fornby song 'I'm waiting by a lamppost at the corner of the street'. Similarly, the theme of the relationship between the two members of a long-standing couple was one of the mainstays of music-hall double-acts (see chapter 2).

Virtually the only critic at the time to grasp Beckett's use of popular techniques for profound purposes was Kenneth Tynan. In his review for the *Observer* of 7 August 1955 he wrote that *Waiting for Godot* 'summoned the music hall and the parable to present a view of life which banished the sentimentality of the music hall and the parable's fulsome uplift. It forced me to re-examine the rules which have hitherto governed the drama; and, having done so, to pronounce them not elastic enough. It is validly new.' As this comment shows, he fully understood the challenge that the play made to contemporary views of the role of theatre in society. Not only did he grasp Beckett's implied suggestion that theatre must refuse its role as provider of uplifting experiences to exclusively middle-class audiences, he also perceived more quickly than most that the play mounted an equally powerful challenge to dramatic conventions as currently understood by everyone in the theatre business.

Hall's attitude from the beginning had been to admit that he hadn't 'the foggiest idea what some of it means . . . but if we stop and discuss every line we'll never open'.[9] He therefore plunged straight into practical rehearsal, which was in fact the way Beckett himself was to work when he came to direct the play twenty years later. His actors were all young and relatively unknown (although he had initially wanted Cyril Cusack for Vladimir). Peter Woodthorpe, who was Estragon, had never played in a professional theatre before and was halfway through a biochemistry degree at Cambridge (which he never completed). Paul Daneman and Timothy Bateson were jobbing actors, willing to perform in anything from Shakespeare to revue. The best known of the actors was Peter Bull. He was the highest paid, receiving £12 a week. When the production transferred to the Criterion Theatre (12 September 1955) he received a weekly wage of £45 while the others were paid £40. Bull was hostile to the play from the beginning: in a radio interview he spoke of his sense of relief when its run ended in 1956.[10]

Neither cast nor director had seen the Paris production. Their attitude varied from the intrigued uncertainty of Hall to the outright hostility of Bull, but they took the play on in a spirit of open-minded experiment; they knew that it had proved a runaway success in Paris, and given that much that was best on the English stage at that time came from Paris it seemed worth a try. Having received little critical recognition for his production of Ionesco's *The Lesson* a few months earlier, Hall did not expect the performance to enjoy a long run: he advised Paul Daneman to accept a contract for the *Punch Review*, which was due to open in September. Daneman followed Hall's advice and when the production transferred to the Criterion Hugh Burden took over as Vladimir.

Hall's preference was not only for continental work. It was also for work of a poetic tendency and which dealt with large themes, as opposed to the drawing-room comedies which dominated the West End stage at the time. Immediately before *Waiting for Godot* he had directed O'Neill's *Mourning Becomes Electra* and the play he was to put on after *Godot* was *The Waltz of the Toreadors* by Anouilh. This interest in plays which probed below the surface realism of English middle-class life helped him to respond to the qualities of Beckett's play, where others had been merely baffled. But it also led him to conceive a production which was considerably more elaborate than that of Blin, and even misled some of the reviewers into describing the play as 'Expressionist'. His set, designed by Peter Snow, was intended to remedy what both director and designer felt to be the excessive sparseness of the text, adding an atmospheric context by visual means. It depicted a country scene in which everything contributed to a sense of picturesque loneliness and decay. Along the back of the stage there was a rostrum covered with a floor cloth suggesting a raised bank, sprouting various bits of scraggy vegetation. On this bank, upstage right, was an extremely substantial tree, fringed by beds of reeds and looking like a gnarled oak in an Arthur Rackham illustration. In front of the tree there was a slope from the raised bank down to stage level. The bank fell more abruptly stage left, with a low mound shaped to serve as a seat. Further left still, on the edge of the stage, there was a tar barrel, a rock and some pieces of stone, as if abandoned by road-menders.[11] Before the play began, and at various points in the action, Hall introduced background music by Bartók to further heighten the sense of strangeness and the feeling of dusk falling on an isolated country road.

The lighting was a more sophisticated version of Blin's lighting in Paris: the backcloth was lit both from above and by a ground row concealed from the audience by the raised rostrum. The general effect for most of the action was of an evening at sunset, with a front wash illuminating the forestage, while the rear was illuminated from behind. When at the end of each act night suddenly falls and the moon rises, a spot was used from behind the backcloth. The costumes were a good deal more stylish and also more theatrical than those worn in the Paris production. Vladimir and Estragon both wore old pinstripe trousers that had once been smart; Vladimir had a waistcoat to match with a morning coat over the top, while Estragon had an old black jacket. Pozzo looked decidedly ridiculous in a very loud check suit (with a check waistcoat of a different design); the trousers of the suit were plus fours and Peter Bull's ample calves were encased in gaiters. His overcoat was also of checked cloth and he wore a cravat beneath a starched white wing-collar. Round his neck was a ribbon with a monocle and his watch-chain was very evident. Like Vladimir and Estragon, he had a bowler hat, although his was of smart, new, brown felt, whereas theirs were both black and battered. Lucky had an ancient stovepipe hat, and a black jacket over porters' dungarees with a collarless shirt.

One result of the cluttered design was that audiences and critics alike assumed Estragon and Vladimir to be tramps, especially since Hall directed Vladimir to emerge from the tar barrel at the beginning of the second act, implying that he had spent the night there. The tar barrel became a focal point for the action, with Vladimir and Estragon frequently coming downstage to sit on it, side by side. In point of fact, the idea that they should be seen as tramps only emerged in the course of rehearsals. At the first rehearsal, possibly influenced by reports of Blin's production, Hall had announced that Vladimir and Estragon were clowns in a circus show,[12] but he gradually came to the conclusion that tramps were closer to the mark. His own summing up of the production many years later was that although there was too much scenery, and although the music was a mistake, the main thrust of the performance was about right: 'It had humanity without sentimentality and a bleakness that coexisted with tenderness. It was also funny.'[13] In his programme note for his second production, which took place at the Old Vic in 1997, he wrote that the importance of the play was that 'it freed the theatre from detailed naturalism. Metaphor once again filled the stage. And the way had been made straight for Harold Pinter, Joe Orton, Edward Bond and several generations to follow.' He went on to argue that the first night of *Godot* was as important as, if not more important than, *Look Back in Anger* the following year in 'the re-invention of British theatre'. This latter judgement seems amply justified. Both productions challenged the generally accepted limits of what could then be presented on stage. But Osborne's originality was limited to the voice of Jimmy Porter; dramaturgically, his play remained within the established limits of contemporary playwriting. Beckett, on the other hand, introduced both a significant new voice and a challenge to the formal conventions of the playwright's craft as it was then practised and understood.[14]

After an uncertain start, the production at the Arts Theatre met with the same kind of cult success as Blin's had enjoyed in Paris eighteen months earlier. A transfer was arranged to the Criterion Theatre, where the play continued to do well throughout the 1955/6 season, concluding with a tour of provincial theatres in March and April 1956. At that time it was unusual for a play which was not a classic revival, with a cast full of stars, to transfer from a small theatre such as the Arts to a long run in a West End theatre. After its long-running success in France, the play was demonstrating what the subsequent half-century has confirmed: that as well as being one of the most challenging twentieth-century plays in its approach to dramatic form it is also one of the biggest crowd-pullers.

The style of Hall's production was very different from Blin's, how-ever. It was much less controlled and had to make do with a much shorter rehearsal period (although Hall insisted on seven weeks, which was three weeks longer than usually allotted). Given that neither Hall nor his cast had any knowledge of the French avant-garde perfor-mance tradition in which Roger Blin had been steeped, they had to find some other point of reference for their work on Beckett's un-familiar dialogue. The audio recording which exists shows that while certain passages were played for pathos the actors more often fell back on the long tradition of English nonsense writing, speaking sections of the text rather in the manner of someone reciting a work by Edward

Lear or Lewis Carroll. Ample use was made of modulations in tone and speed, and they particularly relished the passages of word play, such as the game of insults in Act II.

Five and a half years after the first performance, the four principal actors came together to record a radio discussion about their experiences in the first run of the play. This was broadcast on the BBC Third Programme on 14 April 1961 under the title 'Waiting for What?'.[15] All the actors agreed that Beckett had rendered their task unusually hard. Paul Daneman explained that he and his fellow-actors were inclined to view the audience as 'a large, amiable but sulky dog, which needed to be kept in its place'. Most playwrights, he went on, give actors material with which they can control this creature. *Godot*, however, in their view, failed to give them the all-important levers of control, so they invented a few for themselves. He gave some examples: charging a seemingly innocuous line with the significance normally reserved for *King Lear*, speeding up and slowing down at unexpected points, and, most successful of all, what he called 'suspended bathos'. By this term he meant inserting a long pause between a question and the reply which followed it. 'This technique,' he said, 'can now be seen in the work of messers Simpson, Ionesco, Wesker and Pinter. It is to be hoped that it will soon pass into the curriculum of the Royal Academy of Dramatic Art.' This comment may have been intended flippantly, but it correctly prophesied the advent of what is now known as 'the Pinter pause' (rather than being specially associated with Beckett, or indeed with Wesker). In fact the pauses were seen to be central to the strangeness of the new dramatic style and hostile to the audience.

Being used to a realistic style of playing, both actors and audience found the pauses an embarrassment. In the 1950s, theatre audiences were not as polite or respectful as they are today.[16] The pauses were often taken as opportunities for the audience to make their own comments. On one occasion, after the play had transferred to the Criterion Theatre, when the actors reached the lines, 'We are happy. What shall we do now, now that we are happy?' (Faber 60), a voice called out, 'Well I'm not happy – I've never been so bored in my life.'

Hugh Burden (who had taken over from Paul Daneman as Vladimir) responded by adding an improvised line, 'I think that was Godot', which raised a laugh and calmed the 'sulky dog' for a while.[17] However, the actors rarely invented lines of their own in this way, because they soon discovered two things: in the first place, it made them forget where they were in the text, which was, in any case, particularly hard to memorise, being so full of repetition and echo; secondly, they found that Beckett's verbal patterns had a kind of authority, even when they failed to understand them fully, and Timothy Bateson remembered the cast developing a respect for the play as the run continued throughout the 1955/6 season.[18] Peter Hall would return regularly to the auditorium of the Criterion Theatre, and Bateson remembered that his comment to the cast afterwards was invariably, 'Don't *explain* it to the audience – just do it.' By this he meant that they should curb their desire to bring out the meaning of the play (under the pressure of audience expectation), simply allowing Beckett's words to weave their spell.

One thing clear to director and actors was that the play had its roots in the traditions of the variety show, which depended, as the name suggests, on the alternation of different kinds of 'turn'. The changes would be rung on a series of short acts which would include solo- and double-acts, songs and dances, juggling and acrobatics. The emotions appealed to in the audience would alternate between laughter and pathos. Beckett's play exhibits just such alternation. It starts and ends as a double-act, but in between it includes solo performances by both Pozzo and Lucky, comic routines such as the exchange of hats and pratfalls of various different kinds, including the major collapse in Act II when all four characters end up on the same heap. A production photograph taken at the Arts Theatre in 1955 shows Paul Daneman standing on a raised tree stump with his hat off and his arm extended in a gesture of triumph for the line 'all mankind is us', a pose which strongly suggests the self-conscious showman.

The play's debt to the traditions of variety and clowning was evident to those who saw the Arts Theatre production, but it found expression in the relationship between Pozzo and Lucky rather than

2. The first English production by Peter Hall, Arts Theatre, London, 1955. 'All mankind is us.' Standing left to right: Paul Daneman (Vladimir), Peter Woodthorpe (Estragon). Sitting: Peter Bull (Pozzo). Lying: Timothy Bateson (Lucky).

in that between Vladimir and Estragon. In Paris, the actor playing Vladimir (Raimbourg) had been a music-hall comedian, and we have seen that he had to be restrained from making too much use of his funny walk. All the Parisian critics commented on the comic disparity between the physical shapes of Raimbourg's Vladimir and Latour's Estragon. In London, Paul Daneman and Peter Woodthorpe did not strike spectators as an inherently comic couple: it was Peter Bull, in the role of Pozzo, who had the greatest experience of acting comic parts and seemed almost grotesque. Blin, the first Paris Pozzo, had never performed comic parts and concentrated on giving him a brutal edge. Peter Bull was capable of putting on a fierce exterior, and he developed a special booming voice for Pozzo, but there was something childishly exaggerated about his manner of performing, which made him very difficult to take entirely seriously. Even at his most domineering, his chubby shape and stiffly held arms suggested an Edward Lear caricature rather than a cruel landowner.

Timothy Bateson, as Lucky, was at the opposite extreme from Peter Bull, thus contributing to the comic contrast between the pair. His appearance was thin and bent, an impression he reinforced by getting the stage manager to fill his bags with books so that they were, in reality, extremely heavy to carry. He described his dance as being very feeble, though with a hint of former glories, 'like Fred Astaire aged one hundred and eighty', and remembered that it often got a laugh from the audience. His 'Think' was also performed for comedy, and began with a series of stammering, inarticulate sounds before he launched himself at top speed into the first words: 'Given the existence as uttered forth in the public works of Puncher and Wattmann of a personal God quaquaquaqua . . .'. His way of approaching the speech was to imagine a relationship between Lucky and Pozzo in which Lucky had once had a real understanding of truth and Pozzo had been unable to resist hearing him 'tell the truth' while at the same time hating what he heard, so that he had beaten Lucky even while he went on begging him to 'think'.[19]

The effect of the way the two couples were played was to emphasise the opposition between Pozzo and Lucky to the point where it became so extreme as to seem more clown-like than frightening. At the same time, the relatively straight playing of Vladimir and Estragon tended to emphasise their status as victims and so increase the sense of pathos aroused in those audiences who were not driven from the theatre by the unfamiliarity of the lack of action. The treatment of the boy who comes on at the end of each act only served to emphasise the sense of the play as presenting a mystic existentialist image of man abandoned by a mysterious God: when asked where Mr Godot lived, he pointed to the heavens.[20] The plays of Christopher Fry and T. S. Eliot had helped to link modern religious drama with unconventional dramatic writing in the minds of theatre-goers, and contemporary critics were notably more willing to discuss the religious implications of the play than were their Parisian counterparts.

The dynamics of the interplay between the four adult actors also had their part to play in shaping the production. Although the atmosphere at the Arts Theatre was forward-looking and experimental, the professional pecking order among the actors was as strong as in any other theatre of the day. Peter Woodthorpe, in his début professional role, recalls that he called the other three actors 'sir'.[21] Peter Bull, the most senior of the four, certainly set the tone with his dislike of the play's unconventional qualities, tempered by grumpy acceptance that it was undeniably powerful. In 'Waiting for What?' both he and Timothy Bateson acknowledge that their participation in the production boosted their reputations in the profession. Peter Bull recalled that for years afterwards he would be in demand from advertising agencies who needed 'voice-overs' to do his 'Godot-voice'. Although the other actors did not share Bull's open hostility to the play, they admitted to finding it difficult to understand, and the sense of collective puzzlement probably helped them to give Beckett's words the rhythmic or musical delivery they need, as it had helped Raimbourg in Paris.

Many of the differences between the English and the French productions can be explained by the contrast between the personalities (and ages) of the two directors. Where the austere Blin was in his mid-forties, a mature actor and director at the height of his powers, with years of experience in avant-garde theatre behind him, Hall was an optimistic twenty-four-year-old, at the start of his career and very conscious of trying out a wide range of different styles and directions in theatre. By his own admission, Hall lacked the deep understanding of the text which Blin had built up over a long period of reflection and rehearsal. He responded to its poetry and its rhythms, but lacked the professional experience necessary to do them complete justice. As a result, although the stark originality of Beckett's play came through, the use of pauses, rhythmical patterning and so on was rather hit-and-miss. When Beckett came to see the production at the Criterion in the autumn of 1955 he disliked much of what he saw, especially the production's sentimental or religious tendencies, although he praised the freshness of Woodthorpe's Estragon.[22]

Different audiences seem to have responded very differently to the production. At some performances irritated spectators made noisy exits; at others they were spellbound. The actors recalled that on some evenings the audience laughed a great deal, whereas on others it hardly made a noise. There were also several occasions, especially when the play went on tour, when members of the audience shouted their own suggestions, such as at the point when Vladimir and Estragon were discussing whether to hang themselves and a voice called out: 'Give him some rope.'[23] However, many of those who attended the play were in no doubt about its revolutionary novelty. In a way, this was even more apparent in London than in Paris, precisely because the avant-garde tradition out of which the play sprang was *not* so clearly understood. Many authorities have suggested that this production, rather than Osborne's *Look Back in Anger*, was what really divided the old from the new theatre in postwar England. One of the first to suggest this was Alec Clunes, director of the Arts Theatre from 1942 to 1950, who wrote in 1964: 'the dividing line is 1955, *Waiting for Godot* is the play'.[24]

THE PIKE THEATRE, DUBLIN, OCTOBER 1955, DIRECTED BY ALAN SIMPSON

Responses to the first Irish production, which opened in October 1955, a month after the London première, were as uncomprehending as those of most of the London audiences and critics. Alan Simpson, director of the small Pike Theatre club in Dublin (whose audience capacity was 60), had been in correspondence with Beckett about the possibility of an Irish production since 1953, but Beckett was keen not to upset Donald Albery by permitting a production in Dublin to take precedence over the London opening, and so the Pike Theatre had to wait until after the English production had opened before they were able to put the play on. By the time it reached Dublin, reviewers were well aware that the play had made waves in Paris and London; they came prepared to be shocked.

Unlike England, the Irish Republic had no official censorship of theatre, and so they were able to respect the author's wishes and restore the cuts that had been insisted on by the Lord Chamberlain's Office in London. The reviews mostly concentrated on the play's 'negative qualities' (a phrase used in several reviews) or its 'preaching of a philosophy of despair'.[25] Beckett was repeatedly taken to task for ignoring life's positive joys, and although a few critics were able to fall back on an allegorical interpretation of the play in harmony with Catholicism, most saw it as a threat to the prevailing ideology, providing an uncanny foretaste of the way the play was soon to be received in Communist countries. Beckett's status as a voluntary exile from Ireland also complicated their responses. One critic commented that 'it is more French than Irish, though there is a kinship with Synge's tramps',[26] while another wrote that 'the scene – a country road, a tree – is still quite definitely France'.[27] This last reviewer went on to comment on the difference it made to the play hearing it performed with Dublin accents:

> The Dublin voices strangely change the dramatic values of the piece as compared with the London presentation. *Waiting for Godot* seems much less moving here than it did across the water. Its tramps do not make the same impact nor arouse the same pity. They merely look and sound like two over-chatty wayfarers . . . We do not believe them when at the end they threaten to do away with themselves. We know that, as Dubliners, they are merely making talk and are too sensible to do anything so violent.[28]

This reviewer had clearly liked the rather over-emotional tone of the London production (dismissed by Beckett as 'Anglican fervour'). He was not to know that the more down-to-earth delivery and the Dublin voices were closer to the author's intentions, nor that Peter Hall would adopt just these features when he came to do his second London production in 1997.

The production had a successful run of over one hundred per-formances and then transferred to the Gate Theatre. The Dublin accents of Dermot Kelly as Vladimir and Austin Byrne as Estragon were generally admired. This was a vital element in the interpretation of Alan Simpson, the director, who argued that 'Vladimir's whole speech pattern, with its tendency to use – and misuse – long words in the way that misled Peter Hall into his "broken-down professor" interpretation, is typically Dublin.'[29] But the greatest impact was made by Donal Donelly, who played Lucky as a 'shivering symbol of servitude',[30] drooling continuously while on stage. Nigel FitzGerald was criticised by many as a rather weak Pozzo, less of an obvious tyrant than he had been made by Peter Bull. But here again it seems that the interpretation was more in line with more recent approaches to the role. He was presented as an Anglo-Irish squire, not an obvious despot, in fact quite polite on the exterior but with the colonial's arrogance and moral blindness to his own cruel treatment of his Irish slave. The set made a conscious effort to situate the play in the Irish landscape:

> We used cloths, but painted in a mixture of browns and greens in blobs and splodges which, when lit, gave the effect of a continuous vista of what might be bog, with a pathetic little willow in the foreground, its growth weakened and warped, as it would be in such a place, with nothing to shield it from the force of the west wind carrying rain clouds from the Atlantic.[31]

But despite the production's evident qualities, Dublin theatre-goers appeared determined to see it as a difficult, over-intellectual play. Ulick O'Connor, a cultural commentator, compared the play unfavourably with Shakespeare, whose plays, he argued, are capable of being performed 'before an audience of farm hands, which the plays of Fry, Beckett and Eliot are not'.[32] This fundamental misunderstanding of the nature of Beckett's play would be exploded in November 1957, when it was to hold 1,400 Californian convicts spellbound.

CHAPTER 5

EARLY PRODUCTIONS IN THE UNITED STATES

THE COCONUT GROVE, MIAMI, JANUARY 1956, DIRECTED BY ALAN SCHNEIDER

Once *Waiting for Godot* had achieved its London success and transferred to the Criterion Theatre (12 September 55), its producer Donald Albery decided not to take it to the United States. Since none of the actors was known in America, he preferred to license the play to an American producer instead. In the meantime, Beckett had been obliged to turn down several American directors, including Sam Wanamaker and Leo Kerz. Beckett wrote at the time that 'it was bitter to have to say no' to Kerz, in view of his suggested cast: 'Imagine Keaton as Vladimir and Brando as Estragon.'[1] Keaton did, in fact, work with Beckett a few years later, when he agreed to take the central role in Beckett's one and only film, entitled simply *Film*. The producer for *Waiting for Godot* licensed by Albery was Michael Myerberg. Like Albery, he believed that the play needed a star cast. He had seen the London production and had instantly imagined Bert Lahr in the role of Estragon. His conviction that the part was right for him and that Lahr would be capable of putting across the play's mixture of the comic and the tragic became the key to all of his well-meaning but disastrous plans.

The name of director Alan Schneider was suggested to Myerberg by Thornton Wilder, who was a friend of the producer and a strong advocate of the merits of *Waiting for Godot*. Myerberg had enjoyed great success with his production of Wilder's *The Skin of Our Teeth* a decade earlier (1943) and believed that in *Waiting for Godot* he had discovered another risky but potentially profitable play. Having been impressed by the London production he was keen for Schneider to see it as well before he began rehearsals. Both men also hoped that Beckett would allow an interview. Myerberg contrived that Schneider should travel to Europe on the same boat as Thornton Wilder, who was on his way to Italy. Schneider's autobiography records his astonishment as Wilder attempted first to explain then to improve Beckett's work:

> The first thing Thornton did was to make sure that I understood the play. *Godot*, he explained, was an existentialist work about 'the nullity of experience in relation to the search for an absolute' . . . We met regularly to go over the lines. Thornton started with suggestions for changing a few of them; by the time we got to Cannes, he had changed almost every single one, including the whole of Lucky's speech. I listened religiously on each occasion, trying to keep my mouth from falling open.[2]

As a result of these sessions, Schneider acquired a close, detailed knowledge of the play and of what he called 'its inner structure'. Of course, none of Wilder's revisions were accepted by either author or director, but the experience had helped Schneider to clarify exactly which questions he needed to ask Beckett. In retrospect, it would seem that Thornton Wilder had provided Schneider with an invaluable rite of passage into Beckett's radically new dramatic universe. If Wilder had understood the play better and approved of its text completely, he would not have been able to demonstrate, by his attempted redrafting, how different *Waiting for Godot* was from the theatrical avant-garde of the time.

Schneider had in fact seen Blin's Paris production of the play in 1953. His reaction shows how effective that production was at a visual level, since, despite his ignorance of French, he picked up the play's poetic force simply from the patterns of movement:

> My French is just good enough to get me in and out of the American Express. Yet through the entire performance I sat alternately spellbound and mystified, knowing something terribly moving was taking place on that stage . . . Without knowing exactly what, I knew that I had

experienced something unique and significant in modern theater. *Godot* had me in the beginnings of a grip from which I have never escaped.[3]

He was sufficiently moved to try to obtain English language production rights, but abandoned the attempt when he discovered that Donald Albery had signed a contract for a UK production to be directed by Peter Glenville, with an option for the United States.[4]

Once he reached Paris in November 1955 Schneider succeeded in arranging a meeting with Beckett and seems to have hit it off with him immediately. Beckett suggested a visit to London so that they could view the Hall production together.[5] The week in London, when, together with Beckett, he went to see the play every night for five nights, finally cleared away all Schneider's hesitations and uncertainties:

> Through the week, I discovered not only how clear and logical *Godot* was in its essentials, but how human, friendly, and warm Sam really was underneath his basic shyness. When I first met Sam, I wanted primarily to latch on to anything that might help make *Godot* a success on Broadway. When I left him, I wanted nothing more than to please him. I came with respect and trepidation; I left with a greater measure of devotion than I have ever felt for a writer whose work I was translating to the stage.[6]

'Devotion' is a strong word, but it accurately conveys the response Beckett elicited from many theatre professionals. Schneider's devotion to Beckett, which was to last for the rest of his life, ensured that his productions were always as faithful as possible to the author's intentions. He made a virtue of not imposing his own interpretations on the plays he directed, and went to great pains to clear up anything he did not understand in the plays through face-to-face discussion with Beckett. Schneider's belief that the director's job was similar to that of the translator, requiring faithfulness and sensitivity to the original, was the key to his production methods.

His own way of describing his methods was to emphasise the need to be faithful to both 'the local situation' and to Beckett's 'rhythmical and tonal structure'. By 'the local situation' he meant 'who the characters are as human beings, and what their human situation is. What they are doing, wanting, getting, not getting in a given scene.'[7] In order to explain what he understood by rhythm and tone, he quoted George Devine: 'One has to think of the text as something like a musical score wherein the "notes", the sights and sounds, the pauses, have their own interrelated rhythms; and out of their composition comes the dramatic impact.'[8]

Schneider's combination of fascination and trepidation when planning for a production of *Godot* is understandable. The members of the San Francisco Actors Workshop were to experience similar feelings a couple of years later (see below). The American theatre of the time was governed by commercial pressures to an even greater extent than the London theatre. The farces of Moss Hart and George S. Kaufman, the musical comedies of the Gershwins, Rodgers and Hammerstein and Irving Berlin, were guaranteed to bring a return on their investment. But there was very little demand for serious drama, and much of what there was centred on American experience in the war, treated in melodramatic style. William Saroyan had a hit with *The Time of Your Life*, which won a Pulitzer prize in 1939, but his was an isolated example of formal experiment in an otherwise conventional dramatic scene. The Group Theatre, which had nurtured new play-writing talent throughout the 1930s, disbanded in 1941, and the Theatre Guild, which had been set up with similar ambitions in 1919, became little more than a commercial producer, with such notable hits as *Oklahoma!* (1943) and *Carousel* (1945) to its credit. In the late 1940s and early 1950s the few serious dramatists who were able to get their plays performed regularly belonged mostly to the new realist revolution whose powerhouse was the New York Actors Studio, set up in 1947, where Stanislavski-based 'Method' acting was taught.

The high points of this new theatre were Arthur Miller's *Death of a Salesman* in 1949, directed by Elia Kazan, a co-founder of the Actors Studio, and Tennessee Williams' *A Streetcar Named Desire*, also

directed by Kazan in 1947, with performances of powerful psychological realism from Marlon Brando and Jessica Tandy. In such works
a strong strain of allegorical drama was often combined with more
realistic elements – seen most clearly perhaps in the plays of Eugene
O'Neill and Thornton Wilder – but even at their most poetic, these
plays relied on strong plot lines and placed their characters in realistic,
precisely defined social situations. Theatre of a more abstract nature,
such as that of Adamov, Ionesco or Beckett, was virtually unknown on
the professional American stage, although student productions were
sometimes seen in campus theatres.

   Because it was so unlike the normal theatrical fare, any Broadway
production of *Godot* was bound to run into difficulties. These were
compounded by the fact that Schneider, as director, and Bert Lahr, the
star who was to draw in the crowds, saw different things in the play.
Schneider had returned from Paris and London with a strong sense of
the play's ambiguity, its subtle blending of comic and tragic elements.
Lahr, on the other hand, responded to something else which was
equally clearly present in Beckett's text: its use of vaudeville routines
and comic dialogues. The memoirs of these two men, who failed to
understand one another, often give entirely contradictory accounts of
the rehearsal process that led up to the première on 3 January 1956.

   In 1955 Lahr was sixty years old and coming to the end of a career
as a music-hall clown and comedian. He had first made his name
in the 1920s, playing burlesque revue sketches. His most distinctive
characteristics were 'a swollen mass of a nose and two beady blue eyes,
set closely together and supported by two fleshy pouches. His mouth
was large and seldom closed, bellowing and braying and emitting deep
long notes in a comically exaggerated vibrato.'[9] His most famous
vocal trademark was a guttural 'gnong, gnong, gnong', uttered 'to
register amazement or disbelief at the situation in which he found
himself'.[10] His style of comic performance was broad, grotesque and
very theatrical. This meant that although he was a great hit in the
revues and musical comedies which dominated Broadway in the 1930s
and 1940s, he was not successful as a film actor. Nevertheless, it is for

his one big film role that he is remembered today: the Lion in *The Wizard of Oz* (1938).

The idea of casting the ebullient Lahr in the role of Estragon demonstrated a fundamentally mistaken emphasis on Myerberg's part. Beckett's choice would have been for the much more restrained and sad-faced clowning of Buster Keaton. But at least it meant that the extent to which *Waiting for Godot* can be seen as a piece of music hall was thoroughly tested in production. Lahr was fascinated by the play. According to his son's account, he felt drawn to it from the moment he first read it, although he also felt it was 'too intellectual' for him. His son considered him a natural for the part:

> As an actor, he understood the subtleties of the spoken word without ever having read poetry. He never read any other Beckett plays or novels. Lahr . . . [had] an understanding of the pathos and meaning of the play that went beyond critical generalities. Lahr lived with silences; his understanding of language was commensurate with Beckett's precise, philosophical use of it. His appreciation of the playful potential of words went back to his burlesque days and his use of the malaprop.[11]

Like many brilliant stage comics, Lahr was an anxious depressive off stage. He was also terrified of being upstaged. The rehearsals appear to have been a time of enormous pain and anguish for everyone involved. All had different reasons for this. For Lahr, there was the fear that in agreeing to perform in this 'intellectual' piece he had bitten off more than he could chew, and that his habitual audience would not find it sufficiently comic. As a result, he was constantly coming up with ideas to make the play more appealing. Schneider's account of this tendency reveals his irritated frustration with his leading man: 'Bert would come up with the idea of replacing the end of the "Let's go./ We can't./ Why not?/ We're waiting for Godot" sequence with his old vaudeville "Ohnnnngggg" instead of Beckett's "Ah". Or ask me to cut the Lucky speech because noone understood it. And, anyhow, the audience was coming to see him and not the guy playing Lucky, wasn't it?'[12]

For Schneider, the rehearsals were torture because his conviction that the play must balance the comic and the tragic was frustrated by Lahr's determination to stress the comic side and to explore the play's vaudeville roots. Worse, Schneider felt that Lahr was deliberately trying to boost the importance of Estragon at the expense of Tom Ewell's Vladimir: 'Bert kept saying he was the "top banana", and that the "second banana", Tommy, was really the straight man who should be feeding Bert his laughs. Tommy (and I) kept trying to explain to Bert that this show had two bananas.'[13]

Schneider's attempts at balance were further frustrated by the fact that Myerberg had cast inappropriate actors in the parts of Pozzo and Lucky (against advice from Schneider while he was still in Europe, and for reasons of his own which remain unclear). The actor playing Pozzo, Jack Smart, was incapable, according to Schneider, of remembering his words or managing the business required with the props (whip, rope, pipe, chicken, wine, etc.). As for Charles Weidman (Lucky), he was a dancer by training who had never undertaken a speaking part before. According to Schneider, he was 'riveting' in his silent moments but found Lucky's speech an impossible challenge. As rehearsals progressed, 'each day, he would manage to go a sentence or two further into the speech and then, literally shaking, run off stage to hide in the wings'.[14] In the end, he was never able to complete the speech and the first Miami performance was given by Arthur Malet, the understudy. The other star actor, Tom Ewell, who played Vladimir, had the task of putting up with Lahr's determination to get all the laughs. On the first night Schneider remembers 'having to hold onto Tommy's wife to keep her from charging forcibly on stage to hit Bert'.[15]

Myerberg had even meddled with the stage set, which had been agreed between Schneider and the designer Albert Johnson before he left for Europe, but had been transformed during his absence into a raised space made up of different levels. These were built up by means of 'very complicated ramps'[16] which restricted the actors' movements. But more important than any of these factors in sealing the fate of the production was Myerberg's choice of theatre in which it was to take place. The original agreement had been for a short tour to Washington and Philadelphia prior to the New York opening at the Music Box on Broadway. But advance sales for the tour had not been encouraging, and so Myerberg had decided to accept instead a two-week booking in Miami. The booking was for the opening production of a plush, new theatre named the Coconut Grove. It seems that the owner had been counting on the attraction of a couple of Broadway star actors, and Myerberg did everything to encourage him, with advance publicity which ran as follows:

> Bert Lahr, the star of *Burlesque*, and Tom Ewell, the star of *The Seven Year Itch*, in the laugh sensation of two continents – Samuel Beckett's *Waiting for Godot*.[17]

In Schneider's words, the new theatre had 'a fancy restaurant, a fancy foyer with a fountain . . . a fairly conventional eight-hundred-seat auditorium fronting onto a Broadway-sized stage – and no dressing rooms'.[18] The audience for the first and subsequent nights evidently came expecting some light, frothy, escapist entertainment and were completely flummoxed by *Godot*. Some even wrote outraged letters; John Lahr recalls his father receiving the following:

> Dear Mr. Lahr,
> How can a man who has charmed the youth of America as the Lion in *The Wizard of Oz*, appear in a play which is communistic, atheistic and existential?[19]

After the disastrous two weeks in Miami, Myerberg cancelled the New York opening. For Schneider, 'painful as it was, that decision brought a certain kind of relief'.[20] But Lahr still believed in the play and Myerberg was still convinced that he was the right actor for Estragon. He felt that his only mistakes had been to hire Schneider as director and to market the play as a 'laugh sensation'. His strategy when he finally took the play to New York (into the John Golden Theater on Broadway, first night 19 April 1956) was to appeal in the *New York Times* for seventy thousand intellectuals to support an important avant-garde work. He also found a new director, Herbert Berghof. Berghof felt that it had been 'wrong to cast Tom Ewell with Bert [Lahr]. Their type of comedy is too similar – naive, simple, innocent. Bert has this same radiance or innocence.' He suggested E. G. Marshall: 'he had a kind of New England acuteness, a cerebral quality to contrast with Estragon's vulnerability'.[21] Over a four-week rehearsal period he managed to build up Lahr's confidence in his vaudeville approach, allowing him free rein to treat Marshall as the straight man and himself as the one who got all the laughs. He had a good Pozzo in Kurt Kasznar and an excellent Lucky in Alvin Epstein (an actor who had experience of working in France with Etienne Decroux and Marcel Marceau). His approach was to play the comedy for all it was worth but also to stress the grotesque aspects of the play's action. He studied Bosch and Bruegel, since their paintings show people 'doing something very strange and often very silly, but with great intensity and naturalness'.[22]

To everyone's relief, the first night was reasonably well received and the production ran for ten weeks – not a triumph, but a respectable result, especially after the débâcle of the Coconut Grove. It seems that its Broadway success was very much a personal triumph for Lahr. The review by Brooks Atkinson for the *New York Times* treated him as the unequivocal star of the show,[23] and the *New York Post* praised Lahr's ability to engender in his audience a feeling of warmth and humanity:

> Mr. Lahr, in addition to being enormously funny and touching in the role, somehow managed to seem a kind of liaison between the narrative and the audience, a sort of spiritual interpreter whose warmth and humanity extended across the footlights and caught up every spectator in a shared experience.[24]

It is clear that the effect of Lahr's performance was to reduce the bleak anguish of the situation depicted in the play and to emphasise the moments of warmth and comic insight. The allusion to a 'shared experience' in the above review forcefully expresses this quality in the playing. He was making the audience feel good, a natural instinct in the comedy performer, but one which needs to be curbed when performing in Beckett.

But although the production was undoubtedly one-sided, reducing the play's ambiguities and exaggerating its moments of friendly optimism, the creative opportunities it offered to Lahr enabled him to give an exceptional performance, as witnessed by Kenneth Tynan:

> Without him, the Broadway production of Mr. Beckett's play would be admirable; with him it is transfigured. It is as if we, the audience, had elected him to represent . . . our reactions, resentful and confused, to the lonely universe into which the author plunges us. 'I'm going,' says Mr Lahr. 'We can't go,' snaps his partner. 'Why not?' pleads Mr. Lahr. 'We're waiting for Godot,' comes the reply; whereat Mr. Lahr raises one finger with an 'Ah!' of comprehension which betokens its exact opposite, a totality of blankest ignorance. Mr. Lahr's beleaguered simpleton, a draughts player lost in a universe of chess, is one of the noblest performances I have ever seen.[25]

Although it was fraught with difficulties for him, Lahr regarded his role in *Waiting for Godot* as the vital turning point in his career. By the 1950s, vaudeville had died out and Lahr had already failed to break into films; he needed to make the transition to straight theatre if he was to continue to work as an actor. After *Waiting for Godot*, his stock was high with theatre directors, who began to cast him in plays from the classic repertoire. He continued in this new career as a serious actor until his death in 1962.

The history of these first American productions with Bert Lahr demonstrates an important truth about Beckett's play: although it offers wonderful challenges to the actor, it is not, and never can be, a 'star vehicle'. It would, of course, be possible to cut and rewrite it, as so many people from Thornton Wilder to Lahr wanted to. Even Shakespeare was performed in this way for hundreds of years – cut and altered to suit the dimensions of each new star actor. Performed as written, however, *Waiting for Godot* resists the kind of treatment in which a famous actor winks at the audience behind the mask of his character. This is because of the unusual relationship that Beckett has created between the actors and their characters, as discussed in chapter 2. The actor has to be prepared to present himself naked on stage, abandoning the 'tricks of the trade' and enabling the audience to share in 'the perilous zones in the life of the individual, dangerous, precarious, painful, mysterious and fertile, when for a moment the boredom of living is replaced by the suffering of being'.[26] Schneider certainly understood this and avoided the trap of Broadway productions with star names in his subsequent work on Beckett's plays. In the summer of 1956 Schneider returned to Europe, directed a play at the Arts Theatre in London and visited Beckett again in Paris. He and Beckett corresponded throughout the time when Beckett was struggling with the composition of *Endgame*, and Schneider was responsible for its first American production off Broadway in January 1958. It was left to Herbert Blau and the Actors Workshop of San Francisco to show that *Waiting for Godot* is a play that succeeds best when performed by a company with an ensemble spirit.

THE ACTORS WORKSHOP OF SAN FRANCISCO, 1957, DIRECTED BY HERBERT BLAU

The example of the Broadway production demonstrates what can happen when Beckett's work is treated as a commercial property. The second American production of *Waiting for Godot* was done on the opposite side of the continent, and in the opposite spirit: the spirit of the Beat poets and of the experimental avant-garde. The Actors Workshop of San Francisco had been founded in 1952 by Herbert Blau and Jules Irving with the precise aim of challenging New York's dominance. Like many such theatres, it grew out of an interest in avant-garde work on the part of people working in higher education: both Blau and Irving were teaching at the San Francisco State College when they founded their theatre. Blau had travelled in France and

Germany and had been impressed by the company ethos he discovered in theatres such as the Berliner Ensemble and the Théâtre National Populaire. The early work of the Actors Workshop was inspired by the ideals of the Théâtre Populaire, summarised by Blau as follows: 'the utopian ideal of popular theatre was to be doing plays of high intelligence, from the modern and classical repertoires, for an audience of workers, students and intellectuals: in short, the great dream of the century, with a desire at its extremity for a fusion of socialism and surrealism'.[27]

The Actors Workshop put on some plays by established authors: 'what passed for psychological drama in the mainstream of American theater . . . Our gestures in that direction – partly to keep the riskier work afloat – consisted of Miller and Williams.'[28] But their real commitment was to performing new European plays by authors hardly known in America, such as Brecht's *Mother Courage* (Blau directed the first US production of this in 1956), Pinter (the Actors Workshop's production of *The Birthday Party* was the first Pinter to be staged in America) and also Genet, Dürrenmatt, Frisch, Ionesco and John Whiting.[29] The work of Beckett became a particular passion of Blau's; after his production of *Waiting for Godot* in 1957 (revived in 1962) he went on to direct *Endgame* with the Actors Workshop in 1959 and many of Beckett's later plays in other theatres.

Blau had encountered Beckett's work during his travels in Europe, and had been keen to direct *Waiting for Godot* since the appearance of the Grove Press edition in 1954, though was unable to get the performing rights until after the Myerberg production had completed its run. Even after securing the rights, however, he still had to persuade the members of his company that the play was worth doing. Two of the older company members 'simply refused to be in it',[30] and the others decided not to present it as a full-scale production, but to play it on Thursday nights only. As Blau remembered thirty-five years later: 'I think the hardest thing to reconstruct, now that Beckett has been deified among American theater people, particularly academics, is just how startling those plays were.'[31] The Workshop operated a subscription ticket system, and in view of the plays's controversial reputation it was offered to subscribers as an 'alternative' show. In addition, panel discussions were arranged following the Thursday performances, at which not only the director and one of the actors but also a psychiatrist, a professor and other professionals were present to answer questions from the audience. These discussions were cancelled after the first month, because they became somewhat embarrassing. The cause of embarrassment was the number of men in the audience who stood up and said how much they identified with Lucky. Lucky, as played by Jules Irving (and later Alan Mandell), was portrayed as an androgynous figure with 'a very strong feminine quality' and the climate of the time was not one in which people could openly admit to homosexual tendencies.[32]

Very soon, and against the theatre's expectations, the production 'became a kind of cult phenomenon'[33] and was promoted from its Thursday slot to a regular place in the repertoire, where it remained for some years (with a new production, also by Blau, in 1962). It was sufficiently well thought of to be chosen by the State Department to represent the United States at the 1958 World Fair in Brussels, with a six-week season in New York immediately beforehand.[34] This represented a triumph for West Coast experimentalism over East Coast commercialism and it was not welcomed by everyone in New York,[35] but the production drew large audiences in Brussels and encouraged Blau in his plans for a production of *Endgame* the following year.

The key to the success of the Actors Workshop *Godot* was Blau's understanding of the special (and at that time highly original) demands the play makes of its actors. As he put it, Vladimir and Estragon are simply two *performers* stripped of traditional notions of character. He understood perfectly that the desire to ask questions such as 'What does it mean?' had to be resisted and the actors had to be given the confidence to simply trust Beckett's text: 'As for uncertainty of meaning, just perform what he tells you to perform, and you will feel – as if by some equation between doing and feeling – exactly what you need to feel, and in the bones.'[36] This statement of the need for the actors

3. The production by Herb Blau at the San Francisco Actors Workshop, 1957. Alan Mandell in the role of Lucky, which he performed replacing Jules Irving when the production toured to Belgium.

to take an approach of extreme literality points forward to Otomar Krejča's insistence on the need to 'concretise' (see chapter 7). Writing about his own production a few years later, Blau recalled how his actors gradually discovered the exhausting physical effort demanded of them in performing what had at first seemed to them to be a very intellectual play. Encouraged by Blau, they began to explore the need to abandon Stanislavskian notions of sub-text: 'for the actors, identity has to be rehearsed into being. As there is no biography, there is no other way.'[37]

Through rehearsing the play, he came to understand how it is constructed out of concrete rhythms, composed of 'a continuum of crossed purposes and lapsed memory',[38] and that the play of actions, words and silences had to be orchestrated musically: 'The Chekhovian silences, the residue of aimless doing, are measured as carefully as in Webern. It is then, in silence, that the whole emotive tapestry of the theatrical event can be *heard*. The music is the most artful polyphony.'[39] Blau was the first director to see so clearly the musical quality of the play and the way that the actions, as well as the words and silence, were composed as a kind of concrete poetry which had to be performed with a respect for its own internal rhythms. Armed with such insights, he was able to cut through some of the difficulties his actors experienced with the roles, stressing that the characters had no reality outside the dimension of performance, and that the methods of psychological realism would not be helpful.

Blau did not have it all his own way in rehearsals. The notoriety of the play, which was seen, after its difficult beginnings in Miami and New York, as summing up everything that was pessimistic in modern cultural trends, followed it to the Pacific coast. Even in a small company of avant-garde actors, there were some who found it too much for them. A sense of disaster circulated in the company before the opening night; Blau recalls that the actor originally billed to play Vladimir left in revolt, and that his replacement, Eugene Roche, was a Catholic who approached the role with considerable suspicion that he was promoting a philosophy of despair. Blau was able to cope with these obstacles because he understood so clearly where the play's true power lay. He saw that it stood as a silent rebuke to the obligatory optimism of much American culture. In a letter to his actors, he stated: 'We are a culture given to delusive togetherness and the most frightfully egocentric group therapy; we are a culture playing it safe because we know no other way to play it.'[40] And he explained that 'to a country always in danger of floundering in its industry, *Godot* is a marvellous caution'.[41] This approach to the play recovered something of its provocative effect, so admired by Roger Blin (see chapter 3) and entirely lost in the Myerberg production. It also explains why the production was able to have such a profound impact when it was presented for the inmates of the famous San Quentin state prison (see below).

Unlike those of the Miami production, the actors playing Vladimir and Estragon in San Francisco were not engaged in a battle to show who was 'top banana':

> As the two tramps, Robert Symonds and Eugene Roche scored heavily in trying, always-moving roles. Depicting two completely different personalities, they were able to intermingle these entities with such a degree of transparency that at times one became the other. Always weak, always strong. Forever quitting, forever struggling.[42]

Robert Symonds was one of the Workshop's most senior members, and although Roche was a relative newcomer the relationship between them was extraordinarily convincing and made for much of the production's power. Symonds emphasised the child-like qualities of Estragon, capable of being petulant but lovable at one and the same time. Pozzo was played by Joseph Miksak, an actor with a powerful, commanding presence. His costume suggested something of both the circus ringmaster and the Hollywood film director, complete with jodhpurs, boots and whip. Lucky, as performed by Jules Irving, the co-founder of the Workshop (and subsequently by Alan Mandell, its business manager), was given an enormously heavy costume, further weighed down by very heavy bags which were filled with sand (taking literally an exchange between Vladimir and Pozzo in Act II (Faber 89): Vladimir: 'What is there in the bag?' Pozzo: 'Sand').[43] His 'Think' was delivered at a variable pace, now slowing down, now speeding up, as if on an old wind-up gramophone. The actor suggested an inability to get the words out, but that once they began to come they tore out in a wild frenzy. The set, designed by Robin Wagner, had 'a huge black backdrop with raggedly-etched streaks of white and gray cloud ... [a] bare tree bent like a willow. Above two molded levels there was a hint of barbed wire strung from three stakes. They might have been telephone poles on an abandoned road; the perimeter of a junk yard; or a concentration camp; even, vaguely, a circus.'[44] Blau goes on from this evocation of the set to describe the unity of action, scene and voice in the San Francisco production: 'The action, suited to the impeccable bleakness of the open spaces, broke out of deepest melancholy into dance: a gavotte of musing. If nothing were to be done, it could be done with the most meticulously orchestrated activity.'[45]

The sternest test of the production's power occurred in November 1957, when it was invited into the San Quentin prison. The play, which had been branded by many as pessimistic and intellectually difficult, struck an instant chord with the inmates of the prison and changed the lives of some of them in the most unexpected ways. The circumstances were as follows. Alan Mandell was contacted by George Poultney, the Actors' Equity Association representative in San Francisco, who was also a deputy sheriff, responsible for transferring prisoners from one jail to another. Poultney asked if the Workshop would be willing to provide a dramatic presentation inside the San Quentin prison. The response from company members was enthusiastic, and they first suggested performing *The Crucible*, but it became apparent that only the simplest of sets could be accommodated on the makeshift stage in the prison dining hall, and that no females could be allowed to appear in the performance. As the only play in the Workshop's repertoire to consist entirely of male roles, and having the simplest of sets, *Godot* appeared the obvious choice. Despite some reservations about the 'depressing' nature of the play expressed by the prison psychiatrist, the warden of the prison gave his permission for the performance, which took place on 19 November 1957 in the North Dining Hall on an improvised stage in front of 1,400 convicts, with guards posted all around, rifles at the ready.

Rick Cluchey, who was then a young life-serving inmate of San Quentin, has written of the extraordinary impact the performance had on the hall of convicts. Before the play began, the prison band had been playing jazz. When the band finished, Blau made a brief appearance to warn his audience not to look for a conventional story: 'Just like this band playing here,' he said, 'this play has a theme like a piece of jazz, and there will be riffs off the theme, and then you will come back to the theme.'[46] Hoping against hope, most of the men were waiting for the girls to come on stage.

> When the girlies didn't show and nobody gets shot, it was like all the air left the huge room. All of a sudden whamo here comes Pozzo and Lucky, or translated a mean sonofabitch with a whip and hungry look driving his slave. It was a unique moment, as most of us had never seen live theatre. Instantly there was identification with 'Lucky'. He's packing the bosses bags like a good powder monkey. And look man, the dude's got that sucker at the end of his cane. Suddenly there was no confusion about the Warden's role and my own convict dog boy's ass. I too had a lifetime rope around my neck. Everybody in the audience reacted. Waiting, the play was about waiting![47]

The next issue of the prison journal devoted its leader column to an analysis of the play, making it clear how directly it had spoken to the convicts' experience of life behind bars. It concluded with these memorable words:

> We're still waiting for Godot, and shall continue to wait. When the scenery gets too drab and the action too slow, we'll call each other names and swear to part for ever – but then, there's no place to go![48]

So powerful was the effect of the performance on Cluchey and others in the prison that they went to the warden with a request that they be allowed to start a drama group. He agreed that such activity might reduce violence among the prison population and calm the atmosphere, since 'the prison was actually a bombshell of tension as the State was into a rash of very public executions'. Various restrictions were placed on the group, including 'no female impersonations' and 'no plays which held a dark mirror up to the Law, society or the establishment'. They were allowed $25 per year for make-up, and over the next nine years put on a total of thirty-five productions, including seven of Beckett's works.[49]

The first performance put on by the group was their own production of *Waiting for Godot* in 1960. Members of the San Francisco Actors Workshop returned with Alan Mandell to watch the performance and advise the convicts. Mandell quickly realised that their performance was switching back and forth between Acts I and II and on further investigation discovered that they were using a text printed by *Theatre Arts* magazine, in which sections of the dialogue were mixed up. He offered to help them sort it out, and then, as a further consequence, began to make regular visits to teach them acting, directing and stagecraft, and even instituted a series of lectures by visiting experts, one of the first of which was given by Martin Esslin. Mandell's efforts proved a great morale-booster for the inmates, especially when he helped some of those who were released from prison to find professional theatre work. Rick Cluchey was one of these. He received a state pardon in 1966 and joined up with others who had been part of the prison drama group to put on a play he had written called *The Cage*. They continued to use the name 'San Quentin Drama Workshop' and soon decided to return to Beckett's work with a production of *Endgame* in 1974. This was followed by a spell for Rick Cluchey as Beckett's second assistant on his own production of *Warten auf Godot* at the Schiller-Theater in Berlin in 1975. Cluchey went on to develop a close friendship with Beckett, becoming one of the foremost interpreters of his work in English throughout the world.[50]

The San Francisco Actors Workshop production is rightly remembered as one of the first and most convincing demonstrations of the true power of *Waiting for Godot* to reach out to people of all cultures and backgrounds. It showed that, far from being a fashionable statement of pessimistic Parisian existentialism, accessible only to intellectuals, it was a work of depth and power, with universal appeal, provided it was sympathetically performed and not treated as a clown show. Those who mistakenly believed that only a star performer playing for laughs would allow the play to speak to the masses had been proved decisively wrong.

In 1958, on the occasion of the Brussels revival, Blau wrote a long letter to the cast attempting to restate the foundations on which their performances had been built:

> Remember in our first discussions of the play (Gene [Roche] was not there) a drawing by Paul Klee that I showed you, of an Egyptiac-Negroid woman with a rat growing out of her hair? The effect was grotesque and funny at once. I said then that unless you grasp the play's morbidity (seriousness is not the same thing), you'll never gain its humour.[51]

Blau went on to stress the need for the actors to recover their first, rather horrified responses to the play in order to perform it 'with maximum force'. But the way to achieve such force was through abnegation rather than emphasis: 'Without accepting the next-to-nothingness that Beckett gives you, you will never achieve the proper intensity of desperation.'[52] Blau's tone in this letter is more ethical than aesthetic, speaking of the need for selflessness in the actor, and stressing the 'vocation' of the Actors Workshop to reach a level of pure performance. It is a remarkable statement, effectively combining the collective ethos of the Actors Workshop, and its instinctive commitment to those in need (such as the prisoners of San Quentin), with Beckett's equally compassionate but lucid, honest gaze on the human condition.

CHAPTER 6

BECKETT'S OWN PRODUCTION: SCHILLER-THEATER, BERLIN, MARCH 1975

Beckett's own production of *Waiting for Godot* at the Schiller-Theater, Berlin, in 1975 provides the most important key to understanding the play's potential in performance. He dreaded having to direct it, because he considered the play to be undisciplined, but it gave him the opportunity to revise the text and to clarify aspects that he felt were still confused. To his assistant director, Walter Asmus, he described the play as 'a mess' and explained that because of his lack of theatre experience when he was writing it in the late 1940s the play was 'not visualised' to his satisfaction.[1] For the Schiller-Theater production, which used a German translation by Beckett himself, he completely revised both text and stage directions, and these revisions were then incorporated into an English text for subsequent productions by Walter Asmus closely modelled on Beckett's work in Berlin. Published by Faber in 1993, this revised version is now the authoritative English text,[2] while the standard Faber edition of 1965 still reproduces an only partially revised version.

In his work on the play Beckett demonstrated a remarkable understanding of how theatre performance communicates differently from written text. The shaping of the elements identified by Edward Gordon Craig – action, scene and voice – occupied the centre of his attention for the months he spent working on the production, evidence of the development that had taken place in his approach to theatre over twenty-five years. This development began as early as the late 1950s: from *Krapp's Last Tape* (1959) onwards, Beckett's dramatic compositions had demonstrated a new awareness of the visual dimension and of the poetic force of a dramatic situation in which vocal and visual elements depend on one another. It is possible to imagine productions of both *Waiting for Godot* and *Endgame* in a variety of settings.[3] But in all his subsequent plays, Beckett made the setting part of the stage action in such a way that the two are inseparable. The force of *Krapp's Last Tape* lies in the image of an old man trying to recover memories of his earlier life by listening to his own voice on a tape recorder. It would make no sense to perform the play without a tape recorder. *Happy Days* (1962) makes similarly effective use of the image of a woman being buried alive. It would make no sense to perform the play without Winnie's mound in which she has sunk up to her waist in the first half, and up to her neck in the second.[4] After *Happy Days*, every new play he wrote incorporated some striking new visual image in such a way that the stage picture itself summed up and embodied the experience the play had to offer: the urns in which the characters are confined in *Play* (1964), the single spotlit mouth in *Not I* (1974), the obsessively pacing feet of *Footfalls* (1976) or the rocking chair in *Rockaby* (1982).

In *Waiting for Godot* the scenic situation does not have the same sharp originality – the play's originality lies rather in its whole dramatic structure. So part of Beckett's work as director was to supply this. He began by expanding the initial stage direction, which in its original form was: 'A country road. A tree. Evening' ('Route à la campagne, avec arbre. Soir'). This was changed to read 'A country road. A tree. A stone. Evening', and the description of Estragon 'sitting on a low mound' was changed to 'seated on a stone'. In addition, where the original had begun with Estragon alone on stage, Beckett decided to have Vladimir there from the start as well.

By such means, Beckett was looking for opportunities to visualise more intensely the interplay of thematically linked couples or complementary opposites, such as the tree and the stone, with their distant echo of cross and grave. These were used to set up a series of mirror images, cross-references and echoes, giving the final

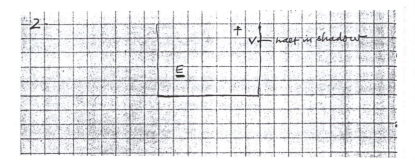

Figure 1. Sketch by Beckett of the stage.

production its poetic complexity. The rather Synge-like country road
has given way to a more general evocation of evening – it is not just the
evening of the day but the evening of life, as the countless references
to death in the play confirm.

Although it was his first attempt at directing the play, Beckett
was by no means a novice in the practicalities of directing. By the
time he agreed to direct *Waiting for Godot* he had acquired considerable experience of theatre production. Not only had he attended
rehearsals for many of his plays, from Roger Blin's first *Godot* onwards, he had also undertaken three productions of his own at the
Berlin Schiller-Theater's small studio theatre named the Werkstatt.
These were of *Endgame* (1967), *Krapp's Last Tape* (1969) and *Happy
Days* (1971). So when he accepted the offer to direct *Godot* on the
main stage of the same theatre he knew what to expect, and evidently enjoyed the challenge of working in German with German
actors. Despite this, he found it a great strain going back over *Godot*,
and instead of approaching the work with the authority of its cre-
ator he assumed his characteristic stance as the artist of failure. As
has been noted, he described the play as 'a mess' and wrote in his
preliminary notebook that his purpose in taking on the production was 'der Konfusion Gestalt geben' ('to give shape to the confusion') (*TN* xi). The key word here is 'Gestalt'. Beckett's production demonstrated his central preoccupation with the way art can

shape experience, drawing out patterns, both visual and musical. The shapes, rhythms, echoes and recurrent patterns on which Beckett laid such emphasis are exactly those elements which are only perceptible in performance and almost impossible to recover after a given production has run its course. But a unique record of Beckett's shaping work as director of his own play survives in the form of his production notebook. This shows how he planned the production, and also, through its erasures and additions, how his direction evolved.

Beckett's notebook is highly original. It does not resemble Brecht's *Modellbucher*, which aimed to give a clear record of a production, since it was written before rehearsals started, as an aid to the director. Nor is it similar to Stanislavski's production notebooks for Chekhov's plays, in which he pasted the text onto one page and then set out, on the facing page, detailed descriptions of what the actors should be doing while speaking the playwright's text. It is more analytical than either of these models and also less exhaustive, since not every line of the play is dealt with. But it does set out the manner in which Beckett visualised his play running its course on stage, both in general outline and in precise details. It shows how Beckett broke the play down into sections for rehearsal purposes and which aspects he picked out for special emphasis in seeking to 'give shape to the confusion'. Its contents are set out below (pp. 126–31), but an initial example will demonstrate his approach. At the beginning of the play Estragon is struggling to remove his boot. When he finally succeeds, he searches in a puzzled way for foreign bodies which might be lodged inside, but can find nothing. While he is engrossed in this, Vladimir removes his hat (as he later says, 'it itched me') and feels around inside, also finding nothing. These two simple actions are repeated throughout the play and seem to echo, in a minor way, the two characters' fruitless quest for Godot. Beckett's notebook shows that he also intended the two actions to echo one another. On page 77 of his notebook, headed 'Inspection hat/boot', he noted '1 boot 3 hat', indicating that where Estragon's painful examination of his boot states the theme, Vladimir's thrice-repeated search inside his hat embroiders variations on this theme. In the course of rehearsals, Beckett developed this idea into a precise notation of the hat inspection in three progressively complex movements as follows:

1. Zuck [shrug]. Look. Shake.
2. "   +   Look. Finger. Tap. Shake. Look.
3. "   ++   Look. Finger. Blow. Tap. Shake. Look. (*TN* 329)

This provides a vivid example of Beckett's approach to the job of directing his play. As he became more interested in and practised at directing for theatre, his tendency to insist on meticulously precise sequences of stage action increased (see, for example, the opening stage directions for *Footfalls*). At the Schiller-Theater in 1975, however, he was not dictatorial. He was revisiting an old play and was conscious of trying things out. He was also conscious of the need to adjust the routines he had imagined to cope with the particular talents and strengths of the actors in his cast. As a result, the inspection of Vladimir's hat as performed by Stefan Wigger did not follow precisely the form given above. (See *TN* 95 for more details).

For anyone attempting to reconstruct the preparations for his production, it is the care that Beckett lavished on every practical detail which stands out first of all. When he arrived in Berlin on 26 December 1974 he had already completed the production notebook mentioned above and had completely revised the German translation, making many hundreds of changes, cuts and revisions in order to bring the text 'closer to the French and English versions and establish more precise verbal repetitions and echoes' (*TN* xi). To facilitate the rehearsal process, he had also committed the German text to memory, leaving him free to concentrate on the actors' work without constant scrabbling in the pages of his copy. The production opened on 8 March 1975, so the rehearsal period lasted more than two months, a great luxury by the standards of most English-speaking

4. The production by Samuel Beckett, Schiller-Theater, Berlin, 1975.
Rehearsal photograph. Left to right: Horst Bollmann (Estragon), Klaus
Herm (Lucky), Stefan Wigger (Vladimir), Carl Raddatz (Pozzo), Samuel
Beckett (director).

theatre. Rehearsals took place in the mornings only (11 a.m. to 3 p.m.)
and were mostly on the main stage. This extended period allowed him
ample opportunity to try out and, where necessary, revise his initial
staging ideas.

Beckett's relationships with the cast were friendly; he had worked
with them before and had been given a free hand to cast any actor
he chose from among the members of the company. He deliberately
picked actors of contrasting body shape for Vladimir and Estragon.
Stefan Wigger, tall and thin, played Vladimir, while Estragon was
taken by Horst Bollmann, who was short and fat. Martin Held, who
had played Krapp in Beckett's 1969 production, was to play Pozzo,
but after two weeks withdrew from the production on grounds of
ill-health and was replaced by Karl Raddatz. Klaus Herm, as Lucky,
showed enthusiasm from start to finish and was judged by Beckett to

be 'a remarkable Lucky. Most moving.'[5] The rehearsal diary kept by
Walter Asmus[6] stresses the friendly atmosphere in which rehearsals
were conducted and the absence of any authoritarian note in Beckett's
dealings with the actors:

> Beckett subjects his own script constantly to critical control in the most
> amazing and sympathetic way. He is also open to suggestions at any
> time, and he even asks for them. He is not at all interested in carrying
> out a rigid concept, but aims for the best possible interpretation of his
> script. Should uncertainty occur, he is ready with a new suggestion the
> next day, always precise and thought-through, even if it does not always
> work immediately.[7]

LUCKY'S 'THINK'

The first thing Beckett chose to tackle when the rehearsals got under
way was Lucky's single long speech in Act I, known as his 'Think'. This
is striking, since it is the last thing a professional director might think
of doing, and we know for a fact that the play's earliest directors, Blin,
Hall and Schneider, all left it till very late in the rehearsal process.
The priority which Beckett gave it perhaps resulted from his own
preoccupations at the time: his dramatic writing over the previous
years had tended more and more towards dramatic monologue. His
most recent play was *Not I*, in which a single voice babbles semi-
incoherently about her life, conveying an impression of fragmentation
which has many similarities to that of Lucky's 'Think'. He had directed
a memorable first production of *Not I* with Billie Whitelaw two years
previously and so he was familiar with the performance problems
posed by long sections of monologue. Moreover, he began to write
Footfalls in Berlin while rehearsing *Godot*, so dramatic monologue was
a continuing preoccupation.

His approach to the 'Think' demonstrates in microcosm his approach to the whole play. He first broke it down into sections. This
had two functions: first, to help Klaus Herm to shape the speech,
and, second, to help the other three actors to shape their reactions to

it. His division of the speech into sections helped to change the way it was understood. Early interpreters had seen it all of a piece, with very little meaning or coherence. Beckett changed all that by showing that, despite the fragmentation of its form, it nevertheless has a clear structure. He divided it into five sections, set out on page 57 of the production notebook. They are as follows:

1. from the start to the first 'but not so fast';
2. to 'waste and pine';
3. to the first 'the facts are there';
4. to 'the facts are there but time will tell';
5. 'I resume alas alas on on' to the end.

Beside section 1 Beckett wrote 'Indifferent heaven'. Sections 2 and 3 were bracketed together with the comment 'Dwindling man'. Sections 4 and 5 carried the comment 'Earth abode of stones & cadenza'. This clear progression from an indifferent heaven through dwindling man to the conclusion of an earth that is the abode of stones give a clear thematic shape to the speech. Two notes added beside section 5 during rehearsals read: 'New elements Skull' and 'Last straw –Tears'.

In addition to these thematic pointers, Beckett's notes indicate the responses of the other three characters. In section 1 Vladimir and Estragon are to be 'concentrated in spite of early shock of quaquaqua-qua and quaquaquaqua', while Pozzo watches attentively for their reactions; in section 2 Pozzo grows increasingly unhappy as the other two become more restive; in section 3 Vladimir and Estragon show 'some interest' in physical culture but lose patience again and make 'audible protestations', while Pozzo has 'fingers in ears bowed forward'; in section 4 it all becomes too much for Estragon and Vladimir, both of whom exit, re-enter and then exit again and only come back again in section 5 on 'the skull'; finally, Beckett notes, 'Cunard Cunard all close in to down L'. In rehearsals this was changed to exclude Pozzo: only Vladimir and Estragon closed in on Lucky and brought him down with a sequence of slow-motion stylised kicks and punches, while Pozzo looked on.

Beckett's advice to Klaus Herm, playing Lucky, showed a keen understanding of how an actor must relate to the part he is playing. He said, for example: '"To shrink and dwindle . . ." will cause bewilderment for the public: but at this point everything will be absolutely clear for Lucky.' He went on to explain that Lucky is anxious to please Pozzo:

> Lucky's thinking isn't as good as it used to be: 'He even used to think prettily once . . .' says Pozzo. Herm could play it that way, watching Pozzo from time to time. And the two others, too. He is not talking simply to himself, he is not completely on his own, says Beckett.
>
> Herm: But he kind of refuses first, he doesn't like the idea of thinking . . .
>
> Beckett: He would like to amuse Pozzo. Pozzo would like to get rid of him, but if he finds Lucky touching, he might keep him. Lucky would like to be successful.[8]

This is an invaluable note for any actor performing Lucky. It shows that for *him* the speech must make some sort of sense, and not be delivered in one great outburst as Jean Martin and Timothy Bateson had done (see chapters 3 and 4). The audience should feel the despair of a man whose pride once lay in the 'pretty' way he could voice his thoughts, but who now finds the control of his words slipping away.

Beckett's notes on Lucky's 'Think' conclude with the words the actor should stress, followed by a list of 'Main shocks'. The words to be stressed show Lucky's desperate attempts to give academic credibility and a meaningful shape to his 'Think'. They begin with 'all research tandems', by which Beckett meant 'Poinçon and Wattman', 'Testu and Conard', 'Fartov and Belcher', 'Steinweg and Petermann', after which he listed the following: 'Hell to Heaven'; 'but not so fast'; 'established' (recurring three times, although each time using a slightly different phrase in the German text); 'waste and pine'; 'shrinks and dwindles'; 'the facts are there'; and 'abode of stones'. Under 'Main shocks' (i.e. the phrases eliciting shocked reactions from Vladimir and Estragon) were: 'quaquaquaqua; quaquaquaqua'; 'Acacacacademy';

'Anthropopopometry'; 'established ter' (i.e. third time); 'As a result ter' (i.e. third time); 'Testew and Cunard'; 'Hockey in the air' (an addition to the German text not present in English editions); 'I resume 3' (crossed out during rehearsals); 'more grave 2 (exit Estragon)'; 'more grave 4 (exit Vladimir)'; 'I resume 4 (re-exit Estragon)'; 'I resume 5 (re-exit Vladimir)'; and 'I resume 8 (Last straw)'.

In the different expressive elements available to the director which Beckett mentions here, we can see an example of three key methods he was to apply to the play as a whole. The first is his subdivision into manageable sections, not only for ease of rehearsing but also to bring out underlying thematic concerns. The second is his emphasis on stress and shock: the expressive dynamics of the speech have been carefully thought out so as to give shape to Lucky's torrent of words. The third is his attention to the positions and moves of the other characters; although he is dealing with a monologue, his concern is for the overall stage picture and for the patterns of movement traced by all four actors. Of course it is not enough to plan these shaping devices in advance: they have to be put into action by performers who have their own concerns and worries. Beckett's handling of his actors is discussed below (pp. 131–4).

DESIGN, SHAPE, THEMES

Knowlson has shown convincingly how much of Beckett's writing was influenced by his knowledge and love of painting. When he began to direct, this influence emerged all the more powerfully. Knowlson comments that 'Lucky is a grotesque who could have existed relatively unremarkably in the world of Bosch, Bruegel or, one of Beckett's favourite painters, Brouwer.'[9] He goes on to cite a specific example where the pattern of stage movement calls to mind a painting by Bruegel, *The Land of Cockaigne*. It is in Act II, where all four figures fall across one another. Beckett paid careful attention to the exact positions in which the actors were to fall. For Pozzo and Lucky, who fall first, he specified: 'Stylize fall as throughout first knees, then forward on face' (*TN* 43). He also added to his stage direction 'They lie helpless among the scattered baggage' the words: 'perpendicular across each other midstage off-centre right'. When a couple of pages later Vladimir and Estragon fall onto the same heap, they were to fall backwards, so as to add angled branches to the perpendicular shape of the cross formed by Pozzo and Lucky. This carefully constructed shape closely resembles the heap of men lying in the left foreground of the painting by Bruegel identified by Knowlson. This was not to be done too realistically, nor too seriously. Beckett said, 'It is a game, everything is a game. When all four of them are lying on the ground, that cannot be handled naturalistically. That has got to be done artificially, balletically.'[10]

Beckett's main efforts were directed towards elaborating shapes and images of this kind, bearers of multiple resonances. He explained his aim as follows:

> To give confusion shape . . . a shape through repetition, repetition of themes. Not only themes in the script, but also themes of the body. When at the beginning Estragon is asleep leaning on the stone, that is a theme that repeats itself a few times. There are fixed points of waiting, where everything stands completely still, where silence threatens to swallow everything up. Then the action starts again.[11]

By following up these 'themes of the body', one can begin to understand how Beckett used this production to extend and develop those aspects of the play that he felt were imperfectly realised in the written text. It is noteworthy that when introducing 'themes of the body' to his actors, Beckett spoke not only of Estragon and his position on stage but also of the 'fixed points of waiting'. These are not indicated in the text, but were introduced by Beckett as he planned the production. He named them *Wartestellen* and used them to punctuate the action in the way that a composer introduces moments of silence between different movements of a musical score. These moments, in which everything stopped and the stage presented a tableau frozen in time, were introduced at the beginning and end of each act and at four further points within each of the acts. On page 75 of the production notebook, headed simply 'W', Beckett had noted 'Opening/close both acts', followed by a list of sixteen points at which a *Wartestelle* might be interpolated. In the course of the rehearsals, he settled on eight of these, four in each act.[12]

His underlying concern was to achieve a clearly defined contrast between the 'themes of the body' as conveyed by Estragon and Vladimir. In rehearsals, he explained that 'Relaxation is a word of Estragon's. It is his dream, to be able to keep calm. Vladimir is more animated.'[13] He also commented that Estragon was close to the ground and belonged to the stone, whereas Vladimir was light, oriented towards the sky, and belonged to the tree.[14] Such indications combined to create a 'theme of the body' in which Estragon's dominant position was slumped on the stone. In order the better to state this theme, Beckett altered the play's opening, as we have seen. Instead of starting on Estragon's feverish attempts to get his boot off, followed by Vladimir's entrance, Beckett placed both actors on stage from the beginning, Estragon sitting on the stone and Vladimir standing near the tree. Vladimir was looking up, listening; Estragon appeared to be half asleep, his head bowed. There was a long moment of silence and stillness, the first of the *Wartestellen* or waiting points. Only after this prolonged pause did Estragon set the action of the play in motion by beginning to pull at his boot. The revised opening enabled Beckett to clarify from the outset the contrasted physicalities of Estragon and Vladimir while also stating the fundamental theme shared by both characters: that of waiting. A similar frozen moment of contrast was achieved at the beginning of Act II, which was also changed so that it began with both characters on stage. The openings found an echo in the *Wartestellen* at the end of the two acts: at the end of Act I, both were sitting on the stone, 'V looking up. E down'; at the end of Act II, they were standing either side of the tree, 'E looking down, V up'.[15]

Given his attention to physical and pictorial detail, the relationship he established with his designer was clearly of primary importance.

5. The production by Samuel Beckett, Schiller-Theater, Berlin, 1975. Left to right: Horst Bollmann (Estragon), Klaus Herm (Lucky), Stefan Wigger (Vladimir).

The designer for this production was Matias Henrioud, known simply as Matias, a French designer who had worked on many previous Beckett productions in Paris as well as designing the three studio theatre productions Beckett had already done at the Schiller-Theater. Matias designed both set and costumes, working closely with Beckett on the project. As might be expected in a production so carefully prepared in advance, set and costumes both make a significant contribution to the images and concepts governing the whole performance. The set was simplicity itself: the stage was completely bare apart from the tree upstage left and the stone downstage right. The stone which replaced the 'low mound' of the original marked an important step in Beckett's attempt to 'give shape to confusion', since it echoes the references to stones in Lucky's 'Think' and, more clearly than the mound, suggests a tomb. Beckett's symbols for sketching the tree and the stone in his notebook were a cross for the tree and a horizontal line for the stone, bearing unmistakeable overtones of cross and tomb. These poetic or symbolic resonances required physical embodiment, as Beckett made plain not just to the actors but to the designer as well: 'Estragon is on the ground, he belongs to the stone. Vladimir is light, he is oriented towards the sky. He belongs to the tree.'[16] In this way, through concrete embodiment of contrasted character-istics, Beckett uses all the expressive means of the stage to develop one of his chief recurring themes: the mystery about why one per-son is favoured while another suffers (explicitly discussed in the first big debate of the play, concerning the two thieves crucified with the Saviour).

Equally important in clarifying the ideas behind the production was the costume design, which made a strong visual statement about the interdependence of the two pairs of characters. This was especially clear in the case of Vladimir and Estragon. Beckett wanted to exploit the difference in height between the short Horst Bollman as Estragon and the tall Stefan Wigger, playing Vladimir. His aim was to build up a paradoxical picture of two people who were very unlike each other and yet depended on each other completely; who were always longing to get away from one another and yet entirely lost without one another; opposites who complemented one another and who were somehow incomplete as individuals if separated:

> Vladimir is going to wear striped trousers which fit him, with a black jacket, which is too small for him; the jacket belonged originally to Estragon. Estragon, on the other hand, wears black trousers which fit him, with a striped jacket which is too big for him; it originally belonged to Vladimir.[17]

In the second act, this arrangement was reversed: Vladimir wore Estragon's black trousers, which were uncomfortably short on him, with the striped jacket that fitted, whereas Estragon had outsize striped trousers beneath a well-fitting black jacket. An incidental benefit of this arrangement was that the final moment of the play, when Estragon's trousers have dropped round his ankles, had a self-evident quality: it was a disaster that had been threatening to happen throughout the act.

Beckett and Matias also developed the leitmotif of complementarity in the costuming of the Pozzo–Lucky couple. Pozzo's trousers and Lucky's waistcoat were made from the same checked material, while Pozzo's jacket was dark grey, matching Lucky's trousers. In this way, their costumes stressed the interdependence of Pozzo and Lucky rather than laying the emphasis on Pozzo's superior social status as landowner. In Walter Asmus' rehearsal diary, Beckett is reported as saying that Pozzo was 'not to be played as a superior figure (as he usually is). Instead, all four characters should be equal. He plays the lord – magnanimous, frightening – but only because he is unsure of himself.'[18] The clothes of both were shabby and broken down.

The lighting design echoed the play's overall theme of repetition with variations. Page 107 of the production notebook lists three lighting states:

> A = 1/2 evening light
> B = full   "   "
> C = Moonlight[19]

Both acts opened and closed with a curtain. After the curtain had risen, in both acts the lighting faded up from nothing to 'A'. In Act I Vladimir's first move towards Estragon (after 'Nothing to be done') brought the light up to 'B' while in Act II it was Estragon's move downstage after Vladimir's 'dog song' which brought it up to 'B'. In both acts it faded down to 'A' again on the departure of Pozzo and Lucky, and then changed to 'C' on the first step back taken by the boy after his conversation with Vladimir. Here again, Beckett was evidently drawing on pictorial inspiration, since page 30 of the notebook bears the name 'K. D. Friedrich' at the point when the moon rises. This refers to Friedrich's painting of two men looking at the moon which Beckett had seen at the art gallery in Dresden.[20] Both acts closed on a five-second *Wartestelle* before the lights were allowed to fade and the curtain came down. After the final curtain the actors took no curtain call because Beckett wanted to avoid breaking the final silence and darkness before the house lights come up.[21]

This careful patterning in the design elements of the production served to emphasise the shaping of the play of repetition and contrast on which Beckett's whole production was structured. A similar shaping could be seen at work in Beckett's indications for actions on stage. Page 73 of the notebook, headed 'INSPECTION PLACE', contains four sketch maps of characters' moves.

The first of these shows Estragon moving all round the stage during his speech 'Charming spot. Inspiring prospects. Let's go' (Faber 13–14). When shortly afterwards Estragon falls asleep, Beckett has Vladimir follow an almost exactly identical pattern of moves before waking him up with his three repeated exclamations of 'Gogo!' (Faber 15). In performance, such repetitions come across extremely clearly and encourage the audience to look for repeated themes or shapes in the movements as much as in the words. The third sketch shows Vladimir making an almost identical round of inspection at the start of the second act, thus establishing the pattern of the second act repeating (with variations) the action of the first act. The fourth sketch shows a movement made by Vladimir after the departure of Pozzo and Lucky in Act II, but it does not completely reproduce the pattern of the three earlier moves, and Beckett has written beside it 'Not properly inspection'. This is consistent with other moves and shaping devices employed, which all tend to decline or fragment or fall apart as the play runs its course.

Similar to the 'inspections' is his treatment of what he called 'Approach by Stages', which is the heading for pages 101–3 of the notebook. These are another example of what Beckett termed 'themes of the body'. Sixteen of them are listed in the notebook, the last of which was deleted in the course of rehearsals. The first two occur early in the first act, on Estragon's speech 'But what Saturday? And is it Saturday? Is it not rather Sunday? Or Monday? Or Friday?' (Faber 15). During this exchange Estragon moved across the stage towards Vladimir in short bursts, stopping between Sunday and Monday

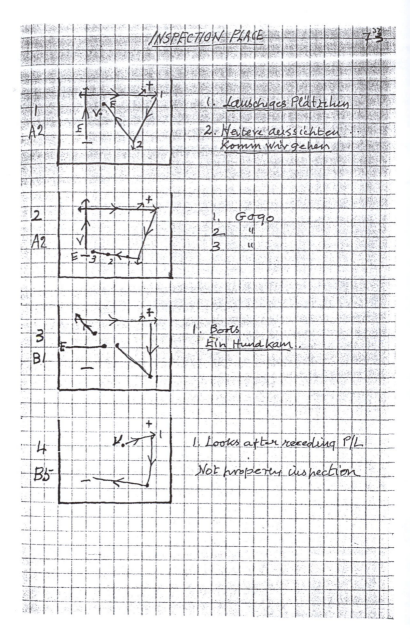

Figure 2. Beckett's sketch for 'Inspection [of] Place'.

and between Monday and Friday. The same pattern of a three-stage approach was then repeated a few lines later for Vladimir's three exclamations of 'Gogo!' mentioned above. Similar moves were given to Pozzo, when, soon after his entrance, he says 'I am Pozzo! (*Silence.*) Pozzo! (*Silence.*) Does that name mean nothing to you?' (Faber 22), and to Vladimir and Estragon as they approach and inspect Lucky (Faber 25). Finally, at the end of the act, the boy's approach and Estragon's angry questioning of him (Faber 49) were accompanied by the same short bursts of movement. In the second act, the motif of the 'approach by stages' was limited to moves by Vladimir and Estragon, being used to particularly good effect in the swearing match (Faber 75).

Beckett himself, in one of his rare comments on directing and how it should be done, complained that 'Producers don't seem to have any sense of form in movement. The kind of form one finds in music, for instance, where themes keep recurring. When, in a text, actions are repeated, they ought to be made unusual the first time, so that when they happen again – in exactly the same way – an audience will recognise them from before.'[22] His use of the motif of 'approach by stages' outlined above shows how he considered such principles ought to be applied. The kind of musical form to which he refers is to be found in the work of most of the great composers in the Western tradition, and is a particular feature of many of the works of Schubert, a composer for whom Beckett felt special affection. At its simplest, it can be seen in sonata form, which works with two fundamental elements: repetition and variation. Beckett is not the only playwright to have used musical form in this way. It is a major strand in Modernist theatre running from Strindberg (who entitled a play *Ghost Sonata*) to Michel Vinaver who has described all of his plays as similar to musical compositions in their use of theme and variations.[23] The principles of repetition and variation emerged especially clearly in the Schiller-Theater production from his design of the actors' movements. These form, in Knowlson's words, 'a whole pattern of moves in semicircles, arcs and chords, horizontals and verticals which create what may be termed a subliminal stage imagery' (*TN* 401). There are no separate headings in the notebook for straight lines and semicircular curves, but the sketches which he included from time to time show how he rang the changes.

Tracing this in detail throughout the production is a monumental task, magnificently achieved in the 465 pages of McMillan and Knowlson's *Theatrical Notebooks of Samuel Beckett*, vol. I, and the reader is referred to that volume's notes for a complete analysis. But one simple example can be extracted to show how different types of movement acquired thematic overtones, especially in respect of the relationships between characters. Pozzo and Lucky were linked in linear fashion. This was apparent from their first entrance, in which the straight line of the rope going like a dog-leash from Lucky's neck to Pozzo's hand was emphasised in Beckett's note. This specified that the rope must be 'just over 1/2 width of stage for P to stop just short of midstage – L to fall just off' (*TN* 197). In other words, the audience witnessed Lucky cross more than half of the stage, dragging the rope behind him, before Pozzo appeared holding the other end, and Lucky had already disappeared offstage on the opposite side from his entrance before Pozzo pulled him up short and the audience heard the clattering of his fall from the wings. Following this, almost all the moves given to Pozzo or Lucky are in straight lines, either from one side of the stage to the other or diagonally across it.

Many of Vladimir and Estragon's moves were also made along straight lines: there was marked use of diagonal movement, for example, when they rushed to and fro in fright and horror at the entrance of Pozzo and Lucky. Beckett varied their patterns of movement, however, by sometimes giving them a curved, semicircular trajectory. This kind of move was often associated with the more contemplative moments of the play. An example is the end of Act I, following the lines 'Are you mad? We must take cover. Come on', where Beckett's revised stage direction reads 'They begin to circle up towards the tree' (Faber 53; *TN* 49, line 1524) and his notebook entry includes a semicircular sketch (*TN* 236). On the page facing the sketch, Beckett has written

'V takes E's left hand or arm as for walks A2'. By this he means that the move should be an echo of earlier 'walks' which also conveyed similar moments of relative quiet or reflection. For example, on page 8 of the notebook he wrote that Vladimir should take Estragon's arm and draw him in a semicircular movement around the stage (also illustrated by a sketch) in the course of the lines following 'Let's wait and see what he says' (Faber 18; *TN* 17, line 307). In this way, through the use of repetition and contrast, particular patterns of movement echo one another, becoming associated in the audience's mind with motifs or moods in the play.

Given Beckett's own comment on musical form, and the experience of echo and counterpoint characteristic of Beckett's use of space, the question of his use of music also seems worth investigating. The second act of the play begins with Vladimir singing a song, and, as Beckett noted on page 38 of the notebook, it is the first of four songs or tunes in Act II. He listed them as:

1. Dog tune
2. Schlafe mein Prinzchen
3. Chopin's Trauermarsch
4. Merry Widow Waltz

McMillan and Knowlson's commentary on this choice of tunes suggests that 'together they may be seen as presenting a musical summary of the situation . . . progressing from the endless verbal circle of the dog song to the physical circle of the hummed tune of the Waltz duet from *The Merry Widow*. Between the two come the crooned first line of the lullaby "Schlafe mein Prinzchen, Schlaf'ein" ("Sleep, My Princeling, go to sleep"), associated with the beginning of life, and the Bom-Bom-ba-Bom of Chopin's Funeral March, associated with its ending' (*TN* 147). The tune used for the dog song was that of 'Carnival in Venice'. It was sung reflectively, with the last two lines spoken very quietly, almost whispered. The lullaby is crooned by Vladimir as Estragon tries to get to sleep about a third of the way through Act II (Faber 70; *TN* 63). The choice of 'Schlafe mein

Prinzchen' (a familiar German song) was made in the course of rehearsals, and other familiar lullabies have been used for performances
in other countries. Chopin's funeral march was hummed by Vladimir
twenty lines later, after Estragon has woken up from a bad dream; he
does so in an attempt to revive Estragon and there is a comic irony
in his coming out with a tune so commonly associated with funeral
processions. Finally, the waltz from *The Merry Widow* came in the
passage where they first insult one another and then make it up again.
It was the climax of their reconciliation:

> VLADIMIR: Come to my arms!
> ESTRAGON: Your arms?
> VLADIMIR: My breast!
> ESTRAGON: Off we go!

At this point, Beckett's original stage direction read 'They embrace',
and for the Schiller production he added: 'Waltz in a full circle humming the Waltz Duet from *The Merry Widow*' (Faber 76; *TN* 69).
Clearly the music was chosen and implemented in such a way as to
underline the circularity of the situation.

THE NOTEBOOKS

There are two notebooks, a preliminary version, known at the Reading University archive where both are housed as the 'green' notebook,
and a final version, known as the 'red' notebook. Beckett had the
red notebook with him throughout rehearsals and made additions or
deletions to it as he worked with the actors. It is this notebook which
is reproduced in *The Theatrical Notebooks of Samuel Beckett*, vol. I. It
begins by breaking the play up into eleven sections, six in Act I and five
in Act II. These are listed as A1–6 and B1–5. Each of these sections has
a few pages devoted to it, giving detailed indications for movements,
gestures and manipulation of props, together with occasional comments on tone of voice or desired effect on the audience. The textual

location of a given move is indicated by a short quotation from the German text, followed by a telegraphic evocation of what movement is to take place. Only the right-hand pages of the notebook are used for these indications, except that Beckett has occasionally filled out his description by drawing a small diagram on the left-hand page, tracing out the pattern of a character's moves using lines and arrows. Apart from these diagrams, the left-hand pages were left blank for alterations or new ideas to emerge in rehearsals, and these were noted by Beckett in red to distinguish them from the black ink used for his preparatory notes. This takes up the first fifty-three pages of the notebook.

The sections are not all the same length and are best seen in musical terms as 'statements' or 'developments' of themes. As we have seen from his treatment of Lucky's 'Think', Beckett approached the play very much with a view to clarifying thematic patterns. A1 runs from the opening to just after Estragon's line 'People are bloody ignorant apes' (Faber 13). Beckett's note at the end of the section reads:

> Thus establish at outset 2 caged dynamics, E sluggish, V restless.
> + perpetual separation and reunion of V/E. (*TN*, 185)

The function of the opening section was thus to bring out the predicament of the two characters, stressing both their opposition and their complementarity.

A2 opens with the first 'inspection of place' and 'approach by stages' of Estragon, mirrored soon after by similar moves on the part of Vladimir. In this section the staging opens out the exploration of the *place* in which they are, but also develops the theme of perpetual separation and reunion, 'like a rubber band, they come together time after time', commented Stefan Wigger in rehearsals.[24] A3 starts from the first sounds of the approach of Pozzo and Lucky. In this section the emphasis is on the encounter between the two couples and their inspection of one another, first Pozzo's inspection of Vladimir and Estragon, and then their inspection of Lucky. It also includes all the elaborate stage business between Lucky and Pozzo as Pozzo enjoys his picnic, and incorporates the third *Wartestelle*, which followed Pozzo's line 'Pan sleeps' (Faber 36). The section ends on the fourth *Wartestelle*, the silence following Pozzo's line 'You see my memory is defective' (Faber 38). Estragon's 'In the meantime nothing happens' opens A5, which includes the build-up to Lucky's 'Think' and the 'Think' itself, and ends with the departure of Pozzo and Lucky. A6 begins with Vladimir's 'That passed the time' (Faber 48), running to the end of the act.

Beckett's notes for A6 show his preoccupation with the lighting and with the precise moves to be taken by the boy. The lighting effect he wanted was for the boy to emerge from deep shadow, and this was achieved in the Schiller-Theater. As for the moves, these were to be a further variation of the theme of 'approach by stages', as the boy moved hesitantly towards Vladimir and Vladimir reciprocated with moves towards the boy. The boy's moves as he exited were to mirror his entry. Vladimir's last words to the boy, 'You did see us, didn't you?', emerged 'as an important motif in Beckett's Schiller production where this despairing cry from Vladimir became something of a climactic moment' (*TN* 143). This was an occasion for another successful lighting effect:

> The Boy's exit was co-ordinated here with the moon which, in Schiller, rose in a perfect arc from the point where Vladimir was standing and stopped above the spot where the Boy had just been. (*TN* 143)

The second act was divided into five sections. B1 runs from the beginning to Vladimir's 'Ah! Que voulez-vous. Exactly' (Faber 65). B2 begins with Estragon's 'That wasn't such a bad little canter' and runs to the point where Pozzo and Lucky enter. B3 and B4 cover the sections of the act in which Pozzo and Lucky are on stage, with the division between B3 and B4 occurring at the fourth *Wartestelle* of Act II after Vladimir's line 'We are men' (Faber 82). Finally, B5 covers the end of the act after Pozzo and Lucky's departure. The staging notes for this act show Beckett developing variations on the patterns of movement he had established in the first act, contrasting straight lines with arcs and circles and echoing the theme of the 'approach by stages'.

The second half of the notebook, from page 54 to page 109, is devoted to a series of twenty analytical headings bringing together recurring themes or actions in the play. Most of these consist simply of lists, devoid of commentary. The first of these headings, 'L's moves A3', catalogues in meticulous detail each step taken by Lucky so as to avoid any confusion about how he carries his burdens and how he responds to Pozzo's stream of commands. These pages of the notebook generally restrict themselves to outlining moves, although there are rare occasions where general principles underlying the moves are alluded to, and some of these have been examined above. The twenty headings are listed as follows on page one of the notebook:

L's moves A3
L's think
E's feet
E's sleeps
Whip
V/E and tree
Inspection Place
W
Inspection hat/boot
Doubts confusions
Komm wir gehen [Let's go]
Help
Was sagte ich noch? [What was I saying?]
Sky
Sleep
Erinnern [Remembering]
approach by stages
Divisions
Lighting
Tree

The most striking thing about this list is Beckett's lack of interest in distinguishing thematic concerns from practical details: the two jostle side by side and give a good insight into his state of mind as he prepared

6. The production by Samuel Beckett, Schiller-Theater, Berlin, 1975. Left to right: Horst Bollmann (Estragon), Klaus Herm (Lucky).

his production. It calls to mind strongly the ideal poet of the stage prophesied by Edward Gordon Craig, who would express himself through an integrated composition of everything that the audience can see and hear on the stage. It is not easy to detect any guiding principle behind the things he has chosen to list. He appears to have started from the matters which worried him, such as how to organise all Lucky's paraphernalia, and then, by working through these, to have arrived at those features of the production which give it underlying consistency and artistic shape. These are either repetitions and echoes (that is, elements that call for special emphasis in performance), or items having symbolic resonance, such as his substitution of a stone for a mound, or aspects of pacing and rhythm, such as the *Wartestellen* he introduced.

BECKETT'S HANDLING OF ACTORS IN REHEARSAL

Walter Asmus' account shows that although Beckett always began with the moves and stage business which he had worked out in advance in his notebook he was ready to adjust them in the light of what appeared most effective in rehearsal. He adopted several of the actors' suggestions, especially those which increased comic impact through the use of repetition. In Act I, for example, when Pozzo is trying to introduce himself to Vladimir and Estragon, they built up a comic repetition of the names 'Bozzo . . . Bozzo', 'Pozzo . . . Pozzo', each actor intercutting his line with that of the other. Again, when Pozzo and Lucky depart, Vladimir and Estragon continued to repeat their 'Adieux' and to raise their hats in a gesture of farewell long after the other two had left the stage. Knowlson points out that Beckett's creative work with the actors in rehearsal cannot be deduced from the notebook, especially the way he encouraged them to build up the physical routines, transforming 'vaudeville movements into something almost balletic'.[25] An examples of this was the 'Three hats for two heads' routine in Act II, when Vladimir and Estragon discover the hat left behind by Lucky, which was based on a sequence from the Marx Brothers' film *Duck Soup*. Asmus' diary thus provides an invaluable additional record of the process of creative work which took place in the course of rehearsals.

Asmus' diary stresses the friendly atmosphere in which the work took place, despite Beckett's intense concern for precision in every-thing that was done on stage. He sums it up as 'an atmosphere of "relaxed tension", which could also be described as an occupation of pleasure'.[26] Beckett was unwilling to discuss the play's meaning or content in discursive terms, but was always ready to help the actors with explanations concerning the characters' motivation at any particular moment. He rejected explanations of the kind commonly associated with the Stanislavskian school of naturalism, such as those relating to background, events that have taken place before the action begins, or sub-textual details only hinted at in the text of the play. On the other hand, he was quite forthcoming on the subject of the complex way in which the characters on stage relate to one another. While he was rehearsing Lucky's 'Think', Asmus reports the following exchange between Beckett and Klaus Herm (playing Lucky):

> Herm: He [Lucky] gives Estragon once, a long look. What do you mean to say with this long look?
> Beckett: It's a kind of look you can't explain in a few words. There is a lot in that look. Lucky wants the piece of bone, of course. Estragon, too. That is a confrontation, a meeting of two very poor people.
> Herm: Something like solidarity, is that in it, too?
> Beckett: Yes, there are so many things in his head. Recognising the other one's situation, that is very important – but also some pride, that he is free to dispose of the bones, as opposed to Estragon. But Lucky does not forget either. The kick in the shin should be interpreted as Lucky's revenge for the fact that Estragon took the bone.[27]

While Beckett may not have wanted his characters to be consid-ered in naturalistic terms, he nonetheless envisaged their reactions to one another being built up from a complex interplay of different motives, and expected his actors to convey a range of very subtle nuance through something as simple as a look.

Sometimes the actors yearned for the naturalistic acting style to which they were accustomed. When Beckett was describing the non-realistic way he wanted Lucky to fall, Stefan Wigger asked, 'But how can one prevent the loss of all human consideration, how can one prevent it from becoming sterile', to which Beckett replied, 'it is a game, everything is a game'.[28] He frequently returned to this asser-tion that the play was a game, albeit a game played in earnest: 'It should become clear and transparent, not dry. It is a game in order to survive.'[29] He was determined to avoid imitation of reality, but he respected the real tensions, desires and frustrations present in the ways people interrelate. An example of this realistic yet playful approach to character emerges from the following description by Asmus:

> Starting with 'Sweet mother earth', the scene is being played in con-text until the exit of Pozzo and Lucky [in Act II]. When Estragon and Vladimir – all lying on the ground – shout 'Pozzo', Beckett slips in a small alteration. Instead of speaking all the time towards the back, towards Pozzo, Estragon should say his 'We might try him with other names' directly to Vladimir. There is thus a small intimate moment of conspiracy created at this point, which is reminiscent of similar moments throughout the play.[30]

The conspiratorial, game-like approach was evident in a number of key sequences of action devised by Beckett for his actors, and helped them to come to terms with the precise, sometimes deliberately artificial patterns of movement which he described as 'balletic'.

As can be seen from the examples given, a move was never permis-sible, as it is in so many productions, simply on the grounds that it made the actor feel comfortable or looked natural. On the contrary, every move had a purpose within the overall structure of the produc-tion; no move was either gratuitous or superfluous. The same was true of the delivery of the lines. This had to respect the reality of the char-acters' emotions, provoked by their relationships and the situations in which they were placed, but also the overall thematic patterning, as we saw in Beckett's handling of Lucky's 'Think'. The effect of the moments of stillness and silence was further enhanced by the speed of much of the dialogue. Beckett's production was timed by Ruby Cohn at seventy minutes for Act I and fifty-five minutes for Act II, which is considerably faster than most. For purposes of comparison, Luc Bondy's production (in 1999 – see chapter 9) ran for more than half an hour longer than this.[31] In Beckett's production, the overall experience for audiences was one of lightness and speed, interspersed with haunting moments of anguish.

CHAPTER 7

'FAIL AGAIN. FAIL BETTER.'

The lightness and speed of Beckett's production analysed in chapter 6 came as a surprise to many: 'It was a merry evening. Critics looked on with astonishment and laymen with enjoyment', wrote Friedrich Luft.[1] Susan Sontag confirmed Luft's statement: 'I was actually quite shocked by his production. To my surprise . . . it was very funny, it was fast, as if someone had taken literally Chekhov's declaration that the *Three Sisters* was a comedy. I found it in short much too amusing.'[2] Although some, like Sontag, had doubts, most of the critics were positive. The production toured Europe, appeared at the Royal Court Theatre in London in 1976 and at the Brooklyn Academy of Music in New York in 1977. Its unerring rhythm, balletic grace and powerful combination of movement, gesture, image and voice made it seem, to many theatre people, the 'definitive' production. Beckett did not share this opinion: he knew better than most that nothing is definitive, least of all a theatre production. As the thousands of productions since 1975 have shown, the simple fact of performing with different actors, in a different theatre, for a different audience and in a different context introduces so large a quantity of variables that no one production can ever claim to have exhausted every performance possibility, any more than this can be true of a performance of a piece of music. Performers can only hope to 'Fail again. Fail better.'[3]

Over the next ten years, Beckett was frequently asked to repeat his production in other theatres, but he always refused. He preferred to authorise Walter Asmus, who had been his chief assistant at the Schiller-Theater, to reactivate the production as he had conceived it. Asmus' first revival was at the Brooklyn Academy of Music in May 1978. Asmus remained a close friend of Beckett's for the rest of his life, directing other plays as well as *Godot*. His most widely seen revival of the Beckett *Godot* was done in 1988 for the Gate Theatre, Dublin, revived for a season of all Beckett's plays at the same theatre in 1991 and toured widely (see chapter 9). Asmus also made two video recordings, one of the French text and one of the revised English text.[4] These are the only video versions of the play authorised by Beckett, who always felt that the play was unsuitable for film and turned down several lucrative offers, including one of $25,000 from Paramount Pictures.[5] The one time that Beckett came close to giving in to demands to re-direct *Godot* was in 1984, when the request came from Rick Cluchey. Cluchey had been present in Berlin throughout the Schiller-Theater rehearsals, acting as Beckett's second assistant, and Beckett had grown extremely fond of him. In 1984 the San Quentin Drama Workshop was invited to perform *Godot* at the Adelaide Festival in Australia, but the funding for the company to attend the festival was dependent on Beckett directing the production in person.[6] Beckett accordingly agreed to help with the production, supervising ten days of rehearsals at London's Riverside Studios, for a production which was, in other respects, directed by Asmus with Cluchey as Pozzo.

For actors and directors who had not had the privilege of working with Beckett, the decision to mount a new production of *Godot* after 1975 raised difficult questions. Should they attempt to copy Beckett's own production and risk producing a pale imitation? Or should they come up with an original staging idea of their own? As explained in chapter 1, the rise of the director in twentieth-century theatre had led to a situation in which the expressive means employed in the staging, acting and so on (the 'scenic writing') were seen as complementing the playwright's work and as having equal importance. The tendency to see the director, or theatre company, as the main creative force, and the author as somewhat secondary, reached its height in the 1970s and 1980s, resulting in a number of attempts to perform Beckett's plays in settings or styles different from those imagined by the author. This was the time of JoAnne Akalitis' notorious production of *Endgame* set in a subway tunnel (1984) and of George Tabori's *Happy Days* set in a bed rather than the author's mound of earth (1986). In 1979 the company of the Théâtre National de Strasbourg, under the direction of André Engel, staged a performance they had devised entitled *Ils allaient obscurs dans la nuit solitaire; d'après 'En attendant Godot' de Samuel Beckett*, in which sections of the dialogue of *Godot* were interspersed with other events, such as a rape and a terrorist attack, in a modern urban setting including cars, a café and shops.

Such experiments can be seen as the logical end point of the theatrical developments outlined in chapter 1, developments which explored the expressive possibilities available when a performance opened up discontinuities between text and staging. These experiments have seldom proved successful when applied to plays by Beckett, however, for a reason which goes to the root of Beckett's dramatic originality. The reason is that devices of discontinuity and contradiction are already built into the very fabric of his work. The most celebrated stage direction in twentieth-century theatre is the identical ending of both acts of *Waiting for Godot* : 'Yes, let's go. *They do not move.*' Contradiction between word and action is fundamental. In his own direction of the play, Beckett sought to extend this principle of exploiting discontinuity to every level of the staging. The mismatch of costumes between Vladimir and Estragon clearly exemplified this, as did many other deliberate incongruities, such as Vladimir's humming of the Chopin funeral march when he is trying to cheer up Estragon. Beckett encouraged the actors to vary abruptly the speed of their delivery and of their moves, to give sudden emphasis to particular words, to separate out words and movements. In all these ways, he was enhancing and leading up to that famous last stage direction.

Such stage devices were chosen by Beckett because they helped to express, and to ring variations on, one of the play's most important themes: the mismatch between expectation and reality. In his notebook, Beckett included a page entitled 'Help' which listed twenty-one appeals for help in the course of the play, fourteen of which are ignored. He also included three pages headed 'Doubts confusions', listing the contradictions between the memories of Vladimir and those of Estragon concerning what they did the day before, what instruction they believed they had received, whether Pozzo and Lucky (in Act II) were the same people they had seen the day before, and a number of other disconcerting gaps in their understanding of the world around them. All of these examples are rooted in the most fundamental discontinuity of all, the one on which the whole play rests: that of identity. In the absence of the long-awaited Godot, how can either Vladimir or Estragon be sure who they are. They long to be seen (and to be reassured that they *have been seen*) by someone, because they feel dimly that this would give them the certainty they long for, making whole their sense of fragmentation and discontinuity. Everything appears discontinuous to them, even a cyclical round-song. The play constantly sets discontinuity in counterpoint against the other dominant shape – that of circularity. And Beckett was keen constantly to set one action/movement/sound/light off against another so as to build up a densely resonant poetic/symbolic texture.

If the main resource of twentieth-century directors was to exploit discontinuities, to open up a space for meaning to emerge between word and action, then they found that Beckett had trumped them at their own game. A new director wanting to play against the text is severely constrained by the extent to which Beckett has already inscribed such 'playing against the text' at the heart of his dramatic enterprise. Equally important, if a production attempts to localise *Godot*, to set it in a particular society, or to suggest real-life models for a character, the play often comes across as rather weak. Any attempt to enhance the play's appeal by making it relevant to a known social context appears, paradoxically, to impoverish it rather than to enrich it (although we shall discover some exceptions to this rule). Beckett's own systematic use of discontinuity is possible precisely because his theatre is not mimetic but presentational; it is concerned with what happens between actors and audiences within the real time of the performance and with 'the impossibility of making believable, event-filled plots at all'.[7] It does not imitate an action (in Aristotle's term); it does not even tell a complete story. There is thus little or no scope for relocating the story or setting the characters in a different environment, as, for example, Richard III may be relocated to the period between the two world wars.[8] 'His writing is not *about* something, *it is that something itself*', as Beckett said of Joyce.[9]

The history of the many productions of *Waiting for Godot* falls into two clear periods: those before and those after the revelation of Beckett's own 1975 production. The years 1949–75 were the pioneering stage, when the play appeared genuinely hard to understand, even a little frightening, and when both actors and audiences often felt baffled by it. As Herb Blau reminds us, 'the hardest thing to reconstruct . . . is just how startling those plays were'.[10] This twenty-five year period coincided with Beckett's developing mastery of theatre, as both playwright and director. As his originality became more apparent, so his interpreters multiplied, and, instead of seeming strange and frightening, his theatre work was acclaimed as profound and innovative. The second stage in the production history was the period after 1975, when it was impossible to undertake a new production without some reference to Beckett's.

Yet the trend of the times, as we have seen, was entirely against respect for the playwright's text: every revival of a well-known play was examined for its director's new interpretation or different slant. In line with this approach, certain directors and designers set aside Beckett's stage directions, inventing different settings, or casting female actors in male roles. Beckett's work proved quite resistant to such approaches, however, and even directors who began by wanting to re-contextualise his plays completely often ended up, almost despite themselves, respecting his stage directions. This chapter will examine some examples of what happened when celebrated theatre directors took on the challenge of reviving *Waiting for Godot*.

THE PRODUCTION BY OTOMAR KREJČA, AVIGNON THEATRE FESTIVAL, 1978

The case of Otomar Krejča is an interesting one to study from the perspective outlined above, because he mounted two very different productions of the play, one before and one after Beckett's 1975 Schiller-Theater production. In 1970, when the Za Branou (Behind the Gate) theatre in Prague (of which he had been co-founder) was at the height of its international reputation, he was invited to produce *Waiting for Godot* for the Salzburg Festival. His designer for this production was Josef Svoboda, and between them they conceived a production that was designed to comment on the play, to open up discontinuities between text and performance in the characteristic style of 'directors' theatre' mentioned above. The setting embroidered lavishly on Beckett's stage direction. Instead of a vague, neutral space, it presented an elaborately theatrical *trompe-l'oeil* image designed to destabilise the spectators' sense of where the auditorium ended and the stage began. Flanking both sides of the stage was a prolongation of the auditorium, set at a slight slant, so that a double row of gilded boxes hemmed the action in on both sides, mirroring the boxes in the auditorium. The theme of self-conscious reflection was reinforced by the back wall of the set, which consisted entirely of one enormous mirror in which the audience caught glimpses of itself from time to time but which mostly mirrored the gnarled old tree placed centre-stage and the actors from behind. The tree consisted of a thick trunk, rising to about eight feet, with a dozen or so pollarded branches growing from its crown. The mirror image, reflecting its upstage side, showed the artificial framework propping it up from behind, which was invisible from the front. This production emphasised the play's self-consciously theatrical quality, using it as a way of commenting on the enclosed world of self-regarding theatre festivals. This is an interpretation which can be justified by certain sections of the play, particularly Pozzo's aggressively self-involved performance in Act I, and which was thoroughly explored by André Brassard in his Quebec production (see chapter 8).

The authorities in Prague had never forgiven Krejča for his role in the brief revolution of 1968, and his anti-realistic tendencies ran directly counter to the officially approved style of Socialist Realism. In 1972, four years after the Soviet invasion had restored them to power, the Czech Communist Party felt in a sufficiently strong position to close down Krejča's theatre. He was without work for two years, and decided to go into exile, working in various European centres until 1989, when he was able to work in Prague once more. During this time, he directed *Waiting for Godot* again at the 1978 Avignon Festival in a production sponsored by the theatre at Louvain in Belgium, where he held the post of artistic director. For this production he dispensed with elaborate design ideas such as those he and Svoboda had used in Salzburg, for reasons we shall examine. Between his 1970 production and the one he did in 1978 he had seen Beckett's own production, and this appears to have modified his whole approach to the play. Finally, after his return to Prague he directed the play once again in Czech in 1991.

For the 1978 Avignon Festival production, the normal French term for production ('mise en scène') was not used. Instead, the programme read as follows:

Régie: Otomar Krejča
Décor: Otomar Krejča et Yves Cassagne

Vladimir: Georges Wilson
Estragon: Rufus
Pozzo: Michel Bouquet
Lucky: José-Maria Flotats
Le garçon: Fabrice Luchini

The more technical term 'régie', which might be translated as 'stage direction', emphasised Krejča's desire to serve the text rather than to impose his own vision on it. The production was hailed as a major event. It toured for two years in France, Italy and Belgium, including a revival at the 1979 Avignon Festival, had a long run at Peter Brook's theatre, the Bouffes du Nord in Paris, in 1980, and saw a further revival at the Atelier theatre five years later. There were minor changes in the cast: the Belgian actor André Burton took over the role of Lucky in 1979, while the boy was played by a number of different actors.

The Avignon production was performed in the main space used by the festival: the courtyard of the papal palace. This vast open-air arena, which can hold an audience of over a thousand, imposes its own dynamic on a production. Any reference to a theatre interior, such as Krejča had used in Salzburg, would be impossible in this space. The courtyard alone would have dictated a different approach, but the main motivation for the design seems to have been the director's experience of Beckett's own production in Berlin. Krejča's way of working with actors was always to resist simple photographic realism, developing outer behaviour by means of intensive work on the interior, psychological and spiritual dimensions of the role. He always attempted to bring out the poetic dimensions in any play he was directing. Beckett's success in achieving just this kind of work at the Schiller-Theater persuaded Krejča to attempt a more open approach to the play. In an interview given during the rehearsals in 1979 he said that when he first read the play, in the 1950s, he had seen it as nothing more than an extremely clever 'anti-play', systematically contradicting all our normal expectations of theatre. Now, however, he found it much more profound, considering it to be 'the great poem of our century'. He added that its power could be attributed to the fact that 'this is not a play which *describes* something, it *is* something'.[11]

This time the setting was designed by Krejča himself. It consisted of a large white oval space, twelve metres across and eight metres from front to back, tilted towards the audience. It was completely bare

7. The production by Otomar Krejča, Papal Palace, Avignon Theatre Festival, 1978. Final curtain call, with view from behind the stage, showing the raised, tilted oval platform and the audience applauding in the Papal Palace courtyard.

except for a skeletal tree with a couple of spindly branches upstage left and a stone downstage right. It was originally to have been covered with foam rubber so as to give the impression of uneven ground,[12] but this idea was discarded at the last moment in favour of a smooth white stage-cloth. Under harsh white light, which hardly varied until the end of each act (at the point where the moon rises), this oval shape appeared to hover a few feet above the ground in the surrounding darkness. The neutral, or abstract, quality of this stage space produced widely different associations in the minds of the critics. It was described as a 'saucer, a [circus] ring, a full moon, a desert island, a sort of planetary huis-clos, an opalescent gulag, a no man's land and an ellipse', and several critics felt that it acquired a 'cosmic dimension'.[13]

The reactions of the critics show that the setting managed, as Beckett had said of the play itself, to 'avoid definition', or, at least, to avoid one single restrictive definition. Like the play itself, it succeeded in being both very concretely no more and no less than what it was — i.e. a stage — as well as suggesting other, more metaphorical associations. In French the word for stage is 'plateau', which can also mean 'tray', to which Estragon draws explicit attention in Act II: 'En effet, nous sommes sur un plateau. Aucun doute, nous sommes servis sur un plateau.'[14] The white, tilted oval certainly looked like a 'plateau', while at a metaphorical level the elliptical shape of the stage clearly mirrored the circularity of the plot of *Waiting for Godot*; the production made use of this by introducing a large number of circular movements. In the passages of rapid dialogue between Estragon and Vladimir the two often moved around the perimeter of the stage, either in opposite directions or in parallel moves, and they also made circular moves around both the tree and the stone. At the end of each act the boy entered from the back but remained just outside the level of the white playing space (and slightly below it since it was raised above the level of the stage itself). As he spoke his words, he described a complete circle around the stage, moving slowly and never stopping until he disappeared into the darkness again, just before Vladimir's despairing cry of 'Tu nous a bien vus, n'est-ce pas?' (Act II: 'Dis, tu es bien sûr de m'avoir vu . . . ') ('You did see us, didn't you?' Act II: 'You're sure you saw me . . . ').

On this stage, the fact that Vladimir and Estragon have nowhere else to go acquired an absolute literality. The moments in the play where actors leave the stage were cut to a minimum. When the lights came up at the beginning they were both on stage, as in Beckett's production, Vladimir near the tree at the top of the ellipse with his back to the audience, Estragon downstage right sitting on his stone. Pozzo and Lucky's entry was made from the centre back, Lucky coming straight downstage and collapsing in full sight of the public, not offstage in the wings. In the second act, at the point when Vladimir and Estragon think they hear someone coming, Estragon did not exit (as in the stage directions) but ran around in terror within the bounds of the 'plateau'. The costumes helped to create the effect of a non-specific space: all were black and at certain moments gave the actors the appearance of silhouettes against the white background of the stage.[15] Vladimir and Estragon both had old black jackets, black trousers and black bowler hats. The materials were all very frayed and broken down. Lucky's costume was the same, with very small variations, and only Pozzo stood out by the elegance of his overcoat, worn over a dinner jacket with a smart white waistcoat, starched shirt-front, well-pressed trousers and patent leather shoes.

This production was the object of a very detailed analysis by Odette Aslan.[16] She summed up the actors' performances as follows: 'neither too philosophical nor too clownish, they present ordinary people of today in whom we recognise ourselves'.[17] Krejča's rehearsal method was to discourage any attempt to 'create a character', encouraging his actors to explore and build on their own natural bodily movements. 'Movement speaks to us', he said. 'Wilson's heavy head, the characteristic restlessness of Rufus. It is with the flesh of the actors that we compose'.[18] Consistent with his overall idea that 'this is not a play which *describes* something, it *is* something', his work as director was focused not on the characters but with the actors as human beings.

Michel Bouquet (Pozzo) described it in the following terms:

> He sets out to work with people as people; he tries to help them to understand the subterranean truths contained within the work, but without defining them. He does not direct the actor, he puts the human being on stage. If the human being is an actor, so much the better, but he does not put the actor on stage. He's a humanist director.[19]

Bouquet also commented that he had never worked with a director who possessed such honesty or such perseverance, nor one who was silent so much of the time.[20]

As such descriptions imply, Krejča did not start out with a prepared notebook, in the manner of Beckett. He sought to keep the rehearsal process as open as possible, and to avoid settling for one univocal interpretation. Rufus (the actor playing Estragon) reported to Odette Aslan that Krejča was concerned throughout the rehearsal process to build up layers of meaning: 'part of each rehearsal was devoted to piling up contradictory meanings, working through an infinity of details, playing with the discontinuities between verbal facets [of the text] irrespective of [the characters'] situation or psychology'.[21] The actors responded favourably to Krejča's strategy, which owed its success to the experience and creativity of his cast. The roles of Vladimir, Estragon and Pozzo were all taken by actors famous on the French stage and at the height of their powers. Georges Wilson, who played Vladimir, is an actor capable of weight and gravity, who had played the great tragic roles, but he was also known for his comic abilities and his commitment to the ideals of 'le théâtre populaire'. He had succeeded Jean Vilar as director of the Théâtre National Populaire in 1963 and was a great favourite with audiences at the Avignon Festival. Rufus had a background in comedy and clowning, but had also performed in straight theatre. Michel Bouquet was a highly respected actor of comic roles but was also well known for his many film appearances. He was not an obviously dominant or brutal choice for Pozzo. José-Maria Flotats was a young actor, less well known than the others, and Fabrice Luchini was entirely unknown (though he has since become celebrated for his eccentricity and ironic, self-deprecating humour).

Krejča's policy of trying to develop and extend the actors' natural physique and style of movement led to a contrast between Vladimir and Estragon not unlike that between Bollmann and Wigger in Beckett's Berlin production. Rufus' performance was very physical, with sudden, abrupt movements. He would change from one physical state to another quite suddenly, with no attempt at a smooth or realistic transition. For example, he was awake one moment and asleep the next, almost in mid-sentence. His phases of energetic movement were followed by sudden lapses into apathy. He was constantly drawn back to his stone, expressing the sense of being earthbound, in contrast to Vladimir's more vertical stance and regular interrogations of the sky. He played 'off' Vladimir a great deal, forcing him to take the lead, to keep the game going. Wilson was the perfect foil to Rufus' Estragon, more verbal, more tense and anguished, less able to slump physically. As a pair, they were more separate than Bollmann and Wigger, less visibly tied to one another. Their separation was not constant, however: there were times when they acted in concert, almost as if they were twins. The fifth 'Vous voulez vous en débarrasser', for example, was said in chorus by both at once.[22]

There were also moments when they went through extremely physical routines of comic interplay in which they seemed to draw strength from their symbiosis. One such moment was the scene at the start of Act II where Vladimir persuades Estragon to try on the boots. Rufus lay on his back, so that Wilson had to place the boots on Rufus' feet as they waved upside down in the air; this he did with a sort of screwing motion, and the whole episode turned into a hilarious interplay of encouragement and reluctance. Other, more traditional moments of clowning, such as Lucky's bag dropping on Estragon's foot as they try to make him stand upright, were all used to great advantage, and the 'three hats for two heads' routine in Act II was performed with great comic verve. These moments of symbiotic clowning were all centred on passages in the play where items of concrete importance to the two were in play – hats, boots, 'the little things of life'. And this emphasis gave the performance a great sense of being rooted in the real world of human beings' struggle for survival, counteracting the abstract, generalising tendency of the stage and costumes. The objects emphasised in this way were all very ordinary; a couple of Pozzo's props, his pipe and his vaporiser, were cut because they were judged to lack the same necessary quality possessed by the other objects.

Perhaps because they were able to achieve this concrete or 'literal' quality in the performance, the contrasting moments when the characters' fear, boredom or anxiety broke through were all the more powerful. Wilson, in particular, was praised by reviewers for his ability to express all the anguish of the world. Equally, the production never indulged in sentimentality.

Both Aslan and the theatre reviewers of the time stress that the performance carefully avoided pathos. In particular, the role of Lucky was interpreted in what was seen as a departure from tradition. Jean Martin's harrowing depiction of a man in the last stages of Parkinson's disease had acquired a kind of iconic status, even for those who had not seen Blin's original production. Flotats broke with this tradition, portraying him as a man who can express 'the contradiction between the pain of the human condition and the powers of the intelligence'.[23] Flotats looked like a young intellectual reduced to silence by the powers of the establishment. Michel Bouquet informed Aslan that 'For Krejča, Lucky is Culture, he is The Poet.'[24] Bouquet's performance as Pozzo was extremely forceful: he used looks and silences in a threatening way, was most emphatic about the orders he gave, and often showed signs of impatience or simmering violence. His moments of weakness were all cunningly feigned. He alternated engaging smiles with unpleasant looks, presenting an insecure but dominant personality who gets into terrible rages. His relationship with Lucky was forcefully established through eye contact, as it had been in Beckett's Berlin production. Bouquet explained that during the rehearsals

Krejča had spoken a great deal about failing statesmen who are terrified of losing their power, and that he was encouraged to think of the role in terms of power play rather than personal psychology.

In the characters' movements, developed in the course of rehearsals, Krejča tried to adopt the principles lying behind the moves invented by Beckett in Berlin, drawing echoes and resonances out of the physical themes in the performance. A move by Estragon around one side of the perimeter of the stage would be echoed by a mirror move round the facing side by Vladimir. Like Beckett, Krejča exploited the contrast between moves made in a straight line and those made in a semicircle (though there were more of the latter in Krejča's production than in Beckett's because of the shape of his stage). A further contrast was established between the predominantly circular moves made by Vladimir and Estragon and the moves of Pozzo and Lucky, which were all in straight lines. Krejča's aim throughout the rehearsal period had been, he said, to achieve the maximum poetic force by concentrating on the concrete physicalisation of the characters – their routines, movements, props. He also stated that his aim in producing the play had been to arrive at a performance whose main quality was its 'openness to many interpretations', so that the audience can 'collaborate' in giving it meaning.[25] According to the résumé of the press reviews conducted by Félie Pastorello,[26] this aim was successful, since many of the reviewers used the word 'ouverture' (openness) to describe that main quality of the production. The other thing to emerge from the reviews is that the production was considered to be a great success in demonstrating the comic qualities of a play hitherto considered rather depressing, and that it had achieved an excellent balance between the comic and the tragic moods.

In November 1989, at the time when the Berlin wall was knocked down and the 'Velvet Revolution' which was to bring Vaclav Havel to power was under way, the slogan 'Godot has arrived' appeared in the streets of Prague. In the minds of many people, endless waiting had been the defining mark of the decades of Soviet rule. Krejča was reinstated at the head of his old theatre Za Branou, where *Waiting for Godot*, in a new translation by Karel Kraus, was one of his first productions (November 1991). He copied his successful Avignon production scrupulously, using the same stage design, costumes and patterns of movement. The production was greeted with respect but not with rapture. To audiences and reviewers it seemed too much like a museum piece and the acting was not of sufficiently high quality. In particular, Vladimir, played by Otomar Krejča junior, was criticised for adopting a rather clinical and monotonous performance style. Shortly before *Godot*, Krejča had directed *The Cherry Orchard*, in which Krejča junior had the role of Trofimov. Far from trying to make Beckett's play relevant to the circumstances of post-Communist Prague, Krejča was attempting to restore a tradition of great theatre works whose power would be seen to transcend particular political circumstances, addressing the state of culture in Europe in more general terms. The weighty programme included much of Aslan's analysis of the Avignon production (translated into Czech) and an unsigned comment headed 'As the spectator sees it', which explicitly made the link between Chekhov and Beckett:

> I can imagine the 'eternal' student Trofimov having shambled, in his decrepit galoshes, into *Waiting for Godot* from *The Cherry Orchard*. Of course, two wars, the holocaust, and all the other achievements of our age have deprived this dangerous idealist of his faith in ideology, his prejudices as a progressive thinker, his reliance on there being one single 'sensible' solution.[27]

This intention was understood by the critics, whose responses conveyed admiration for Krejča's work together with a slight disappointment that his *Godot* was so detached from the great events shaping the new Czechoslovakia. One critic expressed the sense that, while history had moved on, the performance was stuck in the past, with this sentence: 'In *Godot* we can discern the textbook of Havelesque drama.'[28]

THE PRODUCTION BY GEORGE TABORI, MUNICH KAMMERSPIELE, 1984

The production by George Tabori makes an interesting point of comparison with Krejča's second and third productions of the play, since Tabori's starting point was also that of a director wishing to make his production comment on the play,[29] but, like Krejča, he ended up withdrawing as far as possible behind Beckett's text, staging it in the most literal form he could find. His way of doing this was, however, very different from Krejča's. It took great liberties with both setting and text, but it also achieved a truth to the spirit of the play. It received exceptional approval from Jonathan Kalb: 'Only once have I come across a "concept" production in which the director made clear that he understood how Beckett's work departs from the representational norms of most other drama.'[30] The 'concept' referred to by Kalb was to present the play in the form of a rehearsal. The audience came into the theatre to find a total of nine people on stage, including the stage manager, the director and the designer, all drinking coffee as if at the start of a rehearsal.[31] When it was time for the play to start, they left the stage and the stage manager called out the names of the actors. Kalb's account continues:

> Thomas Holtzmann and Peter Lühr (Did and Gogo) enter languidly in what could be slightly aged street clothes and read indifferently from their scripts, one of which is the Suhrkamp paperback edition of the play, as ubiquitous in Germany as the Grove edition is in America. Then they gradually work up to performance tempo, leaving their scripts for longer and longer intervals and becoming more and more spontaneous, until at some point the spectator realises they have embodied the characters, though it is impossible to determine exactly when that transition occurred.[32]

The audience sat on benches and cushions all around the central acting area, which was marked out by a circle of sand. It contained one long table (in fact two tables end to end) with half a dozen wooden chairs such as can be found in rehearsal rooms all over the world.

Vladimir and Estragon sat down, one at each end of the table; each had their cup of coffee and Vladimir was smoking a cigarette. To start the action off, Vladimir picked up the book and read out the first stage direction: 'Landstrasse. Ein Baum. Abend.' He then put on his hat as if donning a complete costume. Estragon followed suit, placed one foot up on a chair, and read his first line. In the first few minutes, both actors varied the tone and tempo considerably, as if trying to find the right voice for the part, and when they reached the first refrain of 'Komm, wir gehen! / Wir können nicht. / Warum nicht? / Wir warten auf Godot' ('Let's go. / We can't. / Why not? / We're waiting for Godot') Vladimir paused for a moment before the last line and held his copy of the book up in the air as if to say 'we have to follow the text'. After this, however, they slipped imperceptibly into embodying the roles, as Kalb explains in the extract quoted above.

Their clothes and gestures remained close, however, to the informality of actors in rehearsal. Both had overcoats and Vladimir wore mittens, as if suffering from the cold. Anat Feinberg-Jütte described them as follows:

> Peter Lühr presented a frail yet vivacious, cynical and childlike Estragon, whose physical agility was supplemented by vocal virtuosity. He entered the acting arena somewhat bent, his white hair unkempt, in an open winter coat, carrying a file with paper sheets under his right arm – an intellectual and a poet, full of childlike eagerness. Thomas Holtzmann's Vladimir was his counterpart, a heavy, broad-shouldered, bespectacled, serious and at times tragic partner.[33]

They fitted closely Tabori's vision that 'Estragon and Vladimir are neither clowns nor tramps but refugees, intellectuals.'[34] Tabori's method for all of his Beckett productions was to ignore the author's stage directions and scenic image, searching rather for a presentation that sprung from Beckett's own underlying emotional and psychic life. This he called 'the subtext', giving the word a rather different meaning from that attributed to it by Stanislavski. He considered everything that Beckett wrote to have been autobiographical, and, especially after reading Deirdre Bair's biography, was convinced that the prototypes of Vladimir and Estragon were Beckett and Suzanne on the run from the Gestapo in the Vaucluse.[35] This notion of what lay behind the play was not taken literally, but used to develop the relationship between Vladimir and Estragon. Tabori is insistent that Beckett's works are not difficult to understand but are about recognisable human conflicts.[36]

The performances of Holtzmann and Lühr suggested a couple who were very close physically. At the point after Vladimir's first exit (to relieve himself) when he returns and Estragon begs him for an embrace, Vladimir ended up stretched full-length over Estragon, who was lying on his back across a couple of chairs. At many other points the two made physical contact of a close and intimate kind and the sense of bodily confinement on stage was suggested in a number of other ways. An example of this can be seen in the treatment of Vladimir's prostate trouble. Many productions have emphasised the pain experienced by Vladimir, especially his fear that if he laughs he will lose control of his bladder, but Tabori's appears to be the only production in which he actually wets himself. This was indicated by Estragon tipping the chair as if to pour off the urine when Vladimir rushes offstage after the joke about the brothel. The physical intimacy of Vladimir and Estragon was echoed by Pozzo and Lucky. Carl Ebert, as Pozzo, did not insist on keeping his distance from Arnulf Schumacher's Lucky as in most productions (and as suggested by Beckett's stage directions). On the contrary, he touched him a great deal. At the point where he speaks of getting rid of him he was actually embracing him tightly, and when Lucky began to weep Pozzo licked his tears before handing Estragon a handkerchief to wipe them away. At other times he climbed on Lucky's shoulders and made him carry him around. His Act I exit was particularly dramatic, running along the table, leaping onto the back of Lucky who carried him offstage. Such moments did not appear crude or gratuitous, since everything they did suggested improvisation, the trying out of different possibilities. In keeping with this rehearsal atmosphere, many of the objects, such as the carrots and radishes, and Pozzo's throat spray, were mimed. Although Lucky had the prescribed rope around his neck and carried a case, a basket and a stool, he did not go through the complicated movements demanded of him by Pozzo. Instead, he simply repeated each command, as if memorising what he would have to do. Pozzo sat on the chairs already there around the table, not on his folding stool, and pulled a bagel out of his pocket rather than taking a chicken bone from the basket. The only additional object on stage, apart from the hats (supplemented in Vladimir's case by an old, broken umbrella), was an alarm clock placed on the table, which went off in the middle of Act I at the point where Vladimir says, 'Time has stopped', and Pozzo replies, 'Don't you believe it'. This alarm clock supplemented Pozzo's constant references to his watch and helped to underline the reality of time passing and of waiting for something to happen in the play.

At other moments the reading of the text comes to a halt for a moment. Just before Pozzo's first entrance, the lines 'His name is Godot? / I think so' were repeated several times before Pozzo appeared, not preceded by a loud cry, as in the stage direction, but silently, as if conjured up by the power of the actors' imaginations, reminding one of the appearance of Madame Pace in Pirandello's *Six Characters in Search of an Author*. For anyone who knew the text well the feeling of improvisation was heightened by the numerous cuts, both of words and of stage business. For example, halfway through Lucky's 'Think' Pozzo removed his hat momentarily as if to see if it would stop him speaking (which it did), and the famous exchange of hats in Act II was cut. Very few of Beckett's pauses were respected – it was as if the actors were simply trying out the text, leaving the adjustment of pauses till later. At various points Vladimir would pick up the book and read out the stage direction for a particular piece of business rather than perform it.

What made the production more than just a clever idea was the quality of the acting and the emotional force it carried. The suggestion of a rehearsal framework gave the actors freedom to bring out the play's special quality analysed in chapter 2 and expressed by Krejča: that is, rather than telling its audience a story *about* waiting, it *is* waiting, or, in Robbe-Grillet's formulation, 'pure presence', and the actors oblige the audience to share their own anguished experience of being there for no certain purpose. Holtzmann and Lühr played far more lines to the audience than in most productions. Many of their statements about Pozzo and Lucky, and about the lack of development in the action, such as Estragon's 'Nothing happens, nobody comes, nobody goes, it's awful.' (Faber 41), were directed almost conspiratorially to the audience, and all their subsequent comments on the situation were done as asides in this manner. The result was a performance which was both extremely self-aware and extremely moving. Kalb expressed this by saying:

> Tabori's production is not merely a mimesis, of an episode either on a 'country road' or in a hypothetical theatre, but a meditation on mimesis. And it is unusually compelling because it makes that meditation central instead of peripheral to a chosen dominant metaphor, such as a subway tunnel or an attic room.[37]

The tone of the dialogue was predominantly dark, with very little clowning in the movements, and the mood became progressively more despairing, especially in the last section of Act II. The audience felt its sympathies powerfully engaged at two levels at once: the plight of the artist, for whom there is 'nothing to express ... together with the obligation to express',[38] and the existential plight of two ordinary human beings like ourselves, conscious of the cruelty of the world and shorn of all former comforts.

THE PRODUCTION AT THE HAARLEMSE TONEELSCHUUR, 1988

Other productions of *Waiting for Godot* have taken far greater liberties with Beckett's text and stage directions than Tabori's, most frequently in the matter of casting. With the increasing empowerment of women in theatre, many attempts have been made to perform *Godot* with an all-female cast. One such was in 1988, in Holland, a society where women's liberation was accepted earlier than elsewhere. The production was the object of a lawsuit, which sheds interesting light on the debate about the director's creative freedom, and has been documented by the Dutch theatre scholar Cobi Bordewijk:

> The stage for this production was almost bare; from left to right a long red corridor-carpet had been unrolled, covering the total length of the stage floor. Three large white cloths provided the background. On the middle one the tree was drawn and covered with a black cloth in the second act. To the left and to the right two monumentally sculptured chairs were placed. In this spot, which could be associated with a corridor in a wealthy castle, Vladimir and Estragon were waiting, dressed in expensive and fashionable oversized trench coats in combination with equally expensive costumes and shoes. Pozzo and Lucky pass by in the same kind of outfit, they are dressed alike, as if they are convertible.[39]

This setting, recalling the 'palais à volonté' of neo-classical French theatre, was another attempt to emphasise the play's self-conscious theatricality, like the design of Svoboda for Krejča's Salzburg production. But the actresses did not attempt to change the text at all, and 'did not play female characters, but impersonated men.'[40] The critical reaction was mixed, but the responses were predominantly positive, praising the teamwork of the cast and especially the comic performances of Truus te Stelle as Estragon and Trudy de Jong as Vladimir. Clearly, they were not able to develop the same sense of an irremediable 'presence' that made for much of the power of both the Krejča and the Tabori productions, but the inventiveness of their acting and clarity of the staging drew plaudits. Beckett, however, felt that a boundary had been overstepped. Through the Société des Auteurs et Compositeurs Dramatiques[41] he sued the Haarlemse Toneelschuur for violation of the author's *droit moral* on the grounds that the performers were all female, contrary to indications in the text, and that he had not been advised of this when he had been asked to grant performance rights. The lawyer for the prosecution argued that this was tantamount to substituting trumpets for violins in the performance of a musical composition. But the judge dismissed the case. He ruled that 'since the play was about the human condition in general, it transcended the sexual identity of men and women.'[42] He found that since the performance kept close to the author's words, and was not distorted for purposes of scandal or to preach a feminist message, there was no case to answer.

The question raised by this case is an interesting one, since Beckett himself consistently argued that the play should not be seen as having a specific location, and so might have been thought to be in sympathy with the arguments of the judge. His one reported explanation ('women don't have prostates') has been written off as facetious, and his attitude decried as sexist. But his remark about prostates, although typically economical and rather puckish, deserves to be taken seriously because of its emphasis on the body. As Krejča pointed out, the play came to life when the actors were able to use their own flesh, avoiding 'impersonating' in favour of 'being'. Moreover, at the time of the trial in 1988 Beckett could point to the large number of roles he had written specifically for female performers. Gender and sexuality, he clearly believed, were part of the inescapable physicality of incarnate existence; men and women could not be seen as interchangeable.

PRODUCTIONS OF *WAITING FOR GODOT* IN JAPAN

The Japanese theatre of the late twentieth century offered especially fertile ground for experimental stagings of Beckett's work. This came about because the *Shingeki*, or naturalistic, Western-oriented theatres of Japan, were looking for ways to escape the restrictions of naturalistic acting. The first performance of *Waiting for Godot* was given in 1960 and others followed. Many critics commented on the links between Beckett's conception of theatre and the tradition of Japanese Noh, and actors began to explore these similarities in practice. One of the first was Hisao Kanze, a Noh actor who was cast as Vladimir in a production which set out to explore the anti-naturalistic form of *Waiting for Godot*, and who 'unexpectedly found in rehearsing the play that necessary physical movements resulted naturally from his training in Noh.' He also discovered that, as in Noh, Beckett's play depends on 'a stylised and abstract balance'.[43] The initial discovery of similarities led on to a period in which Beckett's work was adapted to Japanese performance styles and often extensively rewritten. *Waiting for Godot* was especially popular: for the twenty-year period 1972–92, Mariko Hori Tanako lists sixteen adaptations based more or less loosely on Beckett as opposed to ten straight productions of the play.[44] Even when the play was performed as written, it was frequently cast against gender. One director, Shoji Koukami, defended his decision to cast Vladimir and Estragon as women with the statement that women are used to waiting: 'If men say' "we are waiting for Godot", it sounds unnatural and I fear the whole play loses the reality of life.'[45]

In 1994 the internationally celebrated director Yukio Ninagawa did a twin production with two casts, one all-male and the other all-female. These performed on alternate evenings at the Ginza Saison, a large commercial theatre in Tokyo. The production was unlike Ninagawa's habitual style, which is generally very colourful and theatrically flamboyant. In an interview given when the production (male cast only) was broadcast on television, Ninagawa explained that his aim was to reveal the classic status of Beckett's work, stripped of all theatricality. A play which demanded almost nothing from the director, other than to give close and sympathetic attention to the work of the actors was, for him, an enjoyable novelty. In both male and female versions he was able to cast outstanding performers, and he commented on his pleasure in being able to work with mature actors. Kon Nishimura (the male Vladimir) had, he felt, demonstrated just the quality required by Beckett's plotless play. He described this as 'being able to play to the maximum while at the same time being totally relaxed on stage'. This suggests an approach to the play that was similar to both Krejča's and Tabori's appreciation of the need to emphasise the actors' physical presence on stage. It would seem, however, that Ninagawa's approach was more permissive, and that he was content to allow the actors to 'be themselves' rather than to develop rhythmical patterns of action, or even to evolve close relationships between them. Although undeniably powerful performances, the playing of Nishimura and Toru Emori (Estragon) seemed rather detached and failed to suggest a close or long-standing relationship. The two female performers Etsuko Ichihara (Vladimir) and Mako Midori (Estragon) were more successful in this respect.

The setting (used by both male and female casts) was a raked stage suggesting a road running down from back to front, with a sloping hillside to right and left, strewn with stones. The colour changed subtly in the course of the performance, beginning with a sombre black and culminating in a beautiful deep blue for the moonrise created by means of lighting. The moon was an enormous red disc hovering above the skyline. The stage extended downwards to form a large thrust into the audience and Ninagawa encouraged a good deal of audience involvement, including direct address and exits into the audience whenever Vladimir had to leave the stage.

The costumes were different for male and female casts. They were not chosen with a view to establishing a predominantly Western or Japanese atmosphere, but rather with a view to facilitating the most expressive performances, in theatrical terms, from each of the actors. The male Vladimir and Estragon wore old-fashioned, formal, Western suits with tail coats, but these were rather shabby and covered with patches – a traditional Japanese symbol for poverty. Vladimir had a very neat, stylised white beard (denoting wisdom and experience in Japanese theatre) and Estragon was clean-shaven; neither looked as if they had slept in a ditch. Pozzo contrasted sharply with the worn dignity of Vladimir and Estragon. Pozzo's costume had all the marks of Ninagawa's usual flamboyance. Everything about him suggested bad taste, from his loud, double-breasted suit, two-tone shoes and medallion to his eccentric multicoloured overcoat with the flavour of

a Kabuki costume. To the Japanese spectator, he appeared as a typi-
cal *yakuza* (mafia man) and behaved with a mixture of bluster and
exaggeratedly corny comic gestures. Lucky wore a black-and-white
checked Sumo wrestler's robe, emphasising his physical dependence
on Pozzo.[46] Ryuiji Sawa's performance as Pozzo was full of exaggerated theatricality and his speech about the coming of night was
delivered with a combination of mismatched Kabuki gestures and
crude peasant dance steps. His antics raised much derisive laughter from the audience. Lucky also performed in a crudely physical
manner: his 'Think' was delivered in a monotone, and as it went
on he used the words almost like an aggressive weapon, combined
with forward-lunging Sumo movements (not only at Vladimir and
Estragon, as they tried to stop him talking, but also at the front rows
of the audience).

The mood of the male version continued to be quite grotesque and
comical until near the end, when there was a change of tone, bringing
the play to a close on a quietly tragic note. In the female version there
was more overall unity. The text was not changed, so that the women
performed as if they were men, although they wore female dress.
Vladimir and Estragon had bowler hats to indicate their male status, but their costumes were geisha kimonos, tattered, but (like the
male performers' suits) redolent of former glories. Etsuko Ichihara
as Vladimir and Mako Midori as Estragon were both well-known
character actresses, and their performances were more successful in
achieving the symbiotic relationship between the two than those of
the male performers had been. Pozzo and Lucky also differed from
their male counterparts. In the words of one audience member: 'Pozzo
was played by the foremost artist of the Fujima dancing school, who
impersonated a traditional manipulator of monkey shows in a gor-
geous Kabuki attire, with Lucky, an over-fed female lackey, played as
the manipulated monkey.'[47]

With sold-out performances and a television broadcast, it may
be that Ninagawa succeeded in his aim of making the play better
known in Japan as a modern classic. What is most striking, however,

is that his approach should have been so similar to that of European directors – namely, seeing the play as one in which the actors had to be encouraged to perform as themselves – when one reflects on how different this is from Ninagawa's instincts as a theatre director. Each of the directors and their casts discussed in this chapter have had to face what Xerxes Mehta described as 'the central performance dilemma of these [Beckett's] plays . . . the necessity for the performer to face an audience without any stable identity to rest upon'.[48] Although all of these directors were accustomed to imposing their own ideas upon the plays they directed, all of them discovered in *Waiting for Godot* a kind of theatre in which the actor has somehow to do without fictional characters or preconceived ideas, and to act out for their audiences what it means simply to *be there*. Mehta writes of Beckett's late plays, yet his words are equally applicable to the productions we have examined:

> The bedrock purpose of Beckett's final body of work is to expose the nakedness and terror of human existence by exposing naked and terrified human beings on stage.[49]

CHAPTER 8

GODOT IN POLITICAL CONTEXT

A casualty of *Waiting for Godot*'s classic status has been the *provocative* quality of the play, which seemed so important to Blin (see chapter 3). Too often a production will be mounted precisely because the play has become a *safe* bet, for both theatres and theatre-goers: theatre managers find it safe because the cast is small and the set undemanding; theatre-goers are safe in the knowledge that they are witnessing one of the great plays in the modern repertoire. And yet, despite its reassuring status as a modern classic, the play has not entirely lost its provocative quality, as is demonstrated by a number of cases where it has been performed in situations of political oppression. The quality that held the attention of the San Quentin prisoners – its ability to speak, like a parable, to their particular condition – has repeatedly appeared to lend the play special relevance in oppressive circumstances, such as South Africa under apartheid, Sarajevo under siege by Serbian forces, or Palestine under Israeli occupation.

THE PRODUCTION BY VASILIJE POPOVIĆ, BELGRADE, 1956

Already in the 1950s the play had been banned or considered subversive by regimes as far apart as Catholic Ireland and the Eastern European Communist bloc. A representative example is that of the first Yugoslav production in Belgrade. The text was translated by Andreja Milićević at the suggestion of Dušan Matić, an important Yugoslav writer, who had seen Blin's production in 1953. He then showed it to the director Vasilije Popović, who persuaded Prerag Dinulović, artistic director of the Belgrade Drama Theatre, to allow him to begin rehearsals in January 1954. Dinulović did not include an announcement of the production in the official repertoire of the theatre, however, being nervous of official reaction to a work which was considered 'decadent' by the Communist Party's writers' union, whose job it was to filter influences from the West. Within the theatre itself, opinion was sharply divided about whether the play should be staged.

When the day provisionally set aside for the first performance arrived, the management of the theatre were so nervous that they decided that the performance should go ahead but with no audience present: only employees of the theatre would be allowed into the auditorium. This provoked strong reactions from intellectuals, who gathered in front of the theatre to demonstrate and to protest against the decision. Although security guards had been posted at all entrances to the theatre, some members of the public managed to get in and hid behind the seats in the upper circle until they were spotted and thrown out. Others managed to gain entrance through a window which had been left open and to see the play through to the end. The general effect was to create the impression of a major artistic event taking place in Belgrade, and this in turn persuaded the management to ban all further performances. Their weakness may be explained, if not excused, by knowing that they depended for their livelihood on the approval of the government censor, and that they had recently been forced to withdraw Jean Anouilh's comedy *Le Bal des voleurs* (*Thieves' Carnival*) from the repertoire. The reason given was that Anouilh portrayed his thieves as nice, positive characters, with the result that real thieves who came to see the play would never desire to mend their ways.

But a momentum had built up around the production of *Godot* and the actors kept looking for a way to present the production to those who had not been lucky enough to get in to the one performance at the Belgrade Drama Theatre. In June an offer came from the painter Mica Popović to use his studio for a private performance with no officials present, and so the second performance took place for an invited audience of about a hundred, mainly people from theatrical and literary circles. One writer who was present commented:

> This banned *Godot* was and is the most exciting play I have ever attended. We were all afraid because we were doing something forbidden and we were all happy because we were able to watch something that, we felt then, would become part of our society and of our civilisation.[1]

This performance again created much discussion and demand for more performances. The French Ambassador offered to make space for the performance in the Embassy (which, as 'French territory', fell outside the jurisdiction of the Belgrade authorities), but the director declined, feeling that it should be performed on a Yugoslav stage or not at all. He had to wait a further two years, until the pressures of the Cold War had eased a little and Yugoslavia's policy of opening itself to Western influences was more firmly established. The original production of *Waiting for Godot*, with the same director and actors, was sanctioned as the inaugural production for a new small-scale experimental theatre known as Atelier 212 (after its audience capacity of 212). It took place on 17 December 1956 with the following cast: Vladimir: Ljubivoje Tadić; Estragon: Bata Paskaljević; Lucky: Mica Tomić; Pozzo: Rade Marković; Boy: Ratislav Jović. It was the first production to take place in a country of the Eastern European bloc[2] and enjoyed considerable critical success. Over the following decades it was frequently revived with the same actors in the roles of Vladimir and Estragon.

THE PRODUCTION BY SUSAN SONTAG, SARAJEVO, 1993

The importance of the first Yugoslav production to the intellectuals of Belgrade was not so much located in the meaning of the play itself as in the way it stood for a tradition of experimental work in Western Europe where freedom of thought was guaranteed. But it would not be true to suggest that any other experimental work might have served just as well, since *Godot*'s central strategy of drawing its audience into the existential experience of waiting, and denying them a coherent plot, spoke eloquently to those early audiences of the absurdities and frustration of life under a totalitarian regime. Forty years later, Susan Sontag chose to direct a production of *Waiting for Godot* in Sarajevo for similar reasons: the play seemed to have special resonance for the inhabitants of a town going through the madness of so-called 'ethnic cleansing'. Her production, put on in Sarajevo in August 1993, at the height of the Serb bombardment of the city, poses with peculiar starkness the question of the political relevance that the play may acquire in special circumstances. This production has also been the subject of several articles by Beckett scholars on the play's relationship to political realities.[3]

Sontag chose to direct a play as an act of solidarity with the people of the besieged city: 'It was the only one of the three things I do – write, make films and direct in the theater – which yields something that would exist only in Sarajevo, that would be made and consumed there.'[4] It was seen by her as an act of defiance against a world which appeared content to stand by and watch while all normal conditions of life were destroyed for the Sarajevans – indoors, their sources of electricity and water were cut off and they were subject to constant bombardment while outside there was the added danger of sniper fire. In these circumstances, to put on a theatre performance was to refuse to accept the brutal imposition of cruel conditions by Serbian soldiers. Her principal concern, in the light of this priority, was to involve as many of the local theatre professionals as possible. The siege of their city had brought normal theatre life to a standstill and so they were only too keen to become involved in the project. Despite the difficulties of getting to and from rehearsals each day, and despite their exhaustion from undernourishment and lack of sleep, the play gave them something to take their minds off the dreadful daily struggle for survival. Sontag therefore cast as much according to the actors' needs as to the requirements of the play.

In order to include the maximum number of performers, she decided to have three parallel couples of Vladimir/Estragon on stage:
at the centre were two male actors, but these were 'flanked on the left
side of the stage by two women and on the right by a woman and a
man – three variations on the theme of the couple'.[5] Her Pozzo was
Ines Fančović, described by Sontag as 'a stout older woman wearing a
large broad-brimmed black hat, who sat silently, imperiously, in the
corner of the room', while her Lucky was Admir ('Atko') Glamočak,
'a gaunt, lithe man of thirty whom I'd admired as Death in *Alcestis*'.[6]
The thinking behind Sontag's production was straightforwardly hu-
manistic: she wanted the casting to be gender-blind on the grounds
that the characters are representative figures and thus not limited to
one gender or the other. Rehearsals were held in the dark in the absence of electricity, with candles and flashlights the only source of
illumination. Many of the stage effects were almost invisible and it
was hard for the actors to do 'something as simple as put on or take
off their bowler hats at the same time'.[7]

Everything in Sontag's direction was devised to give added poignancy to the fact that the production was taking place in Sarajevo. She
commented on Lucky's 'Think', for example: 'I wanted Atko to deliver
Beckett's aria about divine apathy and indifference, about a heartless,
petrifying world, as if it made perfect sense. Which it does, especially
in Sarajevo.'[8] Her reason for choosing *Godot* in the first place was
that 'Beckett's play, written over forty years ago, seems written for
and about Sarajevo.'[9] Avoiding the tendency to perform the play in
muted style, she chose to encourage performances that were 'full of
anguish, of immense sadness, and toward the end, violence'.[10] When
the production opened for public performances they still had only
candles to light the stage and so the audience huddled close to the
stage on two rows of benches so as to be able to see something of
what was going on. Only the first act of the play was performed and
two performances were given, at 2 p.m. and at 4 p.m. – it was too
dangerous for anyone, actors or audience, to be out at night. Sontag
summed up the experience by saying, 'People ask me if Sarajevo ever

seemed to me unreal while I was there. The truth is . . . it seems the most real place in the world.'[11]

Sontag's production cannot really be studied for its solutions to the staging problems thrown up by the play, since it was responding to the situation rather than to the play. For everyone concerned in this enterprise, *Godot* was a potent metaphor for the frustrations and hopelessness of their situation. In addition, the play seemed (to Sontag, at least) to be dealing with the stark realities of life reduced to the most fundamental problems of human survival. The significance of the production lay simply in the doing of it, not so much in the artistic solutions chosen. As a result of this, the most interesting questions raised by the production are not whether she was right to truncate the play or to cast female actors or to introduce two extra couples, but concern rather the nature of the play's relationship to political realities and the extent to which any given production may be made to mirror a particular political reality. This question of mirroring is taken up by Elin Diamond, who points out that Lacan published 'The Mirror Phase' in 1949, the same year that Beckett completed *Godot*.[12] She argues that all political activity is rooted in processes of mirroring and identification that produce potentially violent divisions between those who are 'like ourselves' and those who are 'other'. She points out that Pozzo establishes contact with Vladimir and Estragon by recognising them as human beings 'like himself' and that this assimilation persuades the couple to collude in the oppression of Lucky. And so, her argument concludes, it is clear that *Godot* constitutes a serious exploration of political behaviour, but equally clear that to apply one given allegorical interpretation (whether political or otherwise) is to misunderstand its peculiar power and to fall into thought patterns that are just like Pozzo's.

Lois Oppenheim, discussing the same production, gives guarded approval to Sontag's gesture of humanist solidarity, but also quotes the Croatian writer Slavenka Drakulić commenting on interventions by Sontag and other intellectuals: 'I don't doubt their good intentions. All I say is that if attention and understanding alone could save Sarajevo, then it would have been saved long ago.' This is perhaps to say no more than that art works seldom change the course of history, and it is abundantly clear that Beckett himself rejected the theories of *littérature engagée* (committed literature) that were widely discussed in the 1940s and 1950s, when *Godot* was written and first produced. The evidence for this is not only his deliberate 'vaguening' of the plot and characters, but also his repeated refusal even to enter into discussion about allegorical interpretations of the play. To give the play a specific political meaning, it is necessary to alter it, however subtly, and Beckett always insisted that both his words and his stage directions should be respected. An example of the kind of alterations that are needed survives in the form of notes on the play made by Bertolt Brecht. His copy of the play contains cuts and additions designed to anchor the play in concrete social relations. Beside Estragon, he noted 'ein Prolet' ('a proletarian'), beside Vladimir, 'ein Intellektuel' ('an intellectual'), beside Lucky, 'ein Esel als Polizist' ('a donkey as policeman') and beside Pozzo, 'ein Gutbesitzer' ('a landowner'). Brecht also spoke to his assistant, Manfred Wekwerth, of a plan to counterpoint the play's demonstration of the futile waiting imposed on people by the capitalist West with films made in contemporary China, showing the positive developments that could be made by a worker's state.[13]

THE PRODUCTION BY DONALD HOWARTH,
CAPE TOWN, 1980

The additional use of film would clearly have resulted in something quite different from Beckett's play, but Brecht's identification of the four main characters' social status has some validity. A similar classification has been at the root of some extremely successful productions, notably one in Cape Town, South Africa, in 1980, and another in Haifa, Israel, in 1984, though neither of these productions followed a Brechtian interpretation. The first, directed by Donald Howarth for the Baxter Theatre, Cape Town, toured to America and England, and played at the Old Vic in London in February 1981. During the 1970s, at the request of anti-apartheid campaigners in South Africa, Beckett (like many other writers) had specified that his plays could be performed only in multiracial theatres. Cape Town was home to the Space, one of the few theatres which managed to maintain a consistent multiracial policy, and Donald Howarth had directed several plays with multiracial casts there before he was invited to mount *Waiting for Godot* at the university of Cape Town's Baxter Theatre. His key casting decision was to give the roles of Vladimir and Estragon to black actors and those of Pozzo and Lucky to whites. Vladimir and Estragon were played by John Kani and Winston Ntshona respectively, actors who had worked together for many years and who had created, together with Athol Fugard, two exceptionally powerful denunciations of the apartheid regime: *Sizwe Banzi is Dead* and *The Island*. Bill Flynn, who played Pozzo, had also performed in a play by Fugard, *Hello and Goodbye*, and Peter Piccolo, although he had not worked with Fugard, had performed in the same theatres as the others, especially the Space in Cape Town and the Market Theatre in Johannesburg.

The simple fact of the casting, at the height of apartheid in South Africa, made a powerful statement about the relationships between black and white. Winston Ntshona played Estragon as a simple, unemployed worker, while John Kani gave Vladimir a much more intellectual air, carrying a large black Bible and wearing a pair of steel-framed spectacles. Pozzo was a bulky figure, dressed to suggest a Boer farmer, and Lucky was a frail, bent slave, treated with extreme contempt by his master. The setting was a sandy mound, with a spindly tree and a few reeds. It made no attempt to localise the play in South Africa, though it could easily have been taken to represent a dusty corner of one of the 'homelands' in which the apartheid government obliged black South Africans to reside. The main political thrust of the performance, insofar as it had one at all, came from the dignity, warmth and profound humanity revealed in the performances of Ntshona and Kani, in contrast to Pozzo's grossness and the feebleness of Lucky. Donald Howarth, the director, had realised that the play would not benefit from being overly localised when he had discussed it with Beckett before the start of rehearsals:

> I asked Beckett why no traffic passed by on the road, not even a bicycle. Beckett tilted his head to one side. 'It isn't a road,' he said. 'It's a track on wasteland.' Silence. Then, smiling as though seeing the two friends in that place, he leaned back and said, 'They play a series of games. When one has ended, they start another.' His smile lingered.[14]

This was the approach taken by the cast and it resulted in a richly inventive production. The experience of watching it was like witnessing a performance of a well-known piece of music by outstanding players.

THE PRODUCTION BY ILAN RONEN, HAIFA, 1984

The South African production had enormous power and pathos, especially as it did *not* try to impose a political interpretation, force the sympathies of its audience or change Beckett's text in any way. The quality of the ensemble acting was outstanding, the interplay between Vladimir and Estragon, in particular, benefiting from the depth of the relationship between Kani and Ntshona and from their long experience of oppression. It may have been this production which gave Ilan Ronen the idea for his staging at the Haifa Municipal Theatre in November 1984. Ronen cast two outstanding Arab actors, Yussef Abu-Varda and Muhram Khoury, in the roles of Vladimir and Estragon, with Israeli actors Ilan Toren and Doron Tavory taking the roles of Pozzo and Lucky. The Haifa Municipal Theatre's general manager, Noam Semel, and its artistic director, Omry Nitzan, had set up an Arabic stage as part of the complex, with the aim of mounting plays in Arabic for Arab audiences in Haifa. Its first production had been Fugard's *The Island*, with Abu-Varda and Khoury taking the roles created by Kani and Ntshona. Ronen described their qualities:

> Yussef Abu-Varda, whom I chose to cast as Vladimir, has fine rhetorical talent, a strong stage presence, and a very expressive, intense political involvement. In contrast, Muhram Khoury, whom I cast as Estragon, is an actor with the rare comic sense of a sad clown. He is very intuitive, human and warm, moderate in his political stance, very down-to-earth.[15]

Ronen explained that he had decided from the outset to situate the play in the political context of Israel in 1984. This was some years before the start of the 'Intifada' popular uprising against the Israeli occupation of Palestinian territories, and a time when 'the situation of the Palestinians was at its lowest ebb'.[16] His vision of Vladimir and Estragon as Arabs in the state of Israel was prompted by a situation which he described as follows:

> Nearly all the construction workers in Israel were Palestinians from the West Bank or Gaza. Each day, in the early morning hours, they left their homes, travelling in convoys to the cities of Israel. There they sat and waited for contractors and foremen to hire them. This created an absurd situation in which the country, including the Jewish settlements in the occupied territories, was being built almost exclusively by Palestinians under the rule of Israeli occupation.[17]

In order to situate his production within this context, Ronen used a bilingual translation of the play by Anton Shammas, part Arabic, part Hebrew. Vladimir and Estragon spoke Arabic to each other but Hebrew to Pozzo. Lucky was portrayed as an elderly Arab of the old generation, speaking literary Arabic, in contrast to the two construction workers whose language was the vernacular.[18] Pozzo spoke only Hebrew, apart from a few curses and orders to Lucky, given in Arabic. The setting was a construction site, making the identity of Vladimir and Estragon as labourers waiting for a job quite explicit. Upstage centre stood a wire framework emerging from a cement base – it was clearly waiting for more cement to be added in order to form a pillar supporting the next storey of a building under construction. Further downstage were scattered some building blocks. A pile of three of these downstage right became Estragon's seat, standing in for the stone of Beckett's production, just as the wire framework stood in for the tree. Their costumes were realistic garb for construction workers: dirt-stained, baggy work-trousers, with an old army coat and woollen hat for Estragon and an anorak and cloth hat for Vladimir with its brim turned up (in a style reminiscent of Harlequin, according to Ronen, but equally reminiscent of the hat worn by Winston Ntshona in the South African production). Pozzo, by contrast, wore a light linen suit, white shirt and shoes and a panama hat. Lucky, in addition to his white Arab skull cap, wore an old, dusty brown jacket and trousers and was burdened with a gigantic suitcase, a coat on a coat-hanger, a smart brief case (from which Pozzo took his picnic) and several tubular containers of the kind used for architects' drawings and building plans, which he never put down. The performances of Abu-Varda and Khoury (the actors playing Vladimir and Estragon) were full of details designed to remind audiences of the subservient condition of Israeli Arabs. When Vladimir gave Estragon the carrot, for example, he went into a 'stylized pantomime of an Arab waiter bearing a loaded coffee tray'.[19] Similarly, when Pozzo lit his pipe there was a short pantomime sequence in which Pozzo searched vaguely for somewhere to drop his spent match and finally Estragon held out his boot like an ashtray for Pozzo's convenience. Such details were relished by the public, which made its appreciation felt through frequent outbursts of laughter. This production showed how the play *can* become a vehicle for successful clowning performances, especially when an additional tension is present (caused by the references to social inequalities keenly felt by the audience). The actors made much of the minimal means presented to them by Beckett. Early in the first act, for example, when Vladimir finally manages to get his boot off, there was a brisk clowning sequence in which Vladimir, standing behind the seated Estragon, tried to grab the boot, while Estragon juggled it from side to side beneath his raised knees so that Vladimir could not get it. This was 'capped' a few moments later when Estragon got up and Vladimir made a triumphant pounce on the boot, only to be knocked backwards in horror by the smell.

Moments of clowning such as this recurred throughout the performance, but were always focused on objects of central importance to Vladimir and Estragon, such as boots and hats, and were then picked up again and elaborated on at later points in the action in such a way as to create echoes and reminders, albeit of a rather different kind from those achieved in Beckett's own production. By such means the actors achieved a very successfully physicalised performance style in which themes of the body emerged with great clarity, both individually and collectively. An example of the former was Vladimir's prostate: the actor made much of his inability to laugh without suffering terrible pain and repeatedly burst into uproarious laughter only to double up in agony. An example of strong visual impact in a collective realisation of a 'body theme' was the scene in Act II where they all fall in a heap: this was performed with a good sense of the grotesque and raised much laughter from the audience. The interdependence of Vladimir and Estragon came across vividly at various points, especially in the last stages of Act I when they are trying to hang themselves. This was played in three distinct phases. First they danced around one another as each tried to push the other into position so that he could hang himself; next, Estragon grasped Vladimir by the hand and tried to pull him towards the wire scaffold while Vladimir resisted, so that they ended up leaning at forty-five degrees away from each other until the words 'bough break', when Estragon let go and Vladimir fell to the ground; and finally, each lifted the other in order to test their respective weights on the discussion about which of them is the heavier.

The warmth and humour established through the interdependent clowning of Vladimir and Estragon meant that the moments of anguish were less thoroughly realised. Rather than appearing oppressed by the frustration of their situation and the longing for night to fall, their suffering emerged much more strongly in their relationship with

Pozzo. The actor portraying Pozzo carried a very realistic whip, which he flexed repeatedly. His first entry was made with tremendous force and noise, and he used the initial exchange of names to browbeat Vladimir and Estragon, building to a climax of outrage on the words 'on my land', which clearly carried enormous force in the Arab–Israeli context. He continued to behave towards them with extreme condescension and his treatment of Lucky was brutally violent. After Lucky's 'Think', when his hat is finally removed and he collapses on the ground, 'Pozzo goes wild, brutally kicking Lucky in the shin and yelling in Arabic, "Get up, you pig!" while Gogo, the Arab construction worker, begs him to leave his fellow Arab alone, whimpering in Hebrew, "You'll kill him."' This scene, Ronen recalls, was one of those most often cited by critics who claimed that his production was insulting to the Israeli community.[20] However, the overall political meaning to emerge from this production was humanist rather than revolutionary. For Ronen, the political drift was encapsulated in the second act, when all four characters fall in a heap and then, after much uncertainty, help one another up again: 'The suggestion here seems to be that the two people are dependent on each other, for better or worse.'[21]

The production caused a furious public debate and several right-wing members of the Knesset called for it to be banned. Perhaps because of this, Shoshana Weitz decided to conduct an audience survey of those attending the performances. The survey covered three plays in the season's repertoire, all of which related to the socio-political reality in Israel in 1984/5. They were *The Optimist*, a monologue based on a story by the Israeli Arab author Emil Habibi and dealing directly with the personal and national identity of Israeli Arabs, *Freedom of the City* by Brian Friel and *Waiting for Godot*. The inclusion of Beckett's play in a repertoire dealing explicitly with political oppression must have affected audiences' perception of its meaning, especially since Anton Shammas' translation included occasional references to local political realities. The audience survey was devised with several aims, one of which was to gauge the influence of audience members' socio-political circumstances on their response, and especially on their way of interpreting the play: would they see it as referring to the relations between Arabs and Israelis, or would they understand the play on a more abstract, poetic level? Three separate groups of viewers were surveyed: Israeli Jews, Israeli Arabs and Palestinian Arabs. The study found that both groups of Arab spectators clearly perceived Pozzo as exploiter and oppressor of the other characters and related the situation of Vladimir and Estragon to their own circumstances, whereas the Jewish spectators described Vladimir, Estragon and Pozzo as 'anyones' and the location as an abstract, generalised space.[22] What this important and carefully organised audience survey seems to demonstrate is that, even in a production so clearly slanted towards the depiction of socio-political realities, audience responses are always highly selective, mirroring the preoccupations which they bring with them to the theatre. But the enthusiastic responses of Arab audience members also demonstrate that Beckett's play can speak powerfully to those who are conscious of being oppressed, as it did to the San Quentin prisoners.

THE PRODUCTION BY JOEL JOUANNEAU, NANTERRE, 1991

One final example is worth considering because it attempted to raise similar socio-political concerns within a Western democracy. In 1991 Joël Jouanneau directed a production of *En attendant Godot* at the Théâtre des Amandiers, Nanterre. Nanterre is a rather dispiriting suburb to the west of Paris, a ghetto of cheap high-rise housing which seems more than just a few miles from the luxury of central Paris. The theatre's first director, Patrice Chéreau, had given it a reputation for presenting new, often harsh political work: it was here that the early productions of plays by Koltès had taken place. Jouanneau, like Chéreau, was determined to continue to present work which would address the lives of working-class people, especially the young. His starting point for *Godot* was watching a boy in a train station aimlessly kicking an empty can for hours on end. This image seemed to him to sum up the experience of waiting when one was young, unemployed and had nothing to hope for. The set for his production, designed by Jacques Gabel, presented an urban wasteland with an abandoned electrical plant, which lit up with some small green light-bulbs (in place of the leaves) in the second act. Vladimir and Estragon were street dwellers. Jouanneau was quite explicit about this, explaining that he did not want to show a generalised picture of humanity but to give his characters clearly localised, specific qualities: 'restituer l'image de la dérive d'êtres exclus dans la France des années 90' ('to restore the image of drifters, of people excluded from the France of the 1990s').[23] Pozzo and Lucky were presented as cynical bourgeois exploiter and naive immigrant worker.

A further peculiarity of Jouanneau's interpretation was his conviction that the text suggested a difference of ages between Vladimir and Estragon: he saw Vladimir as older, more experienced, a kind of 'older brother' to Estragon, and the play as 'l'histoire d'une initiation à l'attente' ('the story of an initiation into waiting').[24] The casting reflected this: David Warrilow, an experienced Beckett actor, played Vladimir, wearing an old-fashioned *bleu de travail* (workman's overall), whereas Estragon was played by Philippe Demarle, an actor in his twenties, wearing aggressively contemporary clothes: a rollneck jersey, braces, military-looking trousers, Doc Martins and a shaven skull – the skinhead look. The bowler hats were jettisoned, having too much the flavour, for Jouanneau, of 'metaphysical clowns', and instead both characters wore woollen hats. Large cuts were made in the text, and opportunities to update it were taken: in the sequence of insults in Act II, for example, the actors improvised their own in keeping with the street language of 1991.

Reactions to this interpretation were predictably varied. *Le Monde* described it as extraordinarily beautiful, whereas *Libération* called it rather 'distant', and complained that Beckett's special quality of anguished comedy was absent.[25] To some extent these differences of opinion could be reduced to the difference between those who like their classics updated and those who do not. But it is important to distinguish between the interpretation of the director and designer – the wasteland setting – and those of the actors. More striking than the urban setting, in some ways, was the decision to cast actors of two different generations in the roles of Vladimir and Estragon. The young Philippe Demarle's performance as Estragon was nervous, violent, full of aggressive energy, whereas David Warrilow as Vladimir had a quality of serenity, almost of wisdom. This altered the whole balance of the play's central passages. The two could still be seen to depend on one another, but in a very different way from the symbiosis envisaged by Beckett. The critics who wrote about the production saw this relationship less in terms of a social or political comment than as a way of bridging the theatrical generation gap between the men of the 1950s, the years in which the play saw the light of day, and the youth of the 1990s, for whom the concept of 'waiting' was no longer overlaid with wartime memories but had other connotations altogether.

OTHER PRODUCTIONS IN THE CONTEXT OF CULTURAL STRUGGLE

The theatrical self-awareness of Beckett's drama, in other words, proved stronger than the attempt to give it a localised allegorical meaning. An example of a production which attempted to give the play a metaphorical meaning directly related to cultural struggle took place at the Théâtre du Nouveau Monde, Quebec, in January 1992. Where Beckett's stage direction suggests a 'no man's land', the director André Brassard and his designer Stéphane Roy gave it the specific quality of a *cultural* no man's land. In place of the tree and the stone there was a coat-stand and a piano. Estragon, instead of collapsing on his stone, would collapse on the piano stool, and would play it from time to time. While Vladimir and Estragon were costumed to look like contemporary Québecois down-and-outs (or perhaps street entertainers), Pozzo entered in a golden coach pulled by Lucky and wore a magnificent eighteenth-century wig, ruff, frock-coat and breeches, representing the 'prince of culture' defending the French Academic tradition. Lucky was costumed like a medieval king's jester. The interpretation was clear:

> Brassard was playing with politico-cultural disputes by making Beckett's characters into popular performers waiting for the arrival of 'culture' . . . Traditional French culture was shown as decadent and associated with the culture of the Québec bourgeoisie . . . Brassard's actors, poor, alienated, on an abandoned stage, were waiting, like the Québecois, for the key to their destiny: Godot?[26]

Dressed up in the trappings of the cultural debate in Canada (that is, about whether French-speaking Canadians should defer to the traditions of mainland France or try to establish a new Francophone culture of their own), this production was using the powerful metaphor of Godot in similar ways to other, more politicised productions. The great strength of the Godot metaphor for all such productions is precisely its lack of definition. It can stand not for any old thing but for a great many things – different possible solutions to problems which appear insoluble. It strikes a particular chord with audiences in totalitarian regimes where the population is constantly being encouraged to have patience while their leaders construct the promised land. This may explain why the most rigidly controlled regimes were the ones which banned it for longest. In Eastern Europe it was performed (though not without difficulties, as we have seen) in Yugoslavia, also in Poland and Hungary, but not at all in East Germany, in Romania or in Bulgaria until the collapse of the Soviet union in the late 1980s.[27] In China it was similarly regarded as highly dangerous, especially when Gao Xingjian (the winner of the Nobel prize for literature in 2000) wrote a play inspired by *Waiting for Godot* entitled *The Bus-Stop* (*Chezhan*, performed at the People's Art Theatre of Beijing in 1983). This play shows a group of people gathering to catch a bus from their distant suburb to the big city. They keep hoping that the bus will come, but it never does, and in the end they realise they have wasted years in waiting – they would have done better to walk. The author specifies that the play must be performed in the round, so that everyone in the audience becomes implicated in the experience of fruitless waiting.[28] Three years after its production *The Bus-Stop* was denounced as 'the most pernicious play put on since the birth of the People's Republic'.[29]

Part of the hostility of the Chinese authorities stemmed from the fact that everyone who saw it understood it as carrying a reference to Beckett's play, which was not officially available in China but which is nevertheless known in intellectual circles. The fact is that Godot has become a global symbol, recognised all over the world, though loaded with different meanings according to time, place and political circumstances. The word 'Godot' appears in all sorts of unlikely contexts whenever a cartoonist, commentator or broadcaster needs to appeal to his public's sense of the frustrations of waiting for a promised salvation which fails to materialise. This survey of productions of the play demonstrates that Beckett's work retains, at least potentially, the provocative quality picked out by Roger Blin. It continues to make tyrannical or totalitarian regimes uneasy and speaks on behalf of the dispossessed. At the same time, it resists precisely focused political interpretations which attempt to reduce it to an allegorical statement about one particular situation. As Jonathan Kalb has written: 'Beckett's plays often prove stronger than attempts to politicize them.'[30] Because *Waiting for Godot* thrives on ambiguity, the circumstances in which it is played *can* have an enriching effect, but never in a straightforwardly allegorical way. Just as the text achieves its effects, like poetry, by building up layers of meaning and association, so a production will be enhanced by taking place in circumstances where Vladimir and Estragon's plight resonates, for the audience, with things they feel to be profoundly true in their own lives.

CHAPTER 9

PRODUCTIONS AT THE END OF THE TWENTIETH CENTURY

Two productions of the late 1990s provide an opportunity to review attitudes towards *Waiting for Godot* in the English-speaking theatre profession half a century after the play was written. They are Peter Hall's production at the Old Vic in 1997 and Walter Asmus' production for the 'Beckett Festival' at the Gate Theatre in Dublin, seen at the Barbican Theatre in London in 1999.

These productions demonstrated a striking consensus, suggesting that Beckett's creation, both his text and his staging, have effectively achieved 'classic' status. Although they were performed by casts (and directors) of different nationalities, in different contexts, they adopted identical solutions to most of the main questions raised in mounting the play. Both counted on the attraction of seeing well-known actors in a 'modern classic' to draw an audience, and both played to packed houses. Both used the text printed in McMillan and Knowlson's *The Theatrical Notebooks of Samuel Beckett* rather than those available from Faber or Grove,[1] and both borrowed many of the moves and actions in its accompanying stage directions.[2] For Asmus, this was only natural, since he was attempting to recreate the original Beckett production. For Peter Hall it was a conscious choice, since he believed this text to be superior to the earlier versions for theatre performance.[3] Both productions were given on bare stages, with no suggestion of the road or mound mentioned in Beckett's original stage directions. Both designs copied the Schiller-Theater's spindly tree upstage left and single boulder downstage right. Both were played under a bright, unchanging light until the end, when the moon rose, theatrically, at the back of the stage. In both, Vladimir and Estragon spoke with Dublin accents (noticeably more authentic in the Gate production), effectively reclaiming the play for the Irish dramatic tradition.

THE PRODUCTION BY PETER HALL AT THE OLD VIC, LONDON, 1997

Because they had so much in common, the differences between the two productions are of particular interest. In the first place, Peter Hall's aim was quite different from that of Asmus. Hall made it quite clear that his 1997 production was, in part, an attempt to correct the errors of his earlier production, errors which he put down to youthful inexperience. Beckett, he said, had been responsible for setting him on the road toward aesthetic concentration and the belief that 'less is really more in the theatre'.[4] He had seen Beckett's Schiller-Theater production and been impressed by its 'absolute precision, clarity, hardness'.[5] He aimed to achieve the same qualities in his Old Vic production but did not employ the same methods. Hall did not prepare the equivalent of Beckett's notebook. His method was more reliant on the usual processes of give-and-take in the rehearsal room: 'You ask how we did it. We did it as we would do any play. Start by asking what does he mean, what does he want, and how can we express it. Try to start without preconceptions.'[6] He was clear about one thing: that 'you have to approach Beckett like a piece of music . . . There is a rhythm and a tempo written into *Godot* that is palpable . . . The Anglo-Irish lilt releases the rhythm of the text like nothing else.'[7] So Ben Kingsley (Estragon) and Alan Howard (Vladimir) rehearsed from the very beginning in Anglo-Irish accents, guided by Hall's memories of Beckett's own particular accent. Kingsley succeeded well in mastering this 'lilt'; Howard's accent was less consistent.

Perhaps because of this less systematic approach to rehearsals, Hall's production was neither so precise nor so rich in its handling of the shaping devices as that of Asmus. He did not make use of the device of the 'approach by stages' (see chapter 6), nor were the echoes of movements exploited with quite such systematic rigour as in the Gate Theatre production. An example is the opening of each act. At the beginning of both Act I and Act II in Asmus' production (as in Beckett's) both Vladimir and Estragon were on stage. Hall adopted this change from the Faber text at the start of Act I, but when the lights came up on Act II only Vladimir was present, Estragon entering at the end of Vladimir's song about the dog (as in the original Faber text). The latter is more 'natural' if we imagine the two to have spent the night apart. The former is more 'theatrical', emphasising their role as performers on a stage rather than as characters in a realistic story.

Ben Kingsley's performance was singled out for special praise by almost all the critics: Benedict Nightingale (*Times*, 30 June 1997) called it 'a more subtly hilarious Estragon than Robin Williams five years ago'; Robert Butler (*Independent on Sunday*, 6 July 1997) considered that 'Kingsley is more at home [than Howard] with the snappy reversals of Beckett comedy. He has an innocent beadiness, a small man's rapid intensity – almost a Chaplinesque sprightliness at times, as he shadow-boxes enthusiastically while Vladimir takes a leak offstage.' In addition to these qualities, Kingsley emphasised the character's frustration, grief and anger. At the line 'When you think of the beauty of the way. And the goodness of the wayfarers' (Faber 16), a line which actors often treat with humorous irony, he broke down in sobs. In Act II he clutched his head in agony whenever the reminder came that they were waiting for Godot, and in the sequence after he has woken up and before they find Lucky's hat (Faber 71), Kingsley gave vent to real anger. Howard was more querulous, almost bird-like. For Jane Edwardes (*Time Out*, 2 July 1997), he resembled 'a defrocked priest', for Susannah Clapp (*Observer*, 6 July 1997) 'a philosophy don trying to bring rationality to the proceedings', while Benedict Nightingale (*Times*, 30 June 1997) wrote that 'Howard exudes intellectual excitement and dreamy intensity from inside Vladimir's battered grey mac, only occasionally succumbing to his weakness for histrionics.'

The pair made a perfect contrast, Kingsley earthbound, truculently tied to his stone, Howard airily but ineffectually drifting around the

8. The production by Sir Peter Hall, Old Vic, London, 1997. Left to right:
Alan Howard (Vladimir), Ben Kingsley (Estragon).

stage. It was the symbiotic link between the two characters that they
failed to convey with equal conviction. Both seemed too self-involved
to really need the other, and their 'games to pass the time' lacked the
urgent sense that, if they were to falter, the two would somehow cease
to exist. Their costumes did not help. Instead of emphasising their
symbiotic link (as in Beckett's own production), they appeared quite
unrelated and suggested an attempt to depict two realistic tramps.
Estragon wore an old brown suit, torn and dirty, which had seen far
better days, with a collarless shirt, a waistcoat and a flat cap turned
round so that the peak was behind. Vladimir had an old, torn mac,
no jacket, a waistcoat and neckerchief and old, torn, nondescript

trousers, with a battered trilby. At the very end, when Estragon's trousers came down, they revealed a grotesque old pair of long johns.

Pozzo was also costumed (and played, by Denis Quilley) in realistic fashion as an Anglo-Irish squire, in rather the same vein as Nigel FitzGerald, the first Irish Pozzo (see chapter 4). His was a finely modulated performance, giving one a strong sense of the colonial master who considers himself to be very humane in his treatment of the natives, and who is genuinely shocked when told that his behaviour is a scandal (Faber 27). Lucky, dressed as a Dickensian servant with a battered stovepipe hat, was performed by Greg Hicks with the emphasis on the grotesque, dribbling a lot and spraying gobbets of spit when he began to talk. He began the 'Think' slowly, seeming in control, and raising a laugh by looking pointedly at Vladimir and Estragon on 'loves us dearly with some exceptions for reasons unknown' (Faber 43). As he proceeded he became louder, faster and higher, roaring out the word 'skull' in grotesque fashion, and collapsed full-length on his face when his hat was finally removed. This performance of the 'Think' was offered as a kind of *tour de force* and received a round of applause in performance.[8] Like this speech, the whole production was received with great enthusiasm by Old Vic audiences. Eric Prince noted that 'the sense of enjoyment was quite palpable. At the end large sections of the normally reserved Old Vic audience rose to their feet to offer the players a prolonged standing ovation.' But at the same time he explained that 'reservations as to the production's lack of a sense of desperation, the underpinning texture of anguish and isolation, left me not completely satisfied or won over'.[9]

Like the director, the London critics took this production as an opportunity to make up for earlier misunderstandings. The production was given more column-inches than most, as each critic took up the challenge of explaining the play's classic status and the reasons for its mixed reception in 1955. Sheridan Morley spoke for many when he commented that 'the difference now is one of confidence on both sides of the footlights; actors play in the knowledge they are doing a classic, and when the audience laughs it is because they have been empowered by world reaction across almost half a century to do so' (*Spectator*, 5 July 1997). Both he and Charles Spencer in the *Daily Telegraph* proclaimed the production 'definitive'. Indeed, the critics were unanimous in their praise of the production though not one of them mentioned having seen Beckett's own production. It seemed that they were all bent on reclaiming the play for the British (including Irish) stage and on saluting the achievement of Sir Peter Hall. Hall was acclaimed as the enterprising knight of theatre, far-sighted in taking on the first production in 1955, when the play was 'experimental', and now, forty-two years on, magisterial in his direction of this 'classic' vehicle for great actors.

PRODUCTIONS BY WALTER ASMUS, GATE THEATRE, DUBLIN, 1991–1999

The Gate performance (1999) benefited from a longer gestation period and from the fact that the actors had worked together on this and other Beckett projects many times before. Barry McGovern, who played Vladimir, had performed both Estragon and Vladimir at the Gate in the 1980s. In 1991, when the first complete season of Beckett's play was done at the Gate, McGovern played Vladimir to Johnny Murphy's Estragon, with Alan Stanford as Pozzo and Stephen Brennan as Lucky. The same cast appeared at the Lincoln Center, New York, in 1996 and again at the Barbican Theatre, London, in 1999. In a discussion after the performance on 2 September 1999, McGovern expressed the view that he and Murphy had achieved a suppleness in their interpretation in contrast to a certain stiffness in the Schiller-Theater production. He said, 'We've eased into the boot.' An essential part of that 'easing' process, he felt, was the Dublin voices. He was most insistent that Beckett had not translated his French play into English, but had rather rewritten it in Irish English. The performance was rapid, nearly matching the pace of the Schiller-Theater production, where the running time had been seventy minutes for

Act I and fifty-five minutes for Act II. In this performance Act I lasted seventy-five minutes and Act II fifty-four minutes.[10] Possessing a precise record of the timing, moves, gestures and vocal delivery of Beckett's Schiller-Theater performers, as well as details of costumes, lighting and setting, Asmus was able to recreate his production very accurately from the 'score' established by Beckett. The design, by Louis Le Brocquy, presented a bare stage with only a tree (upstage left) and a stone (downstage right). The tree had only two side branches and an extension of the trunk upwards so that it came very close indeed to the shape of a cross; in the second act three small leaves were projected onto the backcloth behind the tree. The backcloth was dark and suggested clouds or mist. This design was very close to that of Matias for the Schiller-Theater, and indeed each time he directed the play, Asmus attempted to maintain the details, the rhythm and the dynamics of that production. His ability to do this was enhanced by an awareness of the dangers of being *too* rigidly faithful to the original. He had seen how Beckett was always on the lookout for ways to improve on his own staging ideas, especially when fresh ideas emerged from the creative talents of his actors, and Asmus attempted to follow him in this, too.[11]

The performance began with a long pause in silence and semi-darkness as Vladimir looks backstage up at the sky (standing, centre) and Estragon looks broodingly down at the ground (sitting on the stone). After a full two minutes, Estragon gives a cry of effort and pain as he tries to remove his boot and this causes Vladimir to turn abruptly, almost in surprise, and walk downstage towards him. Not until he begins this downstage move do the lights come up. In contrast to this frozen, almost dream-like tableau at the beginning, the first passages of dialogue were taken at a brisk pace, and the parallel inspections of Vladimir's hat and Estragon's boot were performed very neatly and precisely: a neat double tap by Vladimir as he says 'nothing' and a parallel double tap by Estragon on the sole of his boot (when he finally gets it off) as he says 'nothing to be done'. This was then followed by Vladimir taking his hat off and blowing into it twice before tapping it twice again in perfect repetition of the previous gesture. Other physical motifs, including the 'approach by stages', were introduced early on, and recurred throughout the performance. For example, Estragon starts out being most emphatic about not wanting too close or emotional a contact with Vladimir, holding up both palms in a particular way, one hand slightly above the other. The dialogue about the crucifixion, which leads up to the second long pause (Beckett's *Wartestelle*), was spoken in a fast, rather dry and unemotional tone: the subject was evidently one which had been gone over many times before.

This opening section was a model exposition. The impression of clarity that it made can be ascribed partly to the brisk yet rhythmical delivery of the dialogue by McGovern and Murphy, but also to the precision with which the 'themes of the body' were articulated. There was little attempt to create the illusion of reality on stage: one's attention was not drawn, for example, to whether Estragon's foot was 'really' swelling or not. Instead, the emphasis was on the choreography of the actors' movements and gestures, Estragon's soulful, smiling yet self-deprecating immobility on his stone contrasted with Vladimir's tendency to look around much more and his agile yet stiff-legged and pigeon-toed shuffle from one place to another. Their ability to establish rhythms and cadences through the synchronising of posture and gesture is well exemplified in the moments when Vladimir and Estragon pause to look at something. The first time they comment on the tree (Faber 14) there was one such moment, as they both looked first towards one another then away towards the opposite sides of the stage, and then, with perfect timing, turned towards the tree so that they were seen in profile, momentarily fixed in expectation. These synchronised looks not only gave a satisfying sense of rhythm and musical shape, but also resulted in a curiously touching effect. Moreover, the perfect synchronicity of their gestures gave the impression of puppets, which, far from making them seem wooden, increased the audience's sympathy for them: it made them seem as if they were being manipulated by some outside force which they could not control. It was a perfectly judged example of what Bert States described as 'the peculiar co-operation of text and metatext' (see chapter 2).

Further evidence of this 'co-operation' emerged in the way everything they did was presented as a routine or game – what Beckett called 'the game in order to survive' (see chapter 6). Although the dialogue moved rapidly, it was constantly interspersed with moments when the whole action appeared to be in danger of drying up. For example, when Vladimir asks Estragon 'What was it you wanted to know?' (Faber 20), there was one such moment of complete stillness before Estragon replies 'I've forgotten'. This raised a laugh in performance, and reinforced the impression of two performers who knew that their only justification was simply to *be there* and yet whose presence was somehow in danger of draining away, as an actor may 'dry' in mid-speech. Estragon, in particular, emphasised his need to feel himself to be really *there*. When eating his carrot, for example, he did a little rock of pleasure from one foot to the other as if to demonstrate how completely taken up he was in the enjoyment of the experience (though this mood left him as abruptly as it had come). Their intensely symbiotic quality was an aspect of this need to keep the game going: when one ran out of inspiration he always turned to the other. Even their requests to be embraced and the ensuing refusals were somehow imbued with the sense of a routine that both depended on for their lives. This was partly a result of the way actions echoed one another so precisely: when Estragon begged Vladimir to embrace him after Vladimir's first exit (Faber 17) he was refused with a gesture which perfectly paralleled that with which he had refused Vladimir at the beginning of the play (Faber 9).

Their costumes reinforced the sense of symbiosis as those at the Schiller-Theater had done, though less emphatically. Estragon's jacket was of a lightish material and too large for him: it matched Vladimir's trousers. Vladimir had a dark jacket that was slightly too small for him and matched Estragon's trousers, worn over lighter trousers matching Estragon's jacket. In the second act these costumes were reversed: Estragon had a dark jacket over baggy, lighter trousers, while Vladimir wore the small, light jacket over dark trousers. Both wore old collarless shirts, both had black bowler hats, and both were very dirty. When Pozzo and Lucky appeared, they too were very obviously playing a game. Pozzo (Alan Stanford) did not come across as a natural bully. Instead his superiority was a carefully constructed act. In the scene where he puts on his coat (Faber 24), for example, he had already taken it from Lucky and was about to put it on himself, when he paused and gave a sly look in the direction of Vladimir and Estragon, as if to say to himself, 'Wait! I must take care to impress these two by showing I am the sort of man who has a servant to put on his coat for him.' He then handed the coat to Lucky who helped him on with it. The Pozzo–Lucky couple was as interdependent as that of Vladimir and Estragon: everything about them suggested complementarity. Their manner of walking exemplified this: Lucky took tiny, shuffling steps, daintily placing one foot before the other with great rapidity, whereas Pozzo did a high-stepping walk, lifting each foot up and placing it in a self-consciously deliberate style. Pozzo wore white kid shoes, dark trousers, a light frock-coat, a striped waistcoat, a cravat and a light grey hat shaped like a soft bowler. Lucky, on the other hand, had dark, broken-down shoes, trousers and waistcoat of faded, muddy greenish material, a slightly smarter jacket made of the same material as Pozzo's waistcoat and a hat similar to Pozzo's.

As Lucky, Stephen Brennan was profoundly bent over, so that he was looking straight down at the ground. There were less than a dozen occasions when he looked up and these were carefully chosen to achieve the maximum effect. He looked up at Pozzo while he ate his chicken, and again when Estragon asked for the bones. After Estragon had been told he must ask Lucky, Lucky deliberately looked away. But after Pozzo says 'Reply! Do you want them or don't you?' (Faber 27), he turned his gaze full on Estragon and the two of them exchanged a long, meaningful look, during which Lucky slowly straightened in a gesture made up in equal parts of pride, defiance and despair, and then he suddenly broke off the look, drooping down again and looking away. He looked up again when forced to, and stared fixedly at Pozzo while Pozzo wept. The other moments when he looked up emphasised a sense of close dependency between the two, a feeling which was touchingly sealed at the point when Lucky is being helped to his feet again (after his 'Think', Faber 45) and Pozzo is replacing his bags in his hands: to make him hold onto the basket, he carefully, tenderly wrapped each of his fingers, one by one, round the basket handle. There was real anguish in Pozzo's voice as he wondered if he was going to be able to get Lucky to walk again and tremulous relief when he succeeded. Finally, when Lucky was standing again and the bags were back in his hands, Pozzo carefully removed a strand of hair that had fallen over his face before stoking his cheeks with some tenderness and forcing him to re-establish eye contact.

Pozzo, in short, appeared more vulnerable than brutal. He was visibly pained at the failure of his efforts to get Vladimir and Estragon into conversation while Estragon devoured his bone, and throughout the scene he appeared in constant danger of being unnerved by the stony stares with which Vladimir and Estragon opposed him. He underlined the theme of time by consulting his watch whenever time was mentioned, even checking it when he explained how he had taken a 'knook' sixty years before. His speech about Night was done for maximum dramatic effect, constantly checking that his audience's attention was still fixed on him. But he was sufficiently imposing for Vladimir and Estragon to feel they really must *not* speak as they struggled to articulate their question as to why Lucky does not put down his bags, and this mime, though not drawn out, was extremely comic. Estragon finished off his mime (Faber 31) by drawing a big question mark in the air which always drew a big laugh, presumably because it hit a central thematic nerve – that of the doubts and confusions listed in Beckett's notebook.[12]

Lucky's 'Think' started very slow and reasonable, only gradually speeding up and deteriorating. Lucky began erect, with big, confident

9. The production by Walter Asmus, Gate Theatre (Dublin) at the Barbican, London, 1999. Left to right: Barry McGovern (Vladimir), Stephen Brennan (Lucky), Johnny Murphy (Estragon).

arm gestures, which also grew gradually less controlled. The speech was not very clearly shaped into the three sections specified by Beckett, however, and this was arguably one of the less successful parts of the performance. On the first lines, Vladimir and Estragon did a double 'approach by stages', moving slowly from the stone towards Lucky in the centre of the stage, but stepping back abruptly a couple of paces in unison each time he came to 'quaquaquaqua'. They put in quite a lot of exasperated reaction, including Estragon going behind his back and making silly faces at him like a naughty schoolboy. Pozzo, meanwhile, behaves like the ostrich, first hiding his head in his hands, then folding his cape over his head, finally getting down on the ground and burying his head beneath the stool. Estragon takes no part in the ending of the 'Think' – it is Vladimir alone who triumphantly tears off Lucky's hat and holds it aloft above his head as if it were some sort of trophy (a change from Beckett's production).

After Pozzo and Lucky's exit, with its prolonged 'adieux', Vladimir and Estragon remained side by side, staring out into the auditorium, and the moment acquired a certain poignancy, especially because they were standing in just the same position as they had been during the long pause twelve pages earlier, after Pozzo's line, 'Listen! Pan sleeps' (Faber 36). In the following page of dialogue, Vladimir's uncertainty as to how Pozzo and Lucky had changed was expressed with urgent and mounting anguish, concluding on the line, 'Unless they're not the same . . . ' (Faber 49), which was followed by a pause as he gazed steadily off to stage right in the direction of Pozzo and Lucky's departure. The entry of the boy was made from upstage left, behind Vladimir, so that he did not see him until he was halfway across the stage. The boy was dressed entirely in white with very blond hair. He spoke in a colourless voice and appeared quite frightened of Estragon, who threatened him roughly, grabbing his arm and twisting it back on 'Tell us the truth' (Faber 50). At the end of his scene he left the stage backwards, reversing his entry movement, and the moon rose as he left. Vladimir and Estragon then made a long circular walk upstage

10. The production by Walter Asmus, Gate Theatre (Dublin) at the Barbican, London, 1999. 'Adieu! Adieu!' Left to right: Barry McGovern (Vladimir) and Johnny Murphy (Estragon).

to the tree, a move which mirrored Pozzo's exit move. The last bits of
dialogue were done either side of the tree, facing front, very symmetrical. Estragon crossed the stage, returning to his stone on the line
'I wonder if we wouldn't have been better off alone', Vladimir joining
him on 'It's not certain' (Faber 53). They sat almost back to back on
the stone, half faced each other but with their eyes not quite meeting
just before 'Shall we go?', then turned away on 'Yes, let's go' and froze
slowly, Estragon's head bowing forward so that he was looking at the
ground, while Vladimir remained looking up at the sky.

The opening of Act II mirrored that of Act I with slight differences.
There was an extraordinary intensity in the way Vladimir questioned
Estragon about where he had spent the night and what it was he
had done that had provoked a beating. Throughout Act II Vladimir
gradually built up a mood of intensely anguished, almost tragic questioning. He really *longed* to understand their situation, and remained
convinced that an explanation might be found if only he tried hard
enough. The routines in this act, such as the trying on of the boots
and the use of songs, were exactly as in the Beckett production. After
Pozzo and Lucky's entry, their fall was done in the precise shape of
a cross, Lucky feet to audience and head upstage, Pozzo feet to stage
right and head to the left. Vladimir's long speech about mankind
(Faber 79–80) was given very fast and emphatically, combined with
a large circular movement right around the stage, and the ensuing
dialogue between him and Estragon was punctuated by a great deal of
movement between the stone and the fallen bodies. When Vladimir
and Estragon fell, they made a symmetrical arrangement, like two
lower, diagonal branches of the cross formed by Pozzo and Lucky,
and appeared relatively comfortable, with their heads pillowed on
Pozzo. Rather than allow his mood to become more and more an-
grily frustrated, as Ben Kingsley had done, Johnny Murphy retained
a deadpan quality in his performance of Estragon, as if nothing could
surprise him. Barry McGovern's Vladimir became gradually more intense and desperate as he puzzled over the changed status of Pozzo and
Lucky.

Once all the characters were upright, the interdependence of Pozzo and Lucky was once again expressed by the way Lucky gave Pozzo the whip. In an echo of the way Pozzo had wrapped Lucky's fingers around the basket handle in Act I, Lucky wrapped the blind Pozzo's fingers round the handle of the whip. Pozzo's great speech 'Have you not done tormenting me with your accursed time!' (Faber 89) was delivered by Alan Stanford on a note of genuine suffering, but was also shaped in such a way as to create an echo of his hollowly rhetorical delivery of the 'Night' speech in Act I, thus undermining any note of pathos. He and Lucky exit on the opposite side from Act I. Vladimir's speech 'Was I sleeping while others suffered?' (Faber 90) was also delivered with considerable feeling, and concluded with Vladimir staring offstage to the left, so that, as in Act I, he did not see the boy entering behind him. After the boy's first line, he did not look at him but down at the floor, as if he did not entirely believe in his existence – as if perhaps it were all a dream. At the end of their dialogue, as the boy exited backwards, Vladimir did not make a sudden move in his direction, but extended his hand as if to seize a ghost, or something he did not believe was materially there. Meanwhile the boy made his slow retreat and the moon rose in synchronicity with the first act. In this way the theme of the dream, already raised a number of times by Estragon, was given a gentle emphasis. The ending was exactly as in Act I, except that this time they remained upstage beside the tree, staring out front, instead of coming down to the stone.

The broad similarities between these two productions demonstrate the extent to which *Waiting for Godot* is now recognised as a masterpiece at *both* the theatrical level (i.e. taking all the expressive elements of the stage into account, as Edward Gordon Craig had demanded) *and* the literary level. The play is seen as having its own peculiar shape and rhythm (encoded to a large extent in Beckett's stage directions for the revised text), and these are understood to be as central to the artistic work we know as *Waiting for Godot* as the words of Vladimir and Estragon, Pozzo, Lucky and the boy. As James Knowlson has pointed out, this is not just a technical matter of interest to theatre people. The idioms of stage performance are as important to Beckett in articulating his themes as the words his characters speak.[13] The success of any given production must be judged according to its ability to manipulate and counterpoint all the idioms of the stage in expressing such key themes as waiting, loneliness, symbiosis and the painful human awareness of being 'irremediably present' yet subject to slow deterioration, building up a layered, poetic effect.

The Gate Theatre production was more satisfying than the one at the Old Vic, for example, because it managed a clearer counterpoint between the moments of absolute stillness, when both audience and characters shared the experience of waiting, and the contrasting bursts of activity, when the characters play their 'games to survive'. Another reason why it appeared more satisfying was that its actors achieved more grace and precision in both their movements and their delivery of the speeches. Because they were not so involved as Howard and Kingsley with giving a realistic portrayal of down-and-outs, McGovern and Murphy were able to concentrate more on giving musical shape and form to their performances. Beckett spoke of the need for 'the kind of form one finds in music, for instance, where themes keep recurring. When, in a text, actions are repeated, they ought to be made unusual the first time, so that when they happen again – in exactly the same way – an audience will recognise them from before' (see chapter 6). The special gesture used first by Murphy and then by McGovern to signify the refusal of an embrace exemplifies just this quality of being 'made unusual'. Since almost all of an actor's training is devoted to helping him or her to cultivate movements that will seem natural, it is very rare to find actors who can create 'unusual' gestures or movements which nevertheless communicate at a poetic and meaningful level.

Even more difficult to achieve is that mood of profound emotion which occurs when a whole audience feels that it has been touched, through art, by reality. Commentators have rightly picked out the theme of Vladimir's long speech over the prone bodies of Pozzo and

Lucky in the second act:

> To all mankind they were addressed, those cries for help still ringing in
> our ears! But at this place, at this moment of time, all mankind is us,
> whether we like it or not. (Faber 79)

The extent to which a production is able to strike a balance between the universal truths of this play and the particular application to
us, the audience, is another criterion of its success. As has been seen
from the analysis of different productions in different places and at
different times, this sense of the play's relevance does not necessarily
derive from its being placed in a specific social or political location.
This *may* help (as in the Haifa production) but it may just as well
hinder. Rather, it is a question of how vividly the concrete details of
the performance itself are managed. So much of the play's action has
to do with the intransigence of the real, physical world we all have to
deal with: difficulties with standing up and sitting down, with boots,
hats, food and other necessities of life, such as the need to urinate
at regular intervals. And this, in turn, is linked to Beckett's choice of
archetypal figures: the two down-and-outs who long to separate while
depending totally upon one another; the master–slave relationship in
which the master is as dependent on his slave as the slave on his master.
It is when a production succeeds in negotiating these fundamental,
concrete relationships and realities with the maximum richness that
it achieves the quality of 'provocation' admired by Roger Blin. The
temptation, since the objects *are* so basic and since the relationships
do possess the simplicity of binary opposites, is to perform everything
at a one-dimensional level. But the play only comes to life through
its contradictions, and it is the performance which can show both
Pozzo's cruelty and his tenderness, both Estragon's truculent cynicism
and his hopeful innocence, that ultimately creates an experience of
emotional profundity for its audience.

Such considerations might lead one to the conclusion that the
problem of how to mount a production of *Waiting for Godot* has been
settled, once and for all, and that one needs only to copy Beckett's

revised stage directions scrupulously. But it is in the nature of dramatic texts that they only live through being embodied anew, and the fact that the stage directions are as important to *Godot* as the words spoken in no way changes this fundamental truth. The fact that *Godot* has this unusually integrated quality does not mean that it must always achieve realisation by means of the same embodied shapes, movements and images, any more than it means that the words must always be spoken with the same intonations. Rather, it points towards the originality of Beckett's dramatic creation and the need for each new production team to understand the nature of the work they propose to embody. It is neither a play in the tradition of naturalism, nor a Brechtian allegory; it is a new type of structure which comes closer to the theatre dreamed of by Artaud than to any other twentieth-century model one might cite.[14] This is also the insight of Pierre Chabert, an actor and director who worked with Beckett on a number of his plays, including the only work Beckett ever directed which was not written by him: Pinget's *Hypothèse* (1975). Chabert expressed in forceful terms the sense that Beckett writes through the body of the actor and the three-dimensional medium of space:

> Once the theory that action and psychology are all-important has been demolished, the emergence of the "stage" and its specific language (the language that, in Artaud's view, has been repressed since the very origins of "Western Theatre") becomes possible. This physical language, linked to space and to the materiality of stage (bodies, objects, movements, sounds, lights . . .) becomes the primary, fundamental material out of which theatre is made. It participates on equal terms with words and action, in a new kind of three-dimensional writing. Space and words are woven into an integral whole, a single theatre work. Space and all the other expressive elements of the stage acquire a role in the dynamics of the play: they speak and act.[15]

Interpreters who have grasped this fundamental quality of Beckett's work do not need to feel themselves limited by the contingencies of, for example, bowler hats. Once the 'three-dimensional writing' out of which the play is constructed has been understood, all kinds of new possibilities will arise for weaving space, objects, bodies and words into an integral whole.

The first necessary stage was for the multi-dimensional nature of the writing to be recognised. The 1997 production by Hall and the regular re-creations of Beckett's production by Asmus have confirmed that recognition, at least within the ambit of the British and American theatre community. What had, for a long time, been thought of as an anti-play, one that denies the whole basis of Western dramatic tradition, has come to be seen as one which might be better described as infolding it, albeit in a critical light, since, as Chabert writes, it demolishes the all-importance of action and psychology. Herb Blau sums it up as follows:

> And with all its pretended anti-drama, we know it is brazenly theatrical – an occasion for Talent: the Noh, the pantomime, the music hall, the circus, the Greek messenger and the medieval angel; the play is a history of dramatic art. There is even the Secret of the well-made play, Sardoodledom's ultimate question: who is Godot? Will he come? But above all, there is Racine, the great dramatist of the closed system and the moral vacuum, salvaging exhausted *données*, illuminating what was at the beginning almost entirely known.[16]

Blau's reference to Racine alerts us to the play's classical quality. Like all great drama of the Western classical tradition, the play enacts a balance, walks a tightrope between the opposing forces of hope and despair, love and hate, vision and blindness, life and death. And like the plays of Racine, or of the ancient Greek classics on whom he depended, it is not just the narrative of the play which enacts this balance, but the whole arrangement of the performers and the stage space.

In order to understand how dramatic space may generate meaning, one needs to refer to theatre practitioners who have experimented with this aspect of the art of theatre, such as Peter Brook or Jacques Lecoq. Lecoq made an important contribution to the understanding of classical tragedy in performance through his exploration of what he called 'the balanced stage'. He demonstrated that in all classical drama there is fundamental equilibrium to be found in the spacing of the actors and chorus.[17] The space of Beckett's stage for *Waiting for Godot* requires just such a balance. In his first version it was hazy, but he clarified it by doing away with the mound in favour of the stone downstage right counterbalancing the tree upstage left. The tree, which seems to speak of budding life (the leaves) and of an upward movement, is paradoxically seen as the instrument of suicide. The stone, suggesting the immutability of minerals and the stasis of the tomb, is nevertheless the one place where Estragon can achieve a brief escape in sleep. Each point has its own force, yet each also implies its own counterbalancing force. The movements made between these two points ring the changes on these opposing yet balanced components of the drama.

THE PRODUCTION BY LUC BONDY, THEATRE VIDY, LAUSANNE, 1999

Two other productions from 1999, one from Switzerland and one from Spain, demonstrate how the play's classical quality is perceived and how it gives rise to new productions employing different imagery. The Swiss production was put on by the Théâtre Vidy at Lausanne, directed by Luc Bondy. It opened in Lausanne in March 1999, after which it toured widely throughout Europe, coming to London in August 2000. Bondy's production was firmly in the tradition of European 'directors' theatre', and he gave a long interview explaining his ideas about the production which made up the larger part of the programme. In this he was bold enough to say that Beckett was not the best director of his own work, and that his Schiller-Theater production had gone too far in denying his actors the sub-text they needed to function well. He saw *Waiting for Godot* not so much as an anti-play but as one which demonstrated the continuity of the

European cultural tradition, although in the form of ruined remains: '*Godot*: remains of men who eat remains of vegetables in the remains of situations'. He expressed the view that Beckett was an extremely realistic writer, not in the same sense as Ibsen or Shaw, but in the sense that his dramas deal with the concrete realities of life – food, clothing and shelter – set in dramatic situations.

In 1999 Bondy was in his early fifties having built up a very successful career as a director of theatre and opera. His hallmark was a spare but powerful visual aesthetic with an emphasis on physicality and movement on stage. This emphasis perhaps derives from his training (as an actor) with Jacques Lecoq. One of his best known productions was *The Hour When We Knew Nothing of One Another*, a full-length play by Peter Handke without a single spoken word, only movements and gestures (1994, Berlin Schaubühne, Paris Festival d'Automne and Edinburgh Festival). When he speaks of realism, it is not in the context of naturalist theatre that imitates real life, but rather in the context of Strindberg, Ionesco, Genet, Bond and Botho Strauss, all of whose work he has directed. He excels in drawing the best out of actors, achieving performances of great power, full of inventive, concrete detail, but set in a context that is nightmarish or overwhelming, bordering on the surreal. He believes that in order to achieve their best actors need to be able to imagine themselves in a concrete situation. For the setting of *Godot* he was inspired by the book of photographs entitled *Beckett's Ireland*, which he showed to his designer, Gilles Aillaud, asking him to provide a 'difficult terrain'. The result was a set evoking a cold, desolate country road, with a slight powdering of snow. It sloped steeply up from front to back and on either side of the road there was the suggestion of moorland with little bumps and hollows across which the characters slithered or rolled at various points in the performance. This setting, though clearly evoking a real space, seemed more dream-like than realistic, partly because of the colour of the moor – a faded blue – and partly because of the openly theatrical lighting and intense blue cyclorama which ran right around the back of the stage.

The performance was given in French, with only the cuts made in Beckett's revised version, Bondy professing complete respect for Beckett's text (including stage directions). He certainly observed each of Beckett's *Wartestellen*, though it is doubtful whether Beckett would have approved of the sound effects he used (a mixture of recognisable sounds, such as dogs barking, and unearthly electronic noises, which recurred both during pauses and under speech). His achievement was to find a new way of giving life to the themes of the body in the play, images of destitution, loss, waiting and dependency as powerful as those imagined by Beckett, though rather different. Just as the Haifa production had achieved a concentrated power by foregrounding the objects and habits that make up the day-to-day reality of two Palestinian construction workers, so Bondy's actors built up a concrete picture of the world of two refugees, waiting on a cold, lonely hillside, in a situation of desperate need. Like Beckett, Bondy emphasised certain recognisable gestures which returned, with variations, in the course of the performance, but these gestures were mostly manifestations of cold or of physical pain. Estragon (Roger Jendly) continued the business with his boots throughout the first act, never quite deciding whether it was more painful to have them on or off. Both he and Vladimir (Serge Merlin) were dressed in contemporary clothes of the type familiar to audiences in 1999 from the ubiquitous television pictures of columns of refugees pouring out of Kosovo. Both wore trousers and waistcoats that must once have belonged to suits, over which Vladimir had an old duffle coat and Estragon an anorak. Vladimir had a black woollen hat and Estragon an old felt trilby.

In the course of rehearsals a number of additional physical 'games' were elaborated. Vladimir's painful prostate caused him to go into an odd contortion, doubling up in pain. Estragon displayed a tendency to take whatever he could get and was a skilful pickpocket. In the scene in which Pozzo cannot find his watch and then comes back after his first departure because he has forgotten his stool, both actions were motivated by Estragon having surreptitiously removed the object in question without Pozzo noticing. The scene of the trying on of the boots in Act II (Faber 69) was built up into an elaborate game, with much giggling and Estragon rolling around on his back while Vladimir struggled to get the boots on (a reference back to Krejča's production, perhaps); both demonstrate their delight that they have at last found something with which to make the time pass, in sharp contrast to the long, agonised pause that preceded this scene. They took a similar approach to the scene where they fear someone is coming (Faber 74), placing themselves on either side of the stage and shouting to one another as if they were miles apart. Vladimir delivered his 'all mankind' speech (Faber 79–80) very loudly and forcefully, moving impatiently back and forth across the stage and shaking his fist at the sky. From this point onwards his interpretation of the role developed a more and more explicit anger towards the heavens, which built up to an agonised, furious and bitter delivery of his last long speech ('Was I sleeping', Faber 90). But despite this emphasis on the anguished undertones, much of the playing was light, rapid and comic. Bondy said in his interview that he had aimed 'to create the impression of a very precise improvisation with just the right mixture of the unexpected and the necessary', and this well describes the overall effect of the performance.

Although its power derived partly from Merlin and Jendly's realistic evocation of cold and pain, despair and boredom, their abrupt mood-swings or sudden changes of temper disrupted any sense of a naturalistic atmosphere. The first time that Estragon fell asleep (Faber 15), for example, he was crying out in pain one second and asleep the next. Both actors regularly came out with a surprising, unexpected or even 'unnatural' gesture or intonation. For example, the phrase in Vladimir's opening speech, 'You haven't yet tried everything', was followed by a wild, rather desperate laugh. Estragon's memory of the maps of the Holy Land, 'I used to say, that's where we'll go for our honeymoon. We'll swim. We'll be happy' (Faber 12), was the cue for him to break down into tears, but his line a couple of pages later about the tree, 'No more weeping' (Faber 14), was delivered on a rising laugh, almost as if he were congratulating himself for having found a poetic phrase. Some of the repeated phrases were also delivered in fresh or unusual ways. Vladimir's regular explanation to Estragon of why they cannot leave, 'We're waiting for Godot', degenerated into an angry mumble, as if to say 'Why do you force me to repeat this again?'

The dream-like atmosphere was strongly reinforced by the entry of Pozzo (François Chattot) and Lucky (Gérard Desarthe), costumed in preposterous garb and behaving as if they were in a different climate altogether. Pozzo wore a dirty tracksuit bottom, a crumpled, white evening-dress waistcoat and shirt with a white bow tie (undone), a smart gold-coloured coat, an improbable leopard-skin hat and equally improbable snake-skin boots. He was large in every way, physically, vocally and in his gestures. The folding stool was quite unequal to the task of supporting his bulk. In the second act, when he fell, he rolled down the road and plunged off the stage headfirst, leaving his legs waving grotesquely in the air. His line 'Sometimes I wonder if I'm not still asleep' (Faber 86) was given special emphasis, as were the other

11. The production by Luc Bondy, Théâtre Vidy, Lausanne, 1999. Standing: Gérard Desarthe (Lucky). Sitting: François Chattot (Pozzo).

lines to do with sleep and dreams. Lucky was dressed in a light, white linen suit. Lucky's 'Think' was delivered not standing, as is customary, but sitting with one leg folded underneath him, almost nonchalantly, like a professor on a summer picnic who is asked to expound some interesting idea. He spoke as if he thought he was totally in control. When the first 'quaquaquaqua' slipped out he just looked slightly surprised at himself and carried on. His talk retained the semblance of sense until the very end; he never slobbered or gibbered, but just became less and less coherent. When Vladimir and Estragon became really frustrated, they went over the brow of the hill and came back with old cabbage stalks and bits of rotten vegetables, which they threw at him. After his hat was removed Lucky really wept for its loss.

Without sacrificing the play's ambiguity or its balancing of opposites, this performance gave an unusually powerful sense of the characters inhabiting a world of loss. In the Act II sequence where they speak of 'all the dead voices' (Faber 62–3), Vladimir and Estragon had been lying on the road, with their ears pressed to the ground. At the very end, Vladimir lay down on its uncomfortable surface once more and Estragon lay on top of him. This final image summed up the paradox of their only hope being a road that leads nowhere, and spoke of the fragmented culture of 'remains' at the end of the twentieth century, referred to by Bondy in his interview.

THE PRODUCTION BY LLUÍS PASQUAL, TEATRE LLIURE, BARCELONA, 1999

A second example of the way a production may depart from Beckett's while still re-creating the complete world of *Godot*, including its physical, spatial and temporal dimensions, was Lluís Pasqual's 1999 production in Catalan for the Teatre Lliure of Barcelona.[18] The production used a set designed by the painter Frederic Amat, a slope covered with a mass of detritus which appeared to have melted into a kind of lava and then frozen solid. Amat explained that this reflected

12. The production by Luc Bondy, Théâtre Vidy, Lausanne, 1999. The final image: Serge Merlin (Vladimir) lies on the road while Roger Jendly (Estragon) lies on top of him.

his 'anxiety to represent emptiness, that road which Beckett said was no-place'.[19] Pasqual called it 'a post-apocalypse geography in black and white'.[20] Like Bondy, Pasqual insisted that his production did not just present the words of the play but the whole theatrical edifice, including stage directions, and that he had respected every one. He went so far as to count them, claiming that 'there are 400 stage directions in the play, 30% of which mark silences or pauses'.[21] In his view one could judge the success of a production by the quality of the actors and by the way in which these silences are filled. He claimed for himself only the status of conductor, guiding performers through a score.

His way of bringing the whole integrated work to the stage was quite different from Bondy's, rejecting the idea of a concrete situation altogether and exploiting the metaphor of performance in a variety of different ways. His characters had no justification whatever for their situation other than the need to be on stage performing. Estragon several times expressed his frustration with this situation by coming down off the stage into the auditorium. His Vladimir was played by a female actor (Anna Lizaran), not, as he explained, to make a statement, but because she was simply one of the best performers in his company. He encouraged his cast to pursue what Kalb called 'acting [which] effectively involves a kind of quest for an indescribable grail inside the author's stage directions and the music of his words, a process, long and torturous to some, of learning to trust the text'.[22] Between them his actors rang the changes on all the different modes of performance and of filling the empty space that one could imagine. This resulted in a performance with more 'gags' than Bondy's, but one which did not neglect the desperation and anguish of the situation.

Kalb summed up the fundamental task of the producers and actors of Beckett's plays as follows:

> For Beckett as for Artaud, artificiality is a natural state, and part of the theater's job is to demonstrate that: the theater is not mendacious when it avoids explicit contact with social issues; it is rather mendacious

and manipulative when it fails to proclaim its duplicity, the essential collusion of its natural and artificial natures. And that collusion is most effectively shown through the actor's body, his physical presence, and not through words.[23]

The use of the actor's body, his physical presence, differed very considerably in each of the four productions mentioned in this chapter, but all of them drew power from the understanding that *Waiting for Godot* is not a play awaiting an 'interpretation' but one demanding the bodily exploration of that physical presence that is the performer's irremediable condition.

CONCLUSION

Beckett's plays succeed in realising Edward Gordon Craig's vision of the 'theatre of the future', drawing on all the expressive idioms of the stage. His plays come to life through the ingenious counter-pointing of Craig's three key elements: action, scene and voice. They escape what was seen for much of the twentieth century as the di-chotomy between Brecht and Stanislavski: they are not controlled by a larger political project, lying outside them, nor do they de-pend on faithful reconstruction of a realistic sub-text, locating them in particular social milieux. Instead they accomplish the Modernist project of constructing a work which is about nothing other than it-self. And yet the plays, especially *Waiting For Godot*, have also proved favourites with audiences. Peter Hall's experience in 1997 was typi-cal of countless others – *Godot* has always done excellent business at the box office. This is because, though neither didactic like Brecht nor realistic like Chekhov or Ibsen, Beckett's work speaks to us of the real world, of the whole human condition. It does this through an entirely original blend of the ambiguous and the concrete. The reason why *Godot* in particular speaks so powerfully to such a wide range of people is that despite its philosophical and poetic profun-dity it remains firmly rooted within the realm of realities faced by every human being: the need for food, shelter, sleep and security, and the frustration of hope deferred and expectations denied. Be-cause of this, it can stand as a powerful metaphor for any situation in which people suffer need, frustration or oppression. It comes close to realising Artaud's dream of a theatre which would lead us to the discovery of deep, painful truths to which our minds are normally closed.

This book has traced the revising and refining of *Waiting for Godot* through Beckett's own direction of the play, demonstrating how it brings together within its austere architecture the concerns of twentieth-century Modernism and the experiments of Dada and Surrealist performance. Its production history shows the play being tested in the crucible of 'directors' theatre' and emerging clearly as a modern classic. The greatest tribute to the play's originality is the general recognition that the stage directions are as significant as the dialogue, that they make up an integrated, indivisible whole. It is rare for a director today *not* to claim that he has respected Beckett's text totally (as did both Bondy and Pasqual), even when their productions end up being quite different from Beckett's own. The long list of playwrights who acknowledge a debt to Beckett or who can be shown to have borrowed from him also bears witness to the innovatory importance of his work. Michael Billington detected the direct influence of *Godot* on Sarah Kane. In his review of *Crave*, he wrote: 'you can actually hear the rhythms of *Godot*'.[1] Lawrence Graver concluded his study of the play with a compelling discussion of its influence on Pinter, Stoppard, Fugard, Shepard and Mamet, and admitted that he might have included many more.[2] At a time when theatre seemed to be in danger of losing its way in irrelevancies and stale repetitions, *Waiting for Godot* established the template for a necessary poetic dramatic style, one which could provide adequate expression for the bleak horrors of twentieth-century experience.

Despite its radical originality, Beckett's theatre did not emerge from a vacuum. The first three chapters of this book demonstrated how much it owed to the experimental works of Dada and Surrealism, to the popular 'turns' and inventions of music hall and to the traditions of clowns and stand-up comedians. Crucially, it owed its life in production to the far-sightedness and great artistry of Roger Blin, and to the existence of the tiny Left Bank experimental theatres during the fifteen years that immediately followed the Second World War. Blin has been quoted as saying that the two most important people in his life were Beckett and Artaud. For Blin, as for many others since,

Beckett's work has much in common with that of Artaud: just as Artaud spoke of an all-engulfing theatrical experience which would achieve a purity beyond conventional plots and characters, so *Godot* provides what Robbe-Grillet called a theatre of 'pure presence' (see chapter 2). Beckett's is a theatre of 'literality', as defined by Artaud and Adamov (see chapter 1), one in which the actor has no secure fictional construct on which to depend, but where 'identity must be rehearsed into being', in Blau's phrase (see chapter 5).

This analysis of a few of the innumerable productions of *Waiting for Godot* to have appeared in the years since 1953 has shown a number of different ways in which this quality of 'literality' may be realised in production. The first of these is the idea of the game. Beckett's own most oft-repeated comment about the play was that the characters are all engaged in playing games: ' "Didi and Gogo are players," he said. "They play games," as do Pozzo and Lucky. "They are role players," in other words actors. "Pozzo need not be a plutocrat. Blin had him played that way, but Pozzo is also a player," and in common with the other characters, "he runs out of games to play." '[3] Next comes the idea of the performance shape. The play is structured like a piece of music, but instead of ringing the changes on musical phrases, it does the same thing with shapes and patterns – of the stage space and movement within it, of gesture and of the spoken word. The third essential element is the passage of real time. Though only one production reviewed here actually put a clock on stage,[4] any production must find a way to immerse its audience in the same experience of waiting fruitlessly in real time that the characters on stage have to undergo. Linked to this is the pace and rhythm with which these different elements are brought together, articulated and layered. Finally, a production must never lose sight of the fact that the seemingly meandering course of the play in fact contains a carefully balanced meditation on a number of themes: symbiosis, equilibrium, the 'fearful symmetry' of the two thieves and of the play's two couples, waiting and the deferral of hope, the painful human awareness of being 'irremediably present' yet subject to slow deterioration. All of these themes find expression through the concrete, physical stage idioms mentioned above. Value judgements on particular productions depend on the richness with which these various idioms are counterpointed and all the expressive elements deployed in the performance contribute to building up a densely textured, layered effect.

From its origins in ancient Greece, Western drama has been an art of balance. Antigone must balance the demands of piety, which compel her to bury her brother, with those of Creon which command her to leave his corpse untended. *Waiting for Godot* also enacts a drama of balance: the 'even chance. Or nearly' to which Estragon refers when debating methods of suicide with Vladimir (Faber 18). But Beckett's balancing act takes place in a climate of doubts and confusions which constantly threaten to engulf everything else. This is what gives the play its special force as 'the great poem of our century', in Krejča's words (see chapter 7). To see these confusions re-enacted on stage is in many ways a comic experience, but the comedy is always tinged with bleakness. A great production of this play will take its audience through the wry laughter at the weary uncertainties of our age and out on the other side to a poetic understanding of deeper and rarely glimpsed moments in their experience. They will find themselves entering what Beckett, in writing about Proust, called 'the perilous zones in the life of the individual, dangerous, precarious, painful, mysterious and fertile, when for a moment the boredom of living is replaced with the suffering of being'.[5]

SELECT PRODUCTION CHRONOLOGY

Théâtre de Babylone, Paris, 5 January 1953
Directed by Roger Blin
Designed by Roger Blin with Sergio Gerstein
Estragon: Pierre Latour
Vladimir: Lucien Raimbourg
Pozzo: Roger Blin
Lucky: Jean Martin
A Boy: Serge Lecointe

Arts Theatre, London, 3 August 1955 (transferred to the Criterion
    Theatre, 12 September 1955, when Hugh Burden replaced Paul
    Daneman in the role of Vladimir)
Directed by Peter Hall
Designed by Peter Snow
Estragon: Peter Woodthorpe
Vladimir: Paul Daneman
Pozzo: Peter Bull
Lucky: Timothy Bateson
A Boy: Michael Walker

Pike Theatre, Dublin, 28 October 1955
Directed by Alan Simpson
Designed by Mira Burgess and Edmund Kelly
Estragon: Austin Byrne
Vladimir: Dermot Kelly
Pozzo: Nigel FitzGerald
Lucky: Donal Donelly
A Boy: Seamus Fitzmaurice

Coconut Grove, Miami, 3 January 1956
Directed by Alan Schneider
Designed by Albert Johnson
Estragon: Bert Lahr
Vladimir: Tom Ewell
Pozzo: Jack Smart
Lucky: Arthur Malet (understudy for Charles Weidman)
A Boy: Jimmy Oster

John Golden Theater, New York, 19 April 1956
Directed by Herbert Berghof
Designed by Albert Johnson (?)
Estragon: Bert Lahr
Vladimir: E. G. Marshall
Pozzo: Kurt Kasznar
Lucky: Alvin Epstein
A Boy: Luchino Solito de Solis

Atelier 212, Belgrade, 17 December 1956 (originally performed once
    at the Belgrade Drama Theatre in February 1954 but banned)
Directed and designed by Vasilije Popović
Estragon: Bata Paskaljević
Vladimir: Ljubivoje Tadić
Pozzo: Rade Marković
Lucky: Mica Tomić
A Boy: Ratislav Jović

Actors Workshop, San Francisco, Spring 1957
Directed by Herb Blau
Designed by Robin Wagner
Estragon: Robert Symonds
Vladimir: Eugene Roche
Pozzo: Joseph Miksak
Lucky: Jules Irving
A Boy: Anthony Miksak

Schiller-Theater, Berlin, 8 March 1975
Directed by Samuel Beckett
Designed by Matias
Estragon: Horst Bollmann
Vladimir: Stefan Wigger
Pozzo: Carl Raddatz
Lucky: Klaus Herm
A Boy: Torten Sense

Brooklyn Academy of Music, New York, May 1978
Directed by Walter Asmus (billed as 'Samuel Beckett's Production')
Designed by Carole Lee Carroll, costumes by Dona Granata
Estragon: Austin Pendleton
Vladimir: Sam Waterston
Pozzo: Milo O'Shea
Lucky: Michael Egan
A Boy: R. J. Murray Jr

Avignon Theatre Festival, July 1978
Directed by Otomar Krejča
Designed by Otomar Krejča with Yves Cassagne
Estragon: Rufus
Vladimir: Georges Wilson
Pozzo: Michel Bouquet
Lucky: José-Maria Flotats
A Boy: Fabrice Luchini

Baxter Theatre, University of Cape Town, 1980 (Old Vic Theatre,
    London, 17 February 1981)
Directed and designed by Donald Howarth
Estragon: Winston Ntshona
Vladimir: John Kani
Pozzo: Bill Flynn
Lucky: Peter Piccolo
A Boy: Silamour Philander

Kammerspiele, Munich, 4 January 1984
Directed by George Tabori
Designed by Kazuko Watanabe
Estragon: Peter Lühr
Vladimir: Thomas Holtzmann
Pozzo: Claus Eberth
Lucky: Arnulph Schumacher
A Boy: Hans Kremer

Adelaide Arts Festival, Australia, 13 March 1984 (San Quentin Drama
    Workshop production)
Directed by Walter Asmus (under the supervision of Samuel Beckett)
Designed by Maher Ahmad (?)
Estragon: Lawrence Held
Vladimir: Bud Thorpe
Pozzo: Rick Cluchey
Lucky: J. Pat Miller
A Boy: Louis Beckett Cluchey

Haifa Municipal Theatre, November 1984
Directed by Ilan Ronen
Designed by Charlie Leon
Estragon: Muhram Khoury
Vladimir: Yussef Abu-Varda
Pozzo: Ilan Toren
Lucky: Doron Tavory
A Boy: unknown

Haarlem Toneelschuur, Holland, 12 April 1988
Directed by Matin van Veldhuizen (dramaturgy: Nan van Houte)
Designed by Jan Joris Lamers
Estragon: Truus te Stelle
Vladimir: Trudy de Jong
Pozzo: Carla Mulder

Lucky: Hedda van Gennep
A Boy: unknown

Gate Theatre, Dublin, 30 August 1988
Directed by Walter Asmus
Designed by Louis le Brocquy
Estragon: Barry McGovern
Vladimir: Tom Hickey
Pozzo: Alan Stanford
Lucky: Stephen Brennan
A Boy: Tom Lawlor

Théâtre des Amandiers, Nanterre, 1 February 1991
Directed by Joël Jouanneau
Designed by Jacques Gabel
Estragon: Philippe Demarle
Vladimir: David Warrilow
Pozzo: Raymond Jourdan
Lucky: Claude Melki
A Boy: Pieral

Za Branou II, Prague, November 1991
Directed and designed by Otomar Krejča
Estragon: Jan Hartl
Vladimir: Otomar Krejča Jr
Pozzo: Bořík Procházka
Lucky: Alexej Okuněv
A Boy: Vít Vencl

Théâtre du Nouveau Monde, Quebec, 21 January 1992
Directed by André Brassard
Designed by Stéphane Roy
Estragon: Rémy Girard
Vladimir: Normand Chouinard

Pozzo: Jean-Louis Millette
Lucky: Alexis Martin
A Boy: Hugolin Chevrette-Landesque

Sarajevo Youth Theatre, July 1993
Directed and designed by Susan Sontag
Estragon I: Velibor Topić; Estragon II: Milijana Zirojević; Estragon
    III: Irena Mulamuhić
Vladimir I: Izudin Bajrović; Vladimir II: Nada Djurevska; Vladimir
    III: Sead Bejtović
Pozzo: Ines Fančović
Lucky: Admir Glamočak
A Boy: Mirza Halilović

Ginza Saison, Tokyo, 1994
Directed by Yukio Ninagawa
Designer: unknown
male Estragon: Toru Emori; female Estragon: Mako Midori
male Vladimir: Kon Nishimura; female Vladimir: Etsuko Ichihara
male Pozzo: Ryuiji Sawa; female Pozzo: Fujima Murasaki
male Lucky: unknown; female Lucky: unknown
male Boy: unknown; female Boy: unknown

Old Vic, London, 27 June 1997
Directed by Sir Peter Hall
Designed by John Gunter
Estragon: Ben Kingsley
Vladimir: Alan Howard
Pozzo: Denis Quilley
Lucky: Greg Hicks
A Boy: Alex Russell

Teatre Lliure, Barcelona, 10 February 1999
Directed by Lluís Pasqual

Designed by Frederic Amat
Estragon: Eduard Fernández
Vladimir: Anna Lizaran
Pozzo: Francesc Orella
Lucky: Marc Martínez
A Boy: Marc Carreras / Bernat Parallada / Joel Roldan

Théâtre Vidy, Lausanne, 18 March 1999
Directed by Luc Bondy
Designed by Gilles Aillaud
Estragon: Roger Jendly
Vladimir: Serge Merlin
Pozzo: François Chattot
Lucky: Gérard Desarthe
A Boy: Xavier Loira

Gate Theatre, Dublin (at the Barbican, London), 1 September 1999
Directed by Walter Asmus
Designed by Louis le Brocquy
Estragon: Johnny Murphy
Vladimir: Barry McGovern
Pozzo: Alan Stanford
Lucky: Stephen Brennan
A Boy: Dan Colley

NOTES

Introduction

1. Roger Blin, *Souvenirs et propos*, ed. Lynda Bellity Peskine (Paris: Gallimard, 1986), p. 87.
2. Quoted in Rosemary Pountney, *Theatre of Shadows: Samuel Beckett's Drama 1956–76* (Gerrards Cross: Colin Smythe, 1988), p. 163.
3. I am indebted to Michael Robinson for pointing this out to me.
4. This production of *Footfalls*, by Deborah Warner with Fiona Shaw, was halted in 1996 at the insistence of the Beckett estate on the grounds that it had made alterations to both text and stage directions.
5. See Peter Thomson, *Brecht: Mother Courage and Her Children* (Cambridge University Press, 1997), p. 82. Beckett did not at first take such a close interest in the manner of his play's production: Peter Hall worked quite independently and Beckett did not even see his production until it had been running for over three months (see chapter 4).
6. Pierre Chabert, 'Singularité de Samuel Beckett' in Jean-Claude Lallias and Jean-Jacques Arnault, eds., *Théâtre Aujourd'hui 3: L'Univers scénique de Samuel Beckett* (Paris: Centre National de la Documentation Pédagogique, 1994), p. 11.
7. See, for example, Edward Braun, *The Director and the Stage* (London: Methuen, 1982).
8. Reprinted in Edward Gordon Craig, *On the Art of the Theatre* (London: Heinemann, 1911).
9. *Ibid.*, p. 138.
10. *Ibid.*, pp. 180–1.
11. *Ibid.*, p. 81. Beckett, as this study will show, displayed a similar wariness of actors, especially actors who followed the latest fashionable trends. To his first biographer, Deirdre Bair, he said, 'Not for me these Grotowskis and Methods. The best possible play is one in which there are no actors,

only the text. I'm trying to find a way to write one.' See Deirdre Bair, *Samuel Beckett* (New York and London: Harcourt Brace Jovanovitch, 1978), p. 513. Deirdre Bair dates this comment 19 June 1973.

12. Peter Hall, the first English director to produce *Waiting for Godot*, has devoted much of his life to directing opera.
13. See Roland Barthes, 'Réponses', *Tel Quel* 47 (1971), pp. 89–107.

1. Beckett before *Waiting for Godot*

1. See James Knowlson, *Damned to Fame: The Life of Samuel Beckett* (London: Bloomsbury, 1996), pp. 42–3. Knowlson's outstanding biography was the only one to be authorised by Beckett before his death; since it appeared it has provided a much-needed factual account of Beckett's life, scrupulously avoiding the tendency to mythologise which had been a feature of much earlier writing about Beckett.
2. See Colin Duckworth, ed., *Samuel Beckett: 'En attendant Godot'* (London: Harrap, 1966). For the English version, Beckett changed 'le Vaucluse' to 'the Macon country' and excised the name of Bonnelly.
3. Knowlson, *Damned to Fame*, p. 351.
4. Stanley E. Gontarski, *The Intent of Undoing in Samuel Beckett's Dramatic Texts* (Bloomington: Indiana University Press, 1985), p. 35.
5. Knowlson, *Damned to Fame*, pp. 56–7.
6. Katharine Worth, *Samuel Beckett's Theatre: Life Journeys* (Oxford University Press, 1999), p. 132.
7. Knowlson, *Damned to Fame*, p. 259.
8. Duckworth, ed., *En Attendant Godot*, p. xiv.
9. Michael Robinson, *The Long Sonata of the Dead: A Study of Samuel Beckett* (New York: Grove Press, 1969), p. 229.
10. *Ibid.*, p. 230.
11. Samuel Beckett, *Molloy; Malone Dies; The Unnamable* (London: Calder, 1959), p. 36.
12. L. R. Chambers, 'Antonin Artaud and the Contemporary French Theatre' in *Aspects of Drama and the Theatre: Five Kathleen Robinson Lectures* (Sydney University Press, 1965), p. 141. Chambers developed this idea in his article 'Beckett's Brinkmanship', reprinted in Martin Esslin, ed., *Samuel Beckett: A Collection of Critical Essays* (Engelwood Cliffs: Prentice Hall, 1965), pp. 152–68.

13. Annabelle Melzer, *Dada and Surrealist Performance*, 3rd edn, (Baltimore and London: Johns Hopkins Press, 1994), p. xiv.
14. Quoted by Melzer in *Dada and Surrealist Performance*, p. 57.
15. For Tzara's 'Dada Manifestoes' see Mel Gordon, ed., *Dada Performance* (New York: PAJ Publications, 1987).
16. Samuel Beckett, *Eleutheria* (Paris: Minuit, 1995), p. 84.
17. Quoted by Melzer in *Dada and Surrealist Performance*, p. 63.
18. *Ibid.*, p. 41.
19. See James Knowlson and John Pilling, *Frescoes of the Skull: The Recent Prose and Drama of Samuel Beckett* (London: Calder, 1979), p. 260.
20. For a fuller discussion, see Knowlson, *Damned to Fame*, pp. 122–6.
21. *Ibid.*, pp. 124–5.
22. *Ibid.*, p. 364.
23. John Fletcher, 'The Private Pain and the Whey of Words: A Survey of Beckett's Verse' in Esslin, ed., *Samuel Beckett: A Collection of Critical Essays*, p. 24.
24. Preface to Arthur Adamov, *La Parodie; L'Invasion* (Paris: Charlot, 1950). This was reprinted in *Ici et maintenant* (Paris: Gallimard, 1964), pp 13–15.
25. Antonin Artaud, *Le Théâtre et son double* (Paris: Gallimard, 1964), p. 80. This is my own translation of Artaud's text. In *The Theatre and its Double* (London: John Calder, 1970), p. 36, Victor Corti translates the same sentence as follows: 'everything in concept and production is valued and only exists through the degree of its objectification on stage'.
26. Adamov, *Ici et maintenant*, p. 14.
27. Samuel Beckett, *Our Exagmination Round His Factification For Incamination Of Work In Progress* (London: Faber [reprint], 1959), p. 14.
28. Quoted by Deirdre Bair in *Samuel Beckett*, p. 405.

2. *Waiting for Godot* – the play

1. Ruby Cohn, ed., *Samuel Beckett: 'Waiting for Godot': A Casebook* (Houndmills: Macmillan, 1987), pp. 16–17.
2. From an expanded version of Esslin's introduction to *The Theatre of the Absurd*, printed in Cohn, ed., *Casebook*, p. 173.
3. Reprinted in Esslin, ed., *Samuel Beckett: A Collection of Critical Essays*, pp. 108–16. This article first appeared in *Critique* (February 1953).

4. *Ibid.*, p. 110.
5. *Ibid.*, p. 111.
6. References to the English text are not to the first (1956) Faber edition, with its cuts imposed by the Lord Chamberlain for the Arts Theatre performance, nor to the first US publication (1954) by Grove Press, but to the revised second edition of the play, first published in 1965 and frequently reprinted by Faber since then. In 2001 this is still Faber's standard text of the play (although, oddly, it is not the text used in the Faber edition of Beckett's *Complete Dramatic Works*, which reverts to the 1956 text, with a few changes). References are given in the form 'Faber 6', which indicates a quotation from page 6 of the 1965 edition. A more recent text does exist, incorporating the revisions made by Beckett after his own Schiller-Theater production in 1975. This was the text used by both Peter Hall and Walter Asmus for the two major recent productions discussed in my last chapter. Sadly, this text is only available in the bulky first volume of *The Theatrical Notebooks of Samuel Beckett* published by Faber in 1993 (see note 15 below), priced at £75.
7. *Ibid.*, p. 112.
8. Speaking to Alec Reid, and quoted by Colin Duckworth in the introduction to his edition of *En attendant Godot*, p. xcvii.
9. Alec Reid, *All I Can Manage More Than I Could: An Approach to the Plays of Samuel Beckett* (Dublin: Dolmen Press, 1968), p. 52.
10. Geneviève Serreau, *Histoire du 'nouveau théâtre'* (Paris: Gallimard, 1966), p. 90.
11. Knowlson, in *Damned to Fame*, p. 417, quotes Peter Woodthorpe, the first English Estragon, who 'remembered asking him [Beckett] one day in a taxi what the play was really all about: "It's all symbiosis, Peter; it's symbiosis," answered Beckett.'
12. Stanley Cavell, *Must We Mean What We Say?* (New York: Scribner, 1969), p. 125.
13. Bert O. States, *The Shape of Paradox: An Essay on 'Waiting for Godot'* (Berkeley: University of California Press, 1978), p. 82.
14. Programme note for his revival at the Old Vic Theatre, 1997.
15. James Knowlson, 'Introduction' to Dougald McMillan and James Knowlson, eds., *The Theatrical Notebooks of Samuel Beckett*, vol. I: *Waiting for Godot* (London: Faber, 1993), p. xix.

16. See the revised text published in McMillan and Knowlson, eds., *The Theatrical Notebooks*, pp. 8–85.
17. See the notes to the revised text in *ibid.*, p. 89.
18. *Molloy; Malone Dies; The Unnamable*, p. 418.
19. John Fletcher and John Spurling, *Beckett: A Study of his Plays* (London: Eyre Methuen, 1972), p. 65.
20. Samuel Beckett, *The Complete Dramatic Works* (London: Faber, 1986), p. 156.
21. Beckett, quoted by Reid in *All I can Manage*, p. 33.
22. See Knowlson, *Damned to Fame*, pp. 411–17.
23. Samuel Beckett, *Théâtre*, vol. I (Paris: Minuit, 1971), p. 28.
24. *Ibid.*, p. 16. Note, however, the views expressed by both Ruby Cohn and Harry Cockerham to the effect that every 'coarsening' of the dialogue in the English can be matched by a crude expression in French being softened in the English translation. For a review of these and other opinions, see Lawrence Graver, '*Godot* in French and English' in his *Beckett: 'Waiting for Godot'* (Cambridge University Press, 1989), pp. 75–84. Graver concludes that Beckett's main aim when translating his French text into English was to enhance its effectiveness in the theatre: 'he did not set out to make the English *Godot* more of one thing than another (except more actable)'.
25. In *Souvenirs et propos*, p. 84, Blin speaks of Beckett being 'doubtless influenced by the English music-hall and by typical Irish humour of masochism'.
26. Quoted by Roger Wilmut in *Kindly Leave the Stage! The Story of Variety 1919–1960* (London: Methuen, 1985), p. 147.
27. See Duckworth, ed., *En attendant Godot*, p. lix.
28. Knowlson, *Damned to Fame*, p. 379. See also Worth, *Samuel Beckett's Theatre*, in which her chapter 7, 'Rhythms', discusses Beckett's debt to O'Casey, Synge, Yeats and other Irish playwrights.

3. The first production: Théâtre de Babylone, Paris, January 1953, directed by Roger Blin

1. Blin, *Souvenirs et propos*, p. 82.
2. Knowlson, *Damned to Fame*, p. 365.

3. Blin, *Souvenirs et propos*, p. 81.
4. *Ibid.*
5. *Ibid.*, p. 87 ('ce don que possède Beckett de la provocation').
6. *Ibid. Les Nègres* and *Les Paravents* are both by Jean Genet; Blin produced the premières of these plays in 1959 and 1966 respectively. Both provoked outrage, which in the case of *Les Paravents* developed into running street-battles and questions in the Assemblée Nationale. He directed the French première of Athol Fugard's *Boesman and Lena* in 1976.
7. *Ibid.*, p. 74 ('prince-clochard').
8. Ruby Cohn, *From 'Desire' to 'Godot': Pocket Theater of Postwar Paris* (Berkeley and Los Angeles: University of California Press, 1987). See also Geneviève Latour, ed., *Petites scènes . . . grand théâtre: Le théâtre de création de 1944 à 1960* (Paris: Délégation Artistique de la Ville de Paris, 1986).
9. Arthur Adamov, *L'Homme et l'enfant* (Paris: Gallimard, 1968), p. 97; translation taken from Cohn, *From 'Desire' to 'Godot'*, p. 103.
10. Blin finally raised the necessary money to hire the Lancry theatre in 1952, where he put on *La Parodie*, but his funds ran out before he could follow it with *Godot*.
11. Beckett quoted by Knowlson in *Damned to Fame*, p. 385.
12. *L'Observateur*, August 1950. Quoted by Cohn in *From 'Desire' to 'Godot'*, p. 104.
13. In *From 'Desire' to 'Godot'*, Ruby Cohn quotes from a number of the critics in her discussion of the reception of *Les Chaises*; see especially p. 128. See also Marie-Claude Hubert, *Eugène Ionesco* (Paris: Seuil, 1990).
14. See Alfred Simon, *Beckett* (Paris: Belfond, 1983), p. 187.
15. See Knowlson, *Damned to Fame*, p. 386.
16. *Ibid.*
17. *Souvenirs et propos*, p. 83 ('Je vais fermer boutique, autant finir en beauté').
18. *From 'Desire' to 'Godot'*, pp. 19–20.
19. The list includes Georges Bataille, 'Le silence de Molloy' in *Critique* 48 (1951), Maurice Nadeau, 'Samuel Beckett ou le droit au silence' in *Les Temps Modernes* 75 (January 1952), and Maurice Blanchot, 'Où maintenant? Qui maintenant?' in *N.N.R.F.* 1: 10 (October 1953).

20. These and other critical reactions are quoted by Cohn in *From 'Desire' to 'Godot'*, pp. 156–9.

21. *Le Figaro Littéraire*, 17 January 1953; quoted by Cohn in *From 'Desire' to 'Godot'*, pp. 157–8.

22. *Combat*, 17 January 1953; quoted by Cohn, ed., *Casebook*, p. 25.

23. *Les Lettres Françaises*, 15 January 1953; quoted by Cohn in *From 'Desire' to 'Godot'*, p. 157.

24. Jean Duvignaud, for example, used the term 'jansénisme', which had often been invoked when discussing Copeau's work, describing the production as 'une révélation: la maîtrise du jeu des acteurs, le jansénisme de la mise en scène mis au service d'un dialogue de vagabonds hallucinés. Un public hébété.' Quoted by Odette Aslan in *Roger Blin: Qui êtes-vous?* (Lyon: La Manufacture, 1990), p. 330. This is the French version of the Cambridge University Press publication cited in the following note.

25. Odette Aslan, *Roger Blin*, trans. Ruby Cohn (Cambridge University Press, 1988), p. 30. The French text of this book, slightly different and with some additional material, appeared two years later (see note 24).

26. Mark Batty, 'Roger Blin – Le point de repère de la rigueur: A study of his methodology through an assessment of his work', PhD thesis, University of Hull, 1995 (no page nos.). (Batty gleaned this information during a conversation with Jean Martin dated 10 January 1995.)

27. *From 'Desire' to 'Godot'*, p. 153.

28. Aslan, *Roger Blin: Qui êtes-vous?*, p. 139.

29. Blin, *Souvenirs et propos*, p. 58 ('Je ne me suis jamais préoccupé de marquer mes mises en scène d'une espèce de permanence Blin').

30. *Ibid.*, p. 83 ('une solidarité entre maigres').

31. *Ibid.*, p. 85. In the 1950s and 1960s the circus metaphor was often uppermost in the minds of interpreters and it was common for Vladimir and Estragon to be described as clowns. This tendency became far less common from the 1970s onwards.

32. *Ibid.*, p. 86.

33. *Ibid.*, p. 95.

34. *Ibid.*, p. 88.

35. *Ibid.*, p. 89.

36. *Ibid.*, p. 88.

37. Quoted by Aslan in *Roger Blin*, p. 35.

38. Quoted by Blin in *Souvenirs et propos*, p. 90.
39. *Ibid.*
40. Aslan, *Roger Blin*, p. 35, supplemented with information from Batty, 'Roger Blin'.
41. The photocopy of the prompt copy can be consulted in the Samuel Beckett Archive at the University of Reading. It shows that Beckett cut material amounting to about four pages in the course of rehearsals. These cuts are discussed in Batty, 'Roger Blin'.
42. Batty, 'Roger Blin'.
43. *Ibid.*
44. Renée Saurel, *Les Lettres Françaises*, 15 January 1953; quoted by Batty, 'Roger Blin'.
45. Beckett, letter to Blin dated 9 January 1953, translated and quoted by Deirdre Bair, *Samuel Beckett*, pp. 428–9.

4. The first productions in English

1. Quoted by Knowlson in *Damned to Fame*, p. 415.
2. *Ibid.*, p. 414.
3. Colin Chambers, *Peggy: The Life of Margaret Ramsey, Play Agent* (London: Nick Hern Books, 1997), p. 56.
4. J. W. Lambert, 'The London Theatre Season' in Harold Hobson, ed., *International Theatre Annual* 1 (London: Calder, 1956), p. 14. I am indebted to Dan Rebellato for pointing this out in his *1956 and All That* (London: Routledge, 1999).
5. Ivor Brown, ed., *Theatre 1955–6* (London: Max Reinhardt, 1956), pp. 7–8.
6. The cuts demanded by the Lord Chamberlain included the references to Christ at the end of Act I from 'But you can't go barefoot' to 'And they crucified quick' and the first fifteen lines of Lucky's 'Think'. Although these deletions were not necessary for the Arts Theatre 'club' production, the offending lines had to be removed when the production transferred to the Criterion, a public theatre. See Knowlson, *Damned to Fame*, p. 412.
7. See Chambers, *Peggy*, pp. 56–7.
8. Quoted by Colin Duckworth in the introduction to his edition of *En attendant Godot*, p. lxxvii.

9. Quoted by Knowlson, *Damned to Fame*, p. 414.

10. See note 15 below.

11. In *Samuel Beckett's Theatre*, Katharine Worth reproduces two startling early set designs by Peter Snow which show a large tree growing through the floor and walls of a room on stage. She notes that Snow's instinct was to move the stage design away from naturalism, but reports that, in the end, he and Hall decided on the rather more realistic tree, bank of reeds and so on as 'a way of helping the actors to meet the formidable challenge presented by a bare stage in 1955' (p. 28).

12. See Stephen Fay, *Power Play: The Life and Times of Peter Hall* (London: Hodder and Stoughton, 1995), p. 76.

13. Peter Hall, *Making an Exhibition of Myself* (London: Sinclair Stevenson, 1993), p. 107.

14. Hall is engagingly frank about the way the success of the play changed his life. It encouraged both Tennessee Williams and Harold Pinter to ask him to direct their work; it led to an offer to direct at Stratford-on-Avon; and it even brought him a wife: 'Because of it, Leslie Caron asked for me as her director when she did *Gigi* in London. We worked together, fell in love and married.' (Quoted from the programme note for the production at the Old Vic in 1997.)

15. 'Waiting for What?', BBC Third Programme, 14 April 1961, National Sound Archive, ref. no. T 5565 W.

16. See Dan Rebellato's discussion of the gradual 'taming' of the audience in the course of the 1950s in *1956 and All That*, pp. 104–13.

17. Recounted in the course of the radio discussion 'Waiting for What?'.

18. Telephone interview with Timothy Bateson (6 March 1998).

19. *Ibid.*

20. As recalled by Alan Schneider in his autobiographical *Entrances: An American Director's Journey* (New York: Viking, 1986), p. 225.

21. Telephone interview with Peter Woodthorpe (14 March 1998).

22. Alan Schneider's account of the experience of watching the production in the company of the author reads as follows (*Entrances*, p. 225):

> My fondest memories are of Beckett's clutching my arm from time to time and, in a clearly heard stage whisper, saying, 'It's ahl wrahng! He's doing it ahl wrahng!' about a particuler bit of stage business or the interpretation of a certain line. He particularly erupted when the Boy

at the end of the second act pointed to the heavens when he was asked by Vladimir where Mr. Godot lived.

James Knowlson records Beckett commenting in a letter to Pamela Mitchell (16 December 1955) that 'Peter Woodthorpe's playing of Estragon, with his natural Yorkshire accent, [was] superb.' (*Damned to Fame*, p. 417.)

23. Several anecdotes of this kind are recounted in 'Waiting for What?'. Knowlson and Duckworth both include others.

24. Alec Clunes, *The British Theatre* (London: Cassell, 1964), p. 73.

25. N. C., 'Philosophy of Despair at the Pike', *Irish Press*, 29 October 1955.

26. R. M. Fox, 'Pike Players in *Waiting for Godot*', *Dublin Evening Mail*, 29 October 1955.

27. J. J. Finegan, 'Dublin Premier of *Waiting for Godot*', *Dublin Evening Herald*, 29 October 1955.

28. *Ibid.*

29. Quoted by Carolyn Swift in *Stage by Stage* (Swords, Co. Dublin: Poolbeg Press, 1985), p. 183.

30. R. M. Fox, 'Pike Players in *Waiting for Godot*'.

31. Swift, *Stage by Stage*, p. 190.

32. Ulick O'Connor, '*Waiting for Godot*', *Dublin Opinion*, January 1956.

5. Early productions in the United States

1. Quoted by James Knowlson, *Damned to Fame*, p. 413.

2. Schneider, *Entrances*, pp. 222–3.

3. Quoted by Ruby Cohn in *From 'Desire' to 'Godot'*, p. 160.

4. See Knowlson, *Damned to Fame*, p. 411.

5. Schneider, *Entrances*, p. 224.

6. *Ibid.*, p. 227.

7. Alan Schneider, ' "Any Way You Like, Alan": Working with Beckett', *Theatre Quarterly* 5: 19 (1975), p. 34.

8. *Ibid.*, p. 35.

9. Stanley Green, *The Great Clowns of Broadway* (New York: Oxford University Press, 1984), p. 104.

10. *Ibid.*

11. John Lahr, *Notes on a Cowardly Lion: The Biography of Bert Lahr* (New York: Limelight Editions, 1984), p. 256.
12. Schneider, *Entrances*, p. 228.
13. *Ibid.*
14. *Ibid.*, p. 230.
15. *Ibid.*, p. 232.
16. Lahr, *Notes on a Cowardly Lion*, p. 274.
17. *Ibid.*, p. 262.
18. Schneider, *Entrances*, p. 229.
19. Lahr, *Notes on a Cowardly Lion*, p. 270.
20. Schneider, *Entrances*, p. 235.
21. Quoted by Lahr in *Notes on a Cowardly Lion*, p. 274.
22. *Ibid.*, p. 276.
23. Brooks Atkinson, 'Beckett's *Waiting for Godot*', *New York Times*, 20 April 1956.
24. Richard Watts, quoted by Lahr in *Notes on a Cowardly Lion*, p. 280.
25. Kenneth Tynan, *Curtains* (London: Longmans, 1961), p. 272.
26. Beckett, *Proust* (London: Calder and Boyars, 1965), p. 19.
27. Herbert Blau in Lois Oppenheim, ed., *Directing Beckett* (Ann Arbor: University of Michigan Press, 1994), p. 50.
28. *Ibid.*
29. *Ibid.*, p. 51.
30. *Ibid.*, p. 52.
31. *Ibid.*
32. The source of this information is a verbal account of the production given to me by Alan Mandell (recorded on audio tape in September 2000).
33. Blau in Oppenheim, ed., *Directing Beckett*, p. 52.
34. Once again, however, the scandalous nature of the production appears to have made the authorities nervous, since they informed the theatre that it would be 'inadvisable' for the company's stage manager, Jim Kershaw, to accompany it to Brussels. This was the era of McCarthy and no further reason was given for the ban on Kershaw.
35. For Blau's account of the performances in New York and the triumphant reception in Brussels see his *The Impossible Theater: A Manifesto* (New York: Macmillan, 1964), p. 236.

36. *Ibid.*, p. 231.
37. *Ibid.*, p. 232.
38. *Ibid.*, p. 231.
39. *Ibid.*, p. 233.
40. *Ibid.*, p. 240.
41. *Ibid.*, p. 232.
42. A report in the *San Quentin News*, 28 November 1957.
43. This information comes from the same verbal account by Alan Mandell (see note 32 above), although Mandell notes that when he later performed the role of Lucky under Beckett's direction for the San Quentin Drama Workshop's production the costume was less elaborate and the bags were light.
44. Blau, *The Impossible Theater*, p. 245.
45. *Ibid.*
46. Quoted by Mandell (see note 32).
47. Letter from Rick Cluchey to the author dated 26 July 2000.
48. Editorial signed 'CB' [C. Bandman], *San Quentin News*, 28 November 1957.
49. Letter from Cluchey quoted above (see note 47).
50. See Knowlson's *Damned to Fame* for a comprehensive account of Cluchey's relationship with Beckett and productions of his work over the following decades.
51. The letter is reprinted in Blau, *The Impossible Theater*, p. 238.
52. *Ibid.*, p. 239.

6. Beckett's own production: Schiller-Theater, Berlin, March 1975

1. See James Knowlson's introduction to McMillan and Knowlson, eds., *The Theatrical Notebooks*, pp. xi–xxiii.
2. *The Theatrical Notebooks of Samuel Beckett*, vol. I: *Waiting for Godot*, edited with an introduction and notes by Dougald McMillan and James Knowlson (London: Faber, 1993). This volume brings together the revised text and a facsimile of Beckett's production notebook and is therefore the principal source for information about Beckett's production. The editorial notes on both text and production notebook are a model

of clarity and completeness, and the volume is thus quite indispensable for anyone interested in the production. It is also particularly useful as it includes comments about subsequent productions of *Waiting for Godot* by Walter Asmus which were modelled on it. The volume will be referred to as *TN* throughout this chapter.

3. Some examples of attempts to situate *Waiting for Godot* in specific, defined locations are discussed in the last chapters of this book.

4. Occasional attempts at changing these fundamental images have been made. See, for example, Anat Feinberg-Jütte's article '"The Task is not to Reproduce the External Form, but to Find the Subtext": George Tabori's Productions of Samuel Beckett's Texts', *Journal of Beckett Studies* 1:1–2 (1992), pp. 95–115. In this she describes a production of *Happy Days* which placed Winnie in bed, attended by a crippled Willie in a wheelchair. Feinberg-Jütte notes that the result was not entirely successful.

5. Quoted by Knowlson in *Damned to Fame*, p. 608.

6. This diary, originally published in *Theatre Quarterly* 5:19 (1975), pp. 19–26, was reprinted in an expanded version in Dougald McMillan and Martha Fehsenfeld, eds., *Beckett in the Theatre* (London: Calder, 1988), pp. 136–48. The wording of the two versions differs slightly, since both are translations from the original German. Quotations will be given with page references to both versions where a passage exists in both, using the abbreviations *TQ* for *Theatre Quarterly* and *BT* for *Beckett in the Theatre*.

7. *TQ*, p. 20; *BT*, p. 136.

8. *TQ*, p. 22; *BT*, p. 139.

9. Knowlson, *Damned to Fame*, p. 609.

10. *TQ*, p. 23; *BT*, p. 140.

11. *Ibid.*

12. The precise location of each of the *Wartestellen* was as follows:
   Act I
   1. Opening
   2. After Vladimir's line, 'At his horse.' (Faber 19/20; *TN* 19, line 377)
   3. After Pozzo's line, 'Pan sleeps.' (Faber 36; *TN* 34, line 944)
   4. After Pozzo's line, 'You see my memory is defective.' (Faber 38; *TN* 36, line 1026)

5. After Pozzo's line, 'The Net. He thinks he's entangled in a net.' (Faber 40; *TN* 38, line 1090) Beckett cut the text following on pages 40 and 41 of the Faber edition down as far as Estragon's line 'Nothing happens, nobody comes, nobody goes, it's awful!'

6. End of the act (the Schiller-Theater production had a five-second pause before the moonlight faded to black)

Act II

1. Opening

2. After the lullaby which Vladimir sings to Estragon (Faber 70; *TN* 63, line 2067)

3. After the dance which Vladimir and Estragon performed together to the waltz duet from *The Merry Widow* and which follows their reconciliation: Vladimir: 'Come to my arms!' Estragon: 'Your arms?' Vladimir: 'My breast!' Estragon: 'Off we go!' (Faber 76; *TN* 69, line 2277)

4. After Vladimir's line 'We are men.' (Faber 82; *TN* 75, line 2508)

5. After the moon rises and before Estragon wakes (Faber 92; *TN* 83, line 2824)

6. End of the act

13. *TQ*, p. 24; *BT*, p. 140.

14. See note 16 below.

15. These are the directions written in the notebook on pages 31 and 53 respectively. In the course of his rehearsals, Beckett sometimes altered or modified the images he had sketched out in his notebook (see Knowlson's commentary in *TN* for details) and this was a case in point. He ultimately decided against this symmetrical arrangement of E looking down while V looked up (the phrases I have quoted from the notebook are scored out with a red line). But Walter Asmus reinstated the symmetrical arrangement in his English-language productions copying Beckett's original, and the device has often been repeated by subsequent directors (see the analysis of the productions by Walter Asmus and Peter Hall chapter 9).

16. *TQ*, p. 21; *BT*, p. 137.

17. *Ibid.*

18. *BT*, p. 141. (Not in *TQ*.)

19. *TN*, p. 389 (the editors note that this is evidently a post-production entry in the notebook).

20. See the following note in *TN*, p. 409: 'K. D. Friedrich is the German Romantic painter, Caspar David Friedrich (1774–1840) whose painting *Zwei Männer betrachten den Mond* in the Gemäldgalerie, Dresden, provided Beckett with a model for the tableaux at the end of each act of his play.'

21. See *TN*, p. 90. This is a particularly telling example of Beckett's concern for the overall mood and poetic atmosphere. It demonstrates his Modernist (as opposed to postmodern) instincts, wanting to preserve not break the dramatic illusion established. Although Vladimir and Estragon constantly refer to their own situation on stage and are conscious, like Hamm, of being part of something 'taking its course', the literality of their situation (see chapter 2) would be diminished by having them reappear as the actors Wigger and Bollmann.

22. Quoted by Ruby Cohn in *Just Play: Beckett's Theater* (Princeton University Press, 1980), p. 231. This comment was recorded by Charles Marowitz in his 'Paris Log', *Encore* (March 1962), p. 44.

23. See, for example, Michel Vinaver, *Ecrits sur le théâtre* (Lausanne: L'Aire, 1982), p. 289.

24. *TQ*, p. 23; *BT*, p. 140.

25. Knowlson, *Damned to Fame*, p. 609.

26. *TQ*, p. 26; cut from *BT* (p. 147).

27. *TQ*, pp. 22–3; *BT*, p. 139.

28. *TQ*, p. 23; *BT*, p. 140.

29. *TQ*, p. 24; *BT*, p. 140.

30. *TQ*, p. 26; *BT*, p. 148.

31. Bondy used the published French text; the programme announced ninety minutes for Act I and seventy-five for Act II, though when it visited the Festival Hall in August 2000 it in fact ran eighty and seventy minutes respectively.

7. 'Fail again. Fail better.'

1. Friedrich Luft, 'Beckett produces Beckett: West Berlin, 1975' in Cohn, ed., *Casebook*, p. 46.

2. Erika Munk, 'Only the Possible: An Interview with Susan Sontag', *Theater* 24:3 (1993), p. 34.

3. Quoted by Knowlson, *Damned to Fame*, p. 674 (Beckett describing his method in beginning work on *Worstward Ho*).

4. The revised English text is available only in McMillan and Knowlson, eds., *The Theatrical Notebooks*. In the video versions the casts are as follows. English – Estragon: Lawrence Held; Vladimir: Bud Thorpe; Pozzo: Rick Cluchey; Lucky: Alan Mandell; Boy: Louis Beckett Cluchey. French – Estragon: Jean-François Balmer; Vladimir: Rufus; Pozzo: Jean-Pierre Jorris; Lucky: Roman Polanski; Boy: Philippe Deschamps.

5. See Knowlson, *Damned to Fame*, pp. 504–5, for an account of Beckett's tangled relationship with film companies.

6. *Ibid.*, p. 690.

7. Jonathan Kalb, *Beckett in Performance* (Cambridge University Press, 1989), p. 153.

8. A successful production of Shakespeare's *Richard III* in which setting and costumes were used to suggest Britain becoming a Fascist state in the 1920s or 1930s was directed by Sir Richard Eyre, with Ian McKellan as Richard, at London's National Theatre in 1994 and later filmed.

9. Beckett on Joyce in *Our Exagmination Round His Factification For Incamination Of Work In Progress* (London: Faber [reprint], 1959), p. 14.

10. Oppenheim, ed., *Directing Beckett*, p. 52.

11. Otomar Krejča, 'Entretien de Denis Bablet avec Otomar Krejča', video-tape (Paris: Serddav/CNRS, 1978).

12. This solution for the stage floor has been adopted for many productions, notably that of Yukio Ninagawa discussed later in this chapter and that of Luc Bondy discussed in chapter 9.

13. Félie Pastorello, 'La Réception par la presse' in Denis Bablet, ed., *Les Voies de la création théâtrale*, vol. X (Paris: Centre National de la Recherche Scientifique, 1982), p. 249.

14. Beckett, *Théâtre*, vol. I, p. 107. This line was cut by Beckett from his original English translation, but reinstated in the revised text: 'No doubt, we're on a plateau, served up on a plateau' (McMillan and Knowlson, eds., *The Theatrical Notebooks*, p. 67).

15. In the 1991 Prague production these costumes looked a little more specific: several critics commented that the costumes called to mind 'the dark, wear-worn clothes of wandering Jews or figures out of Kafka' (*Mladý svět* 2:34 (1992), pp. 42–3).

16. Odette Aslan, '*En attendant Godot* de Samuel Beckett' in Bablet, ed., *Les Voies de la création théâtrale*, pp. 188–237.

17. *Ibid.*, p. 216.

18. *Ibid.*, p. 216.

19. *Ibid.*, p. 237.

20. *Ibid.*, p. 239.

21. *Ibid.*, p. 232.

22. This is a point in the play where a number of interestingly divergent alternatives have been found in production. In the Luc Bondy production analysed in chapter 9, for example, Serge Merlin's repeated 'Vous voulez vous en débarrasser?' became quieter and quieter, as if he despaired of ever getting a reply.

23. Aslan, '*En attendant Godot*', p. 230.

24. *Ibid.*, p. 230.

25. From the videotape cited in note 11.

26. Pastorello, 'La Réception par la presse', pp. 240–50.

27. I am grateful to David Short, of the London University School of Slavonic and Eastern European Languages, for translations of the programme and of other essays on the production in Czech.

28. *Plzeňský denik*, 19 March 1993.

29. Tabori's production was part of what he called his 'Beckett-project', which comprised a number of productions in the course of the 1980s. His broad aim was to 'find the subtext' – see Feinberg-Jütte, '"The Task is not to Reproduce the External Form, but to Find the Subtext"'.

30. Kalb, *Beckett in Performance*, p. 91.

31. This opening was simplified after the opening performances, so as to avoid the necessity of having so many people on stage: the stage manager simply came on and called the names of the actors, who then appeared.

32. Kalb, *Beckett in Performance*, pp. 91–2.

33. Feinberg-Jütte, '"The Task is not to Reproduce the External Form, but to Find the Subtext"', p. 107.

34. *Ibid.*, p. 104

35. See George Tabori, 'Warten auf Beckett', *Theater Heute* 13 (1984), pp. 78–84.

36. In rehearsal with the actors Tabori exploited ideas drawn from Keith Johnstone's book *Impro*, especially his use of 'status games'. A detailed

account of this process is included in a recent doctoral thesis by Antje Diedrich: '"The stage is not a different country, but an extension of the bathroom": George Tabori's theatre practice as an investigation into the relationship between art and life', PhD thesis, Liverpool John Moores University (2000).

37. Kalb, *Beckett in Performance*, p. 92. The subway tunnel is a reference to JoAnne Akalitis's much contested production of *Endgame*.
38. Samuel Beckett, 'Three Dialogues' in *Proust and Three Dialogues with Georges Duthuit* (London: Calder and Boyars, 1965), p. 103.
39. Cobi Bordewijk, 'The Integrity of the Playtext: Disputed Performances of *Waiting for Godot*' in Marius Buning, Sjef Houppermans and Danièle de Ruyter, eds., *Samuel Beckett Today/Aujourd'hui*, vol. 1: *1970–1989* (Amsterdam and Atlanta: Rodopi, 1992), p. 147.
40. *Ibid.*, p. 147.
41. This is the agency which acts on behalf of all French authors, tracing its origins back to the eighteenth century.
42. Bordewijk, 'The Integrity of the Playtext', p. 152.
43. Mariko Hori Tanako, 'Special Features of Beckett Performances in Japan' in Lois Oppenheim and Marius Buning, eds., *Beckett On and On...* (New Jersey, London and Ontario: Associated University Presses, 1996), p. 230.
44. *Ibid.*, p. 237.
45. *Ibid.*, p. 237.
46. Low-class Sumo wrestlers find themselves reduced to being semi-slaves to their patrons. I am grateful to Mika Sato for her help in understanding the version broadcast on Japanese televison.
47. Junko Matoba, '*Waiting for Godot* in Tokyo', *The Beckett Circle (Tokyo) Newsletter*, Spring 1995, p. 3.
48. Xerxes Mehta, 'Ghosts' in Oppenheim, ed., *Directing Beckett*, p. 179.
49. *Ibid.*, p. 181.

8. *Godot* in political context

1. I am indebted to Dina Djurović for her research on this production. The quotation, and much of the information, comes from a book by Felix Pašić, *Kako smo Čekali Godoa Kad su Cvetale Tikue* (Belgrade: Vepar Press, 1992).

2. It was quickly followed, on 25 January 1957, by the first Polish production at the Wspótczesny theatre in Warsaw. At the same time, the Polish text was published in one of the first issues of *Dialog*, a journal which became an influential channel for making Western dramatic work known in Poland.

3. See, for example, Elin Diamond, 'Re: Blau, Butler, Beckett and the Politics of Seeming', *Drama Review* 44:4 (T168, 2000), pp. 31–43, and Lois Oppenheim, 'Playing with Beckett's Plays: On Sontag in Sarajevo and Other Directorial Infidelities', *Journal of Beckett Studies* 4:2 (Spring 1995), pp. 25–46.

4. Susan Sontag, 'Godot Comes to Sarajevo', *New York Review of Books*, 21 October 1993, p. 52.

5. *Ibid.*, p. 55.

6. *Ibid.*, p. 54.

7. *Ibid.*, p. 56.

8. *Ibid.*, p. 56.

9. *Ibid.*, p. 52.

10. *Ibid.*, p. 57.

11. *Ibid.*, p. 59.

12. Diamond, 'Re: Blau, Butler, Beckett and the Politics of Seeming', p. 40.

13. See Klaus Volker, ed., *Beckett in Berlin* (Berlin: Hentrich, Frölich und Kaufmann, 1985), p. 48.

14. Donald Howarth, from the programme for the performance at the Old Vic Theatre, 17 February 1981. Beckett said the same thing to his actors during rehearsals for the Schiller-Theater production; see chapter 6, p. 133.

15. Ilan Ronen, '*Waiting for Godot* as Political Theatre' in Oppenheim, ed., *Directing Beckett*, p. 240.

16. *Ibid.*

17. *Ibid.*

18. Ronen notes that he was approached by Doron Tavory, 'a Jewish actor considered to be the star of the Haifa Municipal Theatre', who wanted to play Lucky, both for the challenge of the monologue and in order to express his political solidarity with the suffering imposed on the Arabs. His mastery of the literary Arabic of Lucky's 'Think' was such that 'even Arab spectators were convinced that they were

watching an Arab actor'. Ronen, '*Waiting for Godot* as Political Theatre', p. 244.

19. Dan Urian, *The Arab in Israeli Drama and Theatre* (London: Harwood, 1999), p. 91.
20. Ronen, '*Waiting for Godot* as Political Theatre', p. 246.
21. *Ibid.*, p. 245.
22. Shoshana Weitz, 'Mr Godot will not come today' in Hannah Scolnicov and Peter Holland, eds., *The Play Out of Context: Transferring Plays from Culture to Culture* (Cambridge University Press, 1989), pp. 186–98.
23. Joël Jouanneau, 'Non pas l'Homme, mais cet Homme' in Lallias and Arnault, eds., *Théâtre Aujourd' hui*, p. 38.
24. *Ibid.*
25. Colette Godard in *Le Monde*, 9 February 1991; Mathilde la Bardonnie in *Libération*, 11 February 1991.
26. Ginette Hébert, 'Entre l'arbre et la patère: le doigt de Brassard', *Jeu* 64 (1992), p. 18 (my translation).
27. The first East German performance was in 1987 and the first Bulgarian performance in 1988. See Werner Huber, 'Godot, Gorba and Glasnost: Beckett in East Germany' in Marius Buning and Lois Oppenheim, eds., *Samuel Beckett Today/Aujourd' hui*, vol. II: *Beckett in the 1990s* (Amsterdam and Atlanta: Rodopi, 1993), pp. 49–57. I am indebted to Anna Ganev for information about the performance in Bulgaria, given by the Theatre of the National Army, and seen by Bulgarians as an important moment in the re-conquest of freedom.
28. For an analysis of this play, see Harry H. Kuoshu, 'Will Godot Come by Bus or through a Trace? Discussion of a Chinese Absurdist Play', *Modern Drama* 41 (1998), pp. 461–73.
29. Quoted by François Hauter, 'Gao, méconnu en son pays', *Le Figaro*, 14/15 October 2000, p. 34.
30. Kalb, *Beckett in Performance*, p. 252.

9. Productions at the end of the twentieth century

1. See chapter 2, note 6.
2. In interviews given at the time of his production, Peter Hall made a point of expressing his disgust that the publishers had not yet brought out an affordable edition of this text.

3. In an interview with Eric Prince, Hall said: 'Having lived with this text now over a period of rehearsal I now know why he did everything he did [meaning the cuts and changes made in the text by Beckett]. You can feel it and understand it. This is a ruthless professional theatre practitioner looking at his own work and saying: that I need, that I do not need; that works, that does not; that needs clarification. It is tight as a drum. It is a wonderful text. It has a Mozartian simplicity and clarity.' Eric Prince, 'Forty Years On: Peter Hall's Godot', *Journal of Beckett Studies* 8:2 (Spring 1999), p. 53.

4. *Ibid.*, p. 52.

5. Goodwin, John, ed., *Peter Hall's Diaries: The Story of a Dramatic Battle* (London: Hamish Hamilton, 1983), p. 230. Hall went so far as to write: 'It is a masterpiece . . . It revived my shaken faith in the theatre.'

6. Prince, 'Forty Years On', p. 54.

7. *Ibid.*, pp. 55–6.

8. This is mentioned by almost all the reviewers.

9. Prince, 'Forty Years On', p. 48.

10. Timed at the Barbican on 2 September 1999. In a discussion with the audience after the performance on 2 September, Asmus claimed that this was quicker than the same production when adapted to (American) English for the San Quentin Drama Workshop in 1984, when it had run for fifteen minutes longer.

11. In the following analysis, the reader should assume that unless otherwise stated the details of Asmus' production were the same as in Beckett's production.

12. See McMillan and Knowlson, eds., *The Theatrical Notebooks*, pp. 332–43.

13. See, in addition to works by Knowlson already cited, 'Beckett as Director: The Manuscript Production Notebooks and Critical Interpretation', *Modern Drama* 30:4 (December 1987), pp. 451–65.

14. For a discussion of Beckett in relation to Artaud, see Kalb, *Beckett in Performance*, pp. 146–9.

15. 'Une fois la toute puissance de l'action et la psychologie battue en brèche, l'émergence de la "scène" et de son langage spécifique – refoulés du "théâtre occidental", dès l'origine, selon Artaud – devient possible. Ce langage physique, lié à l'espace et à toute la matérialité de la scène (corps, objets, mouvements, sons, lumières . . .) devient premier, originaire,

constitutif. Il participe, au même titre que la parole et l'action, à une écriture en volume d'un type nouveau. L'espace et la parole sont tissés dans un même ensemble, un même objet théâtral. L'espace et tous les éléments du langage scénique acquièrent un rôle dans la dynamique de la pièce: ils parlent, ils agissent.' Pierre Chabert, 'Singularité de Samuel Beckett', p. 9 (my translation).

16. Blau, *The Impossible Theater*, p. 232.
17. Jacques Lecoq, *Le Corps poétique* (Arles: Actes Sud, 1997), pp. 141–5; English translation, *The Moving Body* (London: Methuen, 2000), pp. 132–7.
18. This production opened in February 1999, was seen at the festivals of Lisbon, Strasbourg and Sarajevo, and was then revived in Spanish in Madrid in November 2000.
19. *Diari de Tarragona*, 6 February 1999. ('El escenario refleja esa inquietud y angustia para representar el vacío, ese camino que Beckett dijo que era el no-sitio.')
20. *El Periodico*, 5 February 1999.
21. *El Periodico del Lunes*, 8 February 1999.
22. Kalb, *Beckett in Performance*, p. 149.
23. *Ibid.*, pp. 147–8.

Conclusion

1. *Guardian*, 15 August 1998.
2. Graver, *Beckett: 'Waiting for Godot'*, pp. 93–110
3. Mel Gussow, *Conversations with (and about) Beckett* (London: Nick Hern Books, 1996), p. 33 (conversation dated 24 June 1978).
4. That of George Tabori – see chapter 7.
5. Beckett, *Proust*, p. 19.

SELECT BIBLIOGRAPHY

Abbott, H. Porter, *Beckett Writing Beckett: The Author in the Autograph* (Ithaca and London: Cornell University Press, 1996).

Alvarez, A., *Beckett* (London: Collins, 1973).

Aslan, Odette, '*En attendant Godot* de Samuel Beckett' in Denis Bablet, ed., *Les Voies de la création théâtrale*, vol. X (Paris: Centre National de la Recherche Scientifique, 1982), pp. 188–237.

Roger Blin, trans. Ruby Cohn (Cambridge University Press, 1988).

Asmus, Walter, 'Beckett Directs Beckett', *Theatre Quarterly* 5:19 (1975), pp. 19–26.

Bablet, Denis, ed., *Les Voies de la création théâtrale*, vol. X (Paris: Centre National de la Recherche Scientifique, 1982).

Batty, Mark, 'Roger Blin – Le point de repère de la rigueur: A study of his methodology through an assessment of his work' (PhD thesis, University of Hull, 1995).

Ben-Zvi, Linda, *Samuel Beckett* (Boston: Twayne, 1986).

'Samuel Beckett, Fritz Mauthner, and the Limits of Language', *PMLA*, March 1980, pp. 183–200.

Ben-Zvi, Linda, ed., *Women in Beckett: Performance and Critical Perspectives* (Illinois: University of Illinois Press, 1990).

Blau, Herbert, *The Impossible Theater: A Manifesto* (New York: Macmillan, 1964).

Blin, Roger, *Souvenirs et propos*, ed. Lynda Bellity Peskine (Paris: Gallimard, 1986).

Bordewijk, Cobi, 'The Integrity of the Playtext: Disputed Performances of *Waiting for Godot*' in Marius Buning, Sjef Houppermans and Danièle de Ruyter, eds., *Samuel Beckett Today/Aujourd'hui*, vol. I: *1970–1989* (Amsterdam and Atlanta: Rodopi, 1992), pp. 143–52.

Brater, Enoch, *Beckett at Eighty: Beckett in Context* (Oxford University Press, 1986).

Why Beckett? (London: Thames and Hudson, 1989).

Burkman, Katherine, ed., *Myth and Ritual in the Plays of Samuel Beckett* (New Jersey: Associated University Presses, 1987).

Calder, John, *As No Other Dare Fail* (London: Calder, 1986).

Calder, John, ed., *Beckett at Sixty: A Festschrift* (London: Calder and Boyars, 1967).

Chabert, Pierre, 'Beckett as Director', *Gambit* 28 (1976), pp. 41–64.

The Body in Beckett's Theatre (Princeton University Press, 1980).

'Singularité de Samuel Beckett' in Jean-Claude Lallias and Jean-Jacques Arnault, eds., *Théâtre Aujourd'hui* 3: *L'Univers scénique de Samuel Beckett* (Paris: Centre National de la Documentation Pédagogique, 1994), pp. 3–24.

Chabert, Pierre, ed., *Revue d'Esthétique*, special Beckett edition (Toulouse: Editions Privat, 1986).

Chaikin, Joe, *The Presence of the Actor* (New York: Atheneum, 1972).

Chambers, Colin, *Peggy: The Life of Margaret Ramsay, Play Agent* (London: Nick Hern Books, 1997).

Chambers, L. R., 'Antonin Artaud and the Contemporary French Theatre' in *Aspects of Drama and the Theatre: Five Kathleen Robinson Lectures* (Sydney University Press, 1965).

Coe, Richard N., *Samuel Beckett* (London: Oliver and Boyd, 1964; rev. edn, New York: Grove Press, 1968).

Cohn, Ruby, *Back to Beckett* (Princeton University Press, 1973).

The Comic Gamut (New Jersey: Rutgers University Press, 1962).

From 'Desire' to 'Godot': Pocket Theater of Postwar Paris (Berkeley and Los Angeles: University of California Press, 1987).

Just Play: Beckett's Theater (Princeton University Press, 1980).

Cohn, Ruby, ed., *Samuel Beckett: 'Waiting for Godot': A Casebook* (Houndmills: Macmillan, 1987).

Cooke, Virginia, ed., *Beckett on File* (London: Methuen, 1985).

Cousineau, Thomas, *'Waiting for Godot': Form in Movement* (Boston: Twayne, 1991).

Davison, P. H., 'Contemporary Drama and Popular Dramatic Forms' in *Aspects of Drama and the Theatre: Five Kathleen Robinson Lectures* (Sydney University Press, 1965).

Contemporary Drama and the Popular Dramatic Tradition (Houndmills: Macmillan, 1983).

Duckworth, Colin, ed., *Samuel Beckett: 'En attendant Godot'* (London: Harrap, 1966).

Esslin, Martin, *The Theatre of the Absurd*, rev. edn (Harmondsworth: Penguin, 1968).

Esslin, Martin, ed., *Samuel Beckett: A Collection of Critical Essays* (Englewood Cliffs: Prentice Hall, 1965).

Fletcher, John, and Spurling, John, *Beckett: A Study of his Plays* (London: Eyre Methuen, 1972).

Gontarski, Stanley E., *The Intent of Undoing in Samuel Beckett's Dramatic Texts* (Bloomington: Indiana University Press, 1985).

   'Revising Himself: Performance as Text in Samuel Beckett's Theatre', *Journal of Modern Literature* 22:1 (Fall 1998), pp. 131–55.

Gontarski, Stanley E., ed., *On Beckett* (New York: Grove Press, 1986).

Graver, Lawrence, *Beckett: 'Waiting for Godot'* (Cambridge University Press, 1989).

Graver, Lawrence, and Federman, Raymond, eds., *Samuel Beckett: The Critical Heritage* (London: Routledge and Kegan Paul, 1979).

Green, Stanley, *The Great Clowns of Broadway* (New York: Oxford University Press, 1984).

Gussow, Mel, *Conversations with (and about) Beckett* (London: Nick Hern Books, 1996).

Hall, Peter, *Making an Exhibition of Myself* (London: Sinclair Stevenson, 1993).

Huber, Werner, 'Godot, Gorba and Glasnost: Beckett in East Germany' in Marius Buning and Lois Oppenheim, eds., *Samuel Beckett Today/Aujourd'hui*, vol. II: *Beckett in the 1990s* (Amsterdam and Atlanta: Rodopi, 1993), pp. 49–57.

Kalb, Jonathan, *Beckett in Performance* (Cambridge University Press, 1989).

Kennedy, Andrew, *Samuel Beckett* (Cambridge University Press, 1989).

Knowlson, James, *Damned to Fame: The Life of Samuel Beckett* (London: Bloomsbury, 1996).

Knowlson, James, and Pilling, John, *Frescoes of the Skull: The Recent Prose and Drama of Samuel Beckett* (London: Calder, 1979).

Lahr, John, *Notes on a Cowardly Lion: The Biography of Bert Lahr* (New York: Limelight Editions, 1984).

Lallias, Jean-Claude, and Arnault, Jean-Jacques, eds., *Théâtre Aujourd'hui* 3: *L'Univers scénique de Samuel Beckett* (Paris: Centre National de Documentation Pédagogique, 1994).

Levy, Shimon, *Samuel Beckett's Self-Referential Drama: The Three I's* (Houndmills: Macmillan, 1990).

Mahmood, Shaheen M., 'Beckett in Bangladesh' in Marius Buning and Lois Oppenheim, eds., *Samuel Beckett Today/Aujourd'hui*, vol. II: *Beckett in the 1990s* (Amsterdam and Atlanta: Rodopi, 1993), pp. 59–65.

Mercier, Vivian, *Beckett/Beckett* (Oxford University Press, 1977).

McCarthy, Gerry, 'Emptying the Theatre: On Directing the Plays of Samuel Beckett' in Oppenheim, Lois, ed., *Directing Beckett* (Ann Arbor: University of Michigan Press, 1994), pp. 250–67.

McMillan, Dougald, and Fehsenfeld, Martha, *Beckett in the Theatre* (London: Calder, 1988).

McMillan, Dougald, and Knowlson, James, eds., *The Theatrical Notebooks of Samuel Beckett*, vol. I: *Waiting for Godot* (London: Faber, 1993).

McMullan, Anna, *Theatre on Trial: Samuel Beckett's Later Drama* (London: Routledge, 1993).

Oppenheim, Lois, ed., *Directing Beckett* (Ann Arbor: University of Michigan Press, 1994).

Oppenheim, Lois, and Buning, Marius, eds., *Beckett On and On . . .* (New Jersey, London and Ontario: Associated University Presses, 1996).

Pountney, Rosemary, *Theatre of Shadows: Samuel Beckett's Drama 1956–76* (Gerrards Cross: Colin Smythe, 1988).

Rebellato, Dan, *1956 and All That* (London: Routledge, 1999).

Reid, Alec, *All I Can Manage More Than I Could: An Approach to the Plays of Samuel Beckett* (Dublin: Dolmen Press, 1968).

Ricks, Christopher, *Beckett's Dying Words* (Oxford University Press, 1993).

Robinson, Michael, *The Long Sonata of the Dead: A Study of Samuel Beckett* (New York: Grove Press, 1969).

Rojtman, Betty, *Forme et signification dans le théâtre de Beckett* (Paris: Nizet, 1976).

Schneider, Alan, *Entrances: An American Director's Journey* (New York: Viking 1986).

Simon, Alfred, *Beckett* (Paris: Belfond, 1983).

States, Bert O., *The Shape of Paradox: An Essay on 'Waiting for Godot'* (Berkeley: University of California Press, 1978).

Volker, Klaus, ed., *Beckett in Berlin* (Berlin: Hentrich, Frölich und Kaufmann, 1985).

Wilmer, S. E., ed., *Beckett in Dublin* (Dublin: Lilliput Press, 1992).

Worth, Katharine, *Samuel Beckett's Theatre: Life Journeys* (Oxford University Press, 1999).

'Waiting for Godot' and 'Happy Days' (Houndmills: Macmillan, 1990).

Worth, Katharine, ed., *Beckett the Shape Changer* (London: Routledge and Kegan Paul, 1975).

Zilliacus, Clas, *Beckett and Broadcasting: A Study of the Works of Samuel Beckett for and in Radio and Television* (Abo: Abo Akademi, 1976).

INDEX

Abbey Theatre (Dublin), 14
Abbott and Costello, 42
Abu-Varda, Yussef, 170–5
Actors Studio (New York), 89
Actors Workshop (San Francisco), 89,
    96–105
Adamov, Arthur, 21, 22, 23, 31, 42,
    47–50, 52, 59, 64, 70, 90
Adelaide Festival (Australia), 136
Aillaud, Gilles, 201
Akalitis, JoAnne, 137
Albery, Donald, 71, 83, 86, 88
Amat, Frederic, 205
Anouilh, Jean, 69, 72
Antoine, André, 5
Aragon, Louis, 54
Arden, John, 69, 71
Artaud, Antonin, 7, 21, 22, 23, 31, 47,
    48, 59, 198, 207, 209, 210, 211
Arts Theatre (Cambridge), 72
Arts Theatre (London), 67, 70, 71, 72,
    77, 79, 80, 82, 96
Aslan, Odette, 145, 146, 148
Asmus, Walter, 106, 112, 131–3, 135,
    136, 180, 185–95
At the Hawk's Well (Yeats), 14
Atelier theatre (Paris), 142
Atelier, 212 (Belgrade), 164
Atkinson, Brooks, 94
Audiberti, Jacques, 46
Avignon Theatre Festival, 140–8

Bair, Deirdre, 23, 153
Bal des voleurs, Le (Anouilh), 163

Ball, Hugo, 17, 18
Barbican Theatre (London), 185
Barrault, Jean-Louis, 64
Barthes, Roland, 8
Bartók, Bela, 75
Bateson, Timothy, 74–83, 114
Batty, Mark, 64
Baxter Theatre (Cape Town), 169
Beckett, Samuel
    Dream of Fair to Middling Women, 11
    Eleutheria, 13, 15–22, 28, 38, 46, 47
    Endgame, 96, 98, 104, 107, 108
    Film, 86
    Footfalls, 3, 107, 112
    Happy Days, 37, 107, 108, 137
    Innommable, L', 13
    Kid, The, 15, 19, 20
    Krapp's Last Tape, 26, 106, 107, 108
    Malone meurt, 13, 52
    Mercier et Camier, 13
    Molloy, 13, 52
    More Pricks than Kicks, 12
    Murphy, 12
    Not I, 33, 107, 112
    Play, 107
    Rockaby, 107
    Three Dialogues, 15
    Unnamable, The, 33
    Watt, 13
Belgrade Drama Theatre, 162, 163
Berghof, Herbert, 94
Berliner Ensemble, 3, 69, 97
Billington, Michael, 210
Bim and Bom, 42–3

Birthday Party, The (Pinter), 97
Blanchot, Maurice, 49
Blau, Herbert, 96–105, 139, 199, 211
Blin, Roger, 1, 23, 28, 37, 40, 45–66,
    70, 71, 76, 77, 82, 101, 108, 162,
    179, 197, 210
Blind, The (Maeterlinck), 34
Boesman and Lena (Fugard), 46
Bollmann, Horst, 111, 118, 119, 130
Bond, Edward, 71, 77, 201
Bondy, Luc, 200–5, 207, 210
Bordewijk, Cobi, 156
Bosch, Hieronymus, 94, 115
Bouffes du Nord theatre (Paris), 142
Bouquet, Michel, 146–9
Brahm, Otto, 5
Brando, Marlon, 86, 90
Brassard, André, 141, 177, 178
Brecht, Bertolt, 2, 3, 8, 52, 69, 97, 109,
    168, 209
Brennan, Stephen, 185, 189, 190
Breton, André, 21
Brook, Peter, 8, 142, 199
Brooklyn Academy of Music (New
    York), 135
Brouwer, Adriaen, 115
Brown, Ivor, 69
Bruegel, Pieter, 94, 115, 116
Büchner, Georg, 45
Bull, Peter, 61, 74–83, 85
Burton, André, 142
Bus-Stop, The (Gao Xingjian), 178, 179
Butler, Robert, 182
Byrne, Austin, 85

Cage, The (Cluchey), 104
Cantatrice chauve, La (Ionesco), 21, 48
Cavell, Stanley, 31
Cenci, Les (Artaud), 22
Chabert, Pierre, 3, 198
Chaises, Les (Ionesco), 49, 50, 53
Chambers, Colin, 68
Chambers, Ross, 16

Chaplin, Charlie, 14, 19, 35
Chattot, François, 204
Chekhov, Anton, 5, 100, 150, 209
Chéreau, Patrice, 175
Cherry Orchard, The (Chekhov), 150
Chopin, Frédéric, 125, 126, 137
Cid, Le (Corneille), 15, 19
Clapp, Susannah, 182
Cluchey, Rick, 102–4, 136
Clunes, Alec, 72, 83
Cocktail Party, The (Eliot), 70
Coconut Grove (Miami), 86, 93, 94
Cocteau, Jean, 69
Coeur à gaz, Le (Tzara), 18
Cohn, Ruby, 24, 25, 31, 48, 52, 56, 134
Copeau, Jacques, 55
Craig, Edward Gordon, 5, 6, 7, 8, 10,
    15, 29, 32, 34, 36, 106, 131, 195,
    209
Crave (Kane), 210
Crevel, René, 21
Criterion Theatre (London), 74, 82
Cusack, Cyril, 74

Daldry, Stephen, 9
Daneman, Paul, 74–83
Dante, 34
Death of a Salesman (Miller), 89
Decroux, Etienne, 94
Demarle, Philippe, 176, 177
Desarthe, Gérard, 204
Descartes, René, 34
Deschevaux-Dumesnil, Suzanne, 12,
    14, 15, 46, 65, 153
Devine, George, 89
Diamond, Elin, 167
Dido and Aeneas (Purcell), 5
Dinulović, Prerag, 162, 163
Donat, Robert, 70
Donelly, Donal, 85
Drakulić, Slavenka, 167
Dream Play, A (Strindberg), 19, 22
Duchamp, Marcel, 14

Duck Soup (Marx Brothers), 132
Duckworth, Colin, 15, 34
Dumur, Guy, 53
Dürrenmatt, Friedrich, 97

Ebert, Carl, 153
Edwardes, Jane, 182
Eliot, Thomas Stearns, 70, 81, 85
Eluard, Paul, 21
Emori, Toru, 158–60
English Stage Company, 70
Entertainer, The (Osborne), 69
Entrée libre (Vitrac), 18
Epstein, Alvin, 94
Esslin, Martin, 25, 103, 104
Ewell, Tom, 92–4

Fančović, Ines, 166
Feinberg-Jütte, Anat, 152
Fernald, John, 72
FitzGerald, Nigel, 85, 184
Flannagan and Allen, 42
Fletcher, John, 21, 36
Flotats, José-Maria, 146, 148
Flynn, Bill, 169
Fornby, George, 73
Fratellini, Les, 53
Freedom of the City (Friel), 174
Frère, Marcel, 54
Friedrich, Caspar David, 12, 120
Frisch, Max, 97
Fry, Christopher, 69, 70, 81, 85
Fugard, Athol, 169, 210

Gabel, Jacques, 176
Gaîté-Montparnasse theatre (Paris), 45,
    46, 47, 50
Gao Xingjian, 178
Gate Theatre (Dublin), 44, 84, 136,
    185, 196
Gate Theatre (London), 70
Genet, Jean, 97, 201
Georg, Duke of Saxe-Meiningen, 4

Gerstein, Sergio, 55
Geulincx, Arnold, 34
Ghost Sonata, The (Strindberg), 45, 46
Gide, André, 72
Ginza Saison theatre (Tokyo), 158
Giraudoux, Jean, 69, 72
Glamočak, Admir, 166
Glenville, Peter, 88
Gogol, Nicolai, 72
Goldoni, Carlo, 72
Gontarski, Stanley, 13
Grabbe, Christian Dietrich, 45
Grande et la Petite Manoeuvre, La
    (Adamov), 49
Graver, Lawrence, 210
Green, Julien, 72
Grenier-Hussenot company, 46
Group Theatre, 89
Guggenheim, Peggy, 12
Guinness, Alec, 71
Guy, France, 51

Haarlemse Toneelschuur theatre
    (Holland), 155–7
Haifa Municipal Theatre, 170
Hall, Peter, 1, 3, 7, 24, 34, 44, 67, 70,
    71, 74–83, 88, 180–5, 209
Handke, Peter, 201
Hauptmann, Gerhart, 20
Havel, Vaclav, 149
Heidegger, Martin, 25
Held, Martin, 111
Hello and Goodbye (Fugard), 169
Henrioud, Matias, 118, 186
Herm, Klaus, 111, 112, 114, 118,
    130, 132
Hernani (Hugo), 54
Hicks, Greg, 184
Hobson, Harold, 67, 73
Holtzmann, Thomas, 151–5
*Hour When We Knew Nothing of One
    Another, The* (Handke), 201
Howard, Alan, 181–3, 196

Howarth, Donald, 168–70
Huchette, La, theatre (Paris), 48
Hypothèse, L' (Pinget), 198

Ibsen, Henrik, 20, 70, 201, 209
Ichihara, Etsuko, 158, 160
Illusion, The (Corneille), 8
Inspector Calls, An (Priestly), 9
Invasion, L' (Adamov), 49
Ionesco, Eugène, 21, 42, 48–50, 52, 64,
    70, 78, 90, 97, 201
Irving, Jules, 96, 98, 99, 101
Island, The (Fugard), 169, 170

Jacques, ou la Soumission (Ionesco), 21
Jarry, Alfred, 48, 52
Jendly, Roger, 202–6
Jet de sang, Le (Artaud), 18
John Golden Theater (New York), 93
Johnson, Albert, 92
Johnstone, Dennis, 46
Jong, Trudy de, 156
Jouanneau, Joël, 175–7
Jović, Ratislav, 164
Joyce, James, 11, 12, 14, 21, 139
Jung, Carl Gustav, 34

Kafka, Franz, 52, 64
Kalb, Jonathan, 151, 155, 179, 207
Kammerspiele theatre (Munich), 151
Kane, Sarah, 210
Kani, John, 169
Kanze, Hisao, 158
Kasznar, Kurt, 94
Kazan, Elia, 89, 90
Keaton, Buster, 14, 58, 86, 91
Kelly, Dermot, 85
Kerz, Leo, 86
Khoury, Muhram, 170–5
Kingsley, Ben, 181–3, 194, 196
Klee, Paul, 105
Knowlson, James, 13, 14, 19, 44, 115,
    116, 123, 195

Koltès, Bernard-Marie, 175
Koukami, Shoji, 158
Kraus, Karel, 150
Krejča, Otomar, 99, 140–50, 154, 156,
    157, 203, 212

Lacan, Jacques, 167
Lahr, Bert, 86, 90–9
Lambert, J. W., 69
Lancry theatre (Paris), 49
Land of Cockaigne (Bruegel), 115
Langdon, Harry, 58
Latour, Pierre, 50, 57–66
Laurel and Hardy, 35, 40, 42
Le Brocquy, Louis, 186
Lear, Edward, 81
Leçon, La (Ionesco), 48, 72, 74
Lecoq, Jacques, 199, 201
Lemarchand, Jacques, 53
Lincoln Center (New York), 185
Lindon, Jérôme, 13, 39, 51
Littlewood, Joan, 3, 68
Lizaran, Anna, 207
Look Back in Anger (Osborne), 69
Lorca, Federico García, 72
Lucernaire theatre (Paris), 48
Luchini, Fabrice, 146
Luft, Friedrich, 135
Lühr, Peter, 151–5

McGovern, Barry, 185–96
Malet, Arthur, 92
Mamelles de Tirésias, Les (Apollinaire),
    20, 54
Mamet, David, 210
Mandell, Alan, 98, 99, 101–4
Marceau, Marcel, 94
Mariés de la Tour Eiffel, Les (Cocteau),
    18
Market Theatre (Johannesburg), 169
Marković, Rade, 164
Marshall, E. G., 94
Martin, Jean, 50, 61–6, 114, 148

Marx Brothers, 35, 132
Matias *see* Henrioud
Matić, Dušan, 162
Mehta, Xerxes, 161
Melzer, Annabelle, 17, 18
Merlin, Serge, 202–6
Merry Widow (Lehár), 125, 126
Meyerhold, Vsevolod, 6, 7
Midori Mako, 158, 160
Midsummer Night's Dream, A
    (Shakespeare), 8
Miksak, Joseph, 101
Milićević, Andreja, 162
Miller, Arthur, 70, 97
Mills, Nat, and MacCauley, Bobbie,
    40, 41
Minuit, Editions de, 51, 52
Mnouchkine, Ariane, 7
Molière, 20
Moon in the Yellow River, The
    (Johnstone), 46, 50
Morecambe and Wise, 40, 42
Morley, Sheridan, 184
Mother Courage (Brecht), 3, 97
Mourning Becomes Electra (O'Neill),
    75
Murder in the Cathedral (Eliot), 70
Murphy, Johnny, 185–96
Music Box theatre (Broadway), 93
Myerberg, Michael, 86, 87, 91–4,
    97, 101
Mystères de l'amour, Les (Vitrac), 18,
    21, 22

Nègres, Les (Genet), 46, 58
Neveux, Georges, 50, 51
Nightingale, Benedict, 182
Ninagawa, Yukio, 158–60
Nishimura, Kon, 158–60
Nitzan, Omry, 170
Noctambules theatre (Paris), 48,
    49
Ntshona, Winston, 169

O'Casey, Sean, 14
O'Connor, Ulick, 85
Old Vic theatre (London), 169, 181,
    184
O'Neill, Eugene, 70, 90
Optimist, The (Habibi), 174
Oresteia (Aeschylus), 7
Orphée (Cocteau), 18
ORTF (Organisation de la
    Radio-Télévision Française), 51
Orton, Joe, 77
Osborne, John, 71, 77
Oxford Playhouse, 72

Paravents, Les (Genet), 46
Parodie, La (Adamov), 49
Partage des os, Le
    (Ribemont-Dessaignes), 18
Pascal, Blaise, 34, 53
Paskaljević, Bata, 164
Pasqual, Lluís, 205, 206, 210
Pastorello, Félie, 149
Pelorson, Georges, 19
Péron, Alfred, 12
Picabia, Francis, 14, 17
Piccolo, Peter, 169
Pichette, Henri, 46
Pike Theatre (Dublin), 83
Pinter, Harold, 77, 78, 97, 210
Pirandello, Luigi, 2, 20, 35, 52,
    70, 154
Pitoeff, Sacha, 51, 53
Popović, Mica, 163
Popović, Vasilije, 162–4
Poultney, George, 102
Prince, Eric, 184
Professeur Taranne, Le (Adamov), 21
Proust, Marcel, 212

Quilley, Denis, 184

Racine, Jean, 29, 199
Raddatz, Carl, 111

Raimbourg, Lucien, 50, 57–66, 82
Ramsay, Margaret (Peggy), 68, 72
Reid, Alec, 28
Ribemont-Dessaignes, Georges, 21
Richardson, Ralph, 71
Riverside Studios (London), 136
Robbe-Grillet, Alain, 25, 27, 53, 155,
    211
Robinson, Michael, 15, 16
Roche, Eugene, 100, 101, 105
Ronen Ilan, 170–5
Roussillon d' Apt, 12
Roussin, André
Roy, Stéphane, 177
Royal Court Theatre (London), 70, 135
Rufus, 145–9

Salacrou, Armand, 53
Salzburg Festival, 140
San Quentin Drama Workshop, 103,
    136
San Quentin Penitentiary, 2, 101–5
Saurel, Renée, 54, 65
Sawa, Ryuiji, 160
Schiller-Theater (Berlin), 35, 106, 135,
    140, 180, 181, 185, 186, 188, 200
Schneider, Alan, 86–93, 96
Schubert, Franz, 123
Schumacher, Arnulf, 153
Semel, Noam, 170
Serin muet, Le (Ribemont-Dessaignes),
    18
Serreau, Geneviève and Jean-Marie, 28,
    48, 49, 51–4, 72
Seyrig, Delphine, 51
Shakespeare, William, 21, 85, 95
Shammas, Anton, 171
Shaw, George Bernard, 70, 201
Shepard, Sam, 210
Sheridan, Richard Brinsley, 20
Shulman, Milton, 67
Siegfried (Giraudoux), 20
Simpson, Alan, 44, 83–5

Simpson, N. F., 78
Sinclair, Peggy, 11, 12
Six Characters in Search of an Author
    (Pirandello), 2, 53, 154
Sizwe Banzi is Dead (Fugard), 169
Skin of Our Teeth, The (Wilder), 86
Smart, Jack, 92
Snow, Peter, 75
Sontag, Susan, 135, 164–8
Sophocles, 20
Soupault, Philippe, 21
Spencer, Charles, 185
Stanford, Alan, 185, 189, 195
Stanislavski, Konstantin, 5, 6,100,
    109, 209
States, Bert O., 33, 188
Stein, Peter, 7
Stelle, Truus te, 156
Stoppard, Tom, 210
Strauss, Botho, 201
Streetcar Named Desire, A (Williams), 89
Strehler, Giorgio, 8
Strindberg, August, 20, 45, 46, 52, 70,
    123, 201
Svoboda, Josef, 140, 141, 156
Symonds, Robert, 101
Synge, John Millington, 14, 44, 84

Tabori, George, 137, 151–5
Tadić, Ljubivoje, 164
Tanako, Mariko Hori, 158
Tandy, Jessica, 90
Tartuffe (Molière), 7
Tavory, Doron, 170
Teatre Lliure (Barcelona), 205
Théâtre Alfred Jarry, 22
Théâtre de Babylone (Paris), 23, 28, 45,
    51, 52, 54, 63, 64, 72
Théâtre de Poche (Paris), 51
Théâtre des Amandiers (Nanterre), 175
Théâtre du Nouveau Monde (Quebec),
    177
Theatre Guild, 89

Théâtre National de Strasbourg, 137
Théâtre National Populaire, 97, 146
Théâtre Vidy (Lausanne), 200
Theatre Workshop (Stratford East), 68
Time of Your Life, The (Saroyan), 89
Tomić, Mica, 164
Toren, Ilan, 170
Tsingos, Christine, 45, 47
Two Men Observing the Moon
    (Friedrich), 12
Tynan, Kenneth, 67, 69, 73, 95
Tzara, Tristan, 14, 15, 16, 17, 18,
    21, 46

Ubu Roi (Jarry), 54
Uncle Vanya (Chekhov), 51

Valentin, Karl, 12, 14
Victor, ou les Enfants au pouvoir (Vitrac),
    22
Vilar, Jean, 46, 49, 146
Vinaver, Michel, 123
Vitaly, Georges, 46
Vitrac, Roger, 21, 22

Wagner, Robin, 102
Waltz of the Toreadors (Anouilh), 75
Wanamaker, Sam, 86
Warner, Deborah, 3

Warrilow, David, 176, 177
Weber, Carl, 3
Webern, Anton, 100
Wedekind, Frank, 70
Weidman, Charles, 92
Weiz, Shoshana, 174
Wekwerth, Manfred, 168
Well of the Saints, The (Synge), 14, 34
Wesker, Arnold, 69, 78
Whitelaw, Billie, 112
Whiting, John, 72, 97
Wigger, Stefan, 110, 111, 118, 119,
    127, 133
Wilde, Oscar, 70
Wilder, Thornton, 86, 87, 90, 95
Williams, Robin, 182
Williams, Tennessee, 97
Wilson, Georges, 145–9
Wizard of Oz, The, 91, 93
Woodthorpe, Peter, 74–83
Worth, Katharine, 14
Woyzeck (Büchner), 45

Yeats, William Butler, 14, 20, 44

Za Branou theatre (Prague), 140, 150
Zizi de Dada, Le (Ribemont-
    Dessaignes), 18
Zola, Emile, 4